Watchdogs and Gadflies

Activism from Marginal to Mainstream

WATCHDOGS AND GADFLIES

ACTIVISM FROM MARGINAL TO MAINSTREAM

Tim Falconer

PENGUIN

VIKING

VIKING

Published by the Penguin Group

Penguin Books Canada Ltd, 10 Alcorn Avenue,
Toronto, Ontario, Canada M4V 3B2

Penguin Books Ltd, 80 Strand, London WC2R ORL, England

Penguin Putnam Inc., 375 Hudson Street, New York,
New York 10014, U.S.A.

Penguin Books Australia Ltd, Ringwood, Victoria, Australia

Penguin Books (NZ) Ltd, cnr Rosedale and Airborne Roads, Albany,
Auckland 1310, New Zealand

Penguin Books Ltd, Registered Offices: Harmondsworth,
Middlesex, England

First published, 2001

10 9 8 7 6 5 4 3 2 1

Copyright © Tim Falconer, 2001

Printed and bound in Canada on acid free paper ∞

National Library of Canada Cataloguing in Publication Data

Falconer, Tim, 1958–
Watchdogs and gadflies: activism from marginal to mainstream

Includes index
ISBN 0-670-89417-6

1. Political participation—Canada. 2. Political activists—Canada I. Title.

JL148.5.F35 2001   322.4'0971   C2001-901138-5

Visit Penguin Canada's website at **www.penguin.ca**

FOR CARMEN

The hottest places in Hell
are reserved for those who
remain neutral in time of
great moral crisis.
                —Dante Alighieri

CONTENTS

1 It's the End of Politics As We Know It (And I Feel Fine) *1*

2 When the Going Gets Tough, Activists Turn Pro *23*

3 Walter Robinson and the Rise of
Conservative Activism *45*

4 Education: Activists Will Happen *69*

5 Globalization: The Young and the Idealistic *91*

6 Environment: Tools for Radicals *115*

7 Health: The Demonization of Cranks,
Zealots and Left-Wing Nuts *151*

8 Poverty: Fighting Frustration with Small Victories *177*

9 Justice: The Secrets of Success *197*

10 Duff Conacher and the Drive for Democratic Reform *223*

11 Reveille for Citizens *243*

Appendix: Activist Web Sites *261*

Acknowledgements *264*

Index *266*

1

IT'S THE END OF POLITICS AS WE KNOW IT

(AND I FEEL FINE)

TO A DEMOGRAPHER, I am nothing but a baby boomer. Born in 1958, I come from one of the most prolific of post-war years. And yet, to my way of thinking, I have little in common with the leading edge of the boomers. Too young to join in all the fun, I watched the late 1960s and early 1970s on television and truly believed my older cousins would change the world. My television set showed me a generation of young people determined to right every injustice: to stop a ridiculous war, to win racial equality, to get women out from under the thumb of men, to save the planet from choking on our own pollution and to preserve freedom despite Richard Daley, Richard Nixon and the rest of The Establishment. And in the twisted little universe created by the media, these young people were doing all these good things while enjoying unlimited great sex, fun drugs and exciting rock 'n' roll.

The summer I turned 14, a friend gave me a copy of *Do It!* by Jerry Rubin, the 1960s radical who co-founded the Yippie movement and ended up on trial as one of the Chicago Seven. "Danger! This book will become a Molotov cocktail in your very hands," the back-cover blurb read. "*Do It!* is a Declaration of War between the generations—calling on kids to leave their homes, burn down their schools and create a new society upon the ashes of the old." Today, the book seems rather silly, of course, but back then, for a pampered upper-middle-class, private-school boy, it was provocative stuff. I ate it up—and dreamed that I'd soon join the revolution, which was, I was sure, everywhere but around me.

My envy soon turned to resentment as I realized the world wasn't changing—or at least not the way I imagined it would. The idealism of the '60s soon gave way to the self-indulgence of the '70s. By the time I was allowed to go to bars, legally, disco was taking over. And whatever that rather embarrassing era stood for, it wasn't about changing the world for the better. The baby boomers had sold out.

Instead of utopia, I saw a society that continued to decay. True, women were no longer expected to be barefoot and pregnant in the kitchen, though that had as much to do with tech-nology—notably the birth control pill—as with bra-burning demonstrations. And the troops did come home from Vietnam, eventually, but American foreign policy didn't change much. Meanwhile, the racial divide in America grew wider and more destructive (in spite of all the gains made by the civil-rights move-ment), the health of the planet continued to deteriorate, and free-dom became just another word for unfettered corporate profits.

I felt burned. I left high school thinking, What the hell? I might as well be a happy idiot and simply try to get rich. At uni-versity in Montreal, where I initially studied to be a highly paid mining engineer, I treated anyone who joined any protest with cynicism and disdain. And so while others marched for an end to violence against women, chanted for McGill to stop investing in South Africa or agitated for any number of other worthy causes, I remained unmoved. The sex and drugs and rock 'n' roll of the 1960s were fine, but the rest of it was a hoax. It seemed a much better idea to wallow in the self-pitying anger and nihilism of punk music—or to simply while away the hours in the student pub—than to take a chance on activism.

That cynicism was particularly immature, even for me. After all, we have to go back only a century to see a world few of us would be happy living in. Whatever rights we enjoy in democratic societies are not God-given, and regardless of the failings of the '60s generation, equality and justice have only ever been won through some form of protest. That's easy to forget in our ahistorical times. Nowadays, most North Americans take everything—including democracy itself—for granted. And we've forgotten both the importance of democratic dissent and the rich tradition of activism.

If activism had patron saints, they'd include Martin Luther and Martin Luther King, Mohandas Gandhi and Nelson Mandela. Ralph Nader and Saul Alinsky belong on that list, too. Nader, the prototypical watchdog, relies on research and reasoned arguments. This American's tactics aren't provocative, but his ideas often are. Though he continues to work on a variety of issues, his biggest triumphs date from the days when he took on the automobile industry. Today, we don't give padded steering wheels and dashboards, seatbelts or even air bags a second thought, but they all represent Nader victories. Alinsky, who died in 1972, was the classic gadfly. The American community organizer wasn't short on substance—he's the author of two seminal books on activism, *Reveille for Radicals* and *Rules for Radicals*—but he's best remembered as the master of creative tactics. Once, in an effort to ensure that promises made to a Chicago ghetto organization would be kept, he threatened to bring O'Hare Airport to a halt by having supporters occupy all the washroom stalls. After hearing about the plot, City Hall honoured its commitments.

Canada has few similar icons, but that doesn't mean this country hasn't produced plenty of effective activists. A century ago, Nellie McClung dedicated herself to creating a just society. As a member of the Famous Five (Irene Parlby, Henrietta Muir

Edwards, Emily Murphy and Louise McKinney were the others), she supported Edwards's case right up to the Privy Council, which finally declared Canadian women to be persons in 1929. Earlier, McClung had worked at winning the vote for women and fought for dental and health care for schoolchildren and safer working conditions for factory workers. As a prominent member of the Woman's Christian Temperance Union, McClung also helped bring in prohibition (demonstrating, in the process, both her effectiveness and that one person's paradise is another's hell).

Canadian activists also boast international influence. In the 1930s, Grey Owl helped sell people around the world on the idea of conservation, with his movies about beavers and in his speaking engagements. After he died, in 1938, everyone learned that Grey Owl was really English-born Archie Belaney and not a native Indian, but that didn't diminish his message. In 1971 Vancouver environmentalists launched Greenpeace. Though its head office has since moved, the group remains one of Canada's great gifts to the world. Many activists—on the left and the right—study Greenpeace's campaigns and ability to take advantage of the media to sell its message. John Willis, a Toronto consultant and the chair of Greenpeace USA, believes that, in the beginning, the special magic of the group was that, instead of trying to send a message to cabinet ministers, it aimed to get people in the local bar talking.

"Democracy is a system in which the citizens actively control the power, but do they just vote and after that do nothing? Or, at the other end of the spectrum, do they interact from day to day?" asked Willis, who believes many Canadians still have the attitude: "I guess the government should do something about that." "I suppose you could say activism is the attempt to yank it from one end of that spectrum to the other," he said. "From that point of view, it's not surprising that a group like Greenpeace would be founded in Canada."

More recently, Canadians have been prominent in what is currently the highest-profile form of activism: the anti-globalization movement. The 1997 APEC Summit in Vancouver was one of the earliest anti-globalization protests, predating the so-called Battle in Seattle by two years. Maude Barlow, volunteer national chairperson of the Council of Canadians, played a large role in the 1998 defeat of the Multilateral Agreement on Investment, an international pact that would have seen signatory nations give up their rights to set conditions on foreign investment. And Naomi Klein emerged as the movement's intellectual guru—whether she wanted the gig or not—after the success of her book *No Logo: Taking Aim at the Brand Bullies*. First published early in 2000, the bestseller is now available in nine languages.

While the people protesting in the streets of Seattle, Prague and Quebec City have specific concerns about international trade agreements, they are also lashing out at traditional politics in a society they feel is not inclusive. That's true of all activism, and the anti-globalization movement—or pro-democracy movement, as some people now refer to it—is just the most vivid example. Before the April 2001 Summit of the Americas in Quebec City, the politicians and much of the media did their best to paint the protesters as ill-informed and undemocratic. When International Trade Minister Pierre Pettigrew announced that the participants would release the working text of the proposed free-trade agreement between the countries of North, Central and South America, he spoke derisively of anti-globalization activists and denied, unconvincingly, that the decision had anything to do with the planned protests. Then Prime Minister Jean Chrétien captured the contempt leaders have for the plebs when he dismissed the protesters as irrelevant partiers: "They say to themselves, 'Let's go spend the weekend in Quebec City, we'll have fun, we'll protest and blah, blah, blah.'"

Summit organizers created a gated community protected by a 3.8-kilometre fence and 6,000 well-armed riot cops performing the role of a private security force. To the protesters, the fence—or "the wall," as they called it—was a provocation and, inevitably, they tried to pull it down; conference organizers pointed to the handful of violent protesters as proof that the fence was necessary. But once the tear gas finally wafted away, it became clear that the fence was a metaphor, and the two solitudes it separated might as well have been in parallel universes for all their ability to communicate with each other.

Inside, the leaders of thirty-four countries and their delegations met with each other and with the corporate lobbyists who had paid between $75,000 and $1.5 million for the right to attend "networking events." They repeated the mantra that trade is good (perpetuating the fiction that those outside believed trade is bad) and refused to admit there could be anything wrong with international agreements. Outside, tens of thousands of citizens—the vast majority of whom were peaceful—tried to exercise their democratic right to protest in police-state conditions. The protesters may have had legitimate complaints about the proposed Free Trade Area of the Americas, but they had no leader, no common message and no coherent alternative. Predictably, the media paid little attention to the thoughtful activists, preferring to train their cameras on the anarchists who threw paving stones and hockey pucks.

The Summit heightened our awareness of the fragility of democracy. The anti-activist spin only increased the sense that our elected leaders and media commentators believe politics and decision-making are for the rich and powerful, and that the rest of us ought to just amuse ourselves with the latest episode of *Temptation Island*. But more and more people are unwilling to accept that; they are turning to activism to ensure their voices are heard

by those inside the gated political community. Even if those who
cling to traditional politics don't like it, activism represents nothing so much as an informed, passionate and engaged citizenry.

ALTHOUGH I'D LONG noticed a growing contempt for traditional politics, the trend really started to make sense to me when
Pierre Elliott Trudeau died in the fall of 2000. As I read the papers
and watched the television coverage, I wondered what compelled
so many Canadians, including a surprising number who hated his
policies, to react so strongly to the death of an 80-year-old man.
Part of it, I'm sure, was a natural realization of our own mortality:
when someone who always seemed young dies, we must be getting old. But I'm convinced Trudeau's death also reminded us how
far we've come from a time when politics mattered.

We remember those days as a golden era, and it's not simply
the haze of nostalgia. Like a great hockey player, Trudeau made
those around him—even already formidable adversaries such as
René Lévesque and Peter Lougheed—better. These leaders
(and others, including Richard Hatfield, Allan Blakeney and Bill
Davis) were their own men. They weren't packaged by handlers,
they didn't rely on polls for ideas and they didn't test every plank
of their platforms with focus groups. Today's politicians are so
carefully packaged that we half expect to see the puppeteers'
wires during the photo ops. But when Trudeau turned the 1980
referendum around with his famous appearance at Montreal's
Paul Sauvé Arena, he did it with a speech he'd written himself
and then memorized. It's inconceivable that a present-day politician could pull that off.

Back then, our leaders behaved as though they actually
believed Canada was a good idea. It matters not that globalization, technology and the fear of bankruptcy conspired to make

much of what Trudeau believed in obsolete; we miss the idea that a leader could love literature, appreciate the arts, dream of a just society and want to make Canada a better place and not simply a richer one. Today, we suffer with a prime minister who's I-love-Canada schtick is as shallow as it is unimaginative. Worse, politicians at all levels talk to us only as taxpayers and not as citizens. In fact, the word "citizen" rarely crosses their lips.

"The best and the brightest" haven't been going into politics since the 1960s. And I don't blame them. The job is far from lucrative, the intemperate media scrutiny hurts family and friends and, worse, the power to be wielded is highly overrated. "Cabinet has evolved from a decision-making body under Pearson," a senior bureaucrat told Donald J. Savoie, author of *Governing from the Centre: The Concentration of Power in Canadian Politics*, "to a university-type seminar under Trudeau, to a focus group under Trudeau in his later years in office and also under both Mulroney and Chrétien."

The dry rot in our political system is now so bad that the politicians have almost as much contempt for citizens as the citizens have for the politicians. During the 1993 federal election, then prime minister and leader of the Progressive Conservatives Kim Campbell said an election was no place to discuss serious issues. Everyone—opponents, journalists and the public—jumped all over her. But if the 2000 election was any indication, our political parties and the media agreed with her. All the polls showed health care as the most important issue for Canadians, but all we got was mudslinging. Nobody could agree on what two-tier health care means, and no party laid out its position on the issue—except the NDP, which predictably said it would continue to throw a lot of money at the problem. So if crucial issues won't—or can't—be intelligently debated during an election, they'll be decided by an ever-smaller inner circle, most of whom are heavily influenced by paid lobbyists, and the public will have no input, except for a few polls and perhaps some dog-and-pony shows dressed up as public hearings.

As power concentrates at the centre, parties become less connected to their grassroots members and democracy deteriorates. Worse, the idealist who wants to make a difference in politics must win a nomination and an election, be a member of the party that forms the government, hope for an invitation into cabinet and finally rise to the level of at least finance minister. And this idealist needs to do all this before the whiff of power corrupts him—or her. Lotteries, once described by an Italian politician as a tax on imbeciles, look good by comparison. It takes some people a while to figure this out. Lee Morrison, an outspoken and unabashedly politically incorrect member of parliament from Saskatchewan, was so frustrated by his seven years in the House of Commons that he opted not to run in the November 2000 election.

"I will not regret leaving what has become, under Liberal management, a totally dysfunctional institution. I will not miss the thrill of making well-researched speeches in a virtually empty room. I will not miss working long hours on irrelevant ministerially guided committees. I will not miss the posturing. I will not miss the emasculated government members howling because they do not understand the difference between intelligent heckling and boorish noise," the Canadian Alliance member said in his last parliamentary speech. "I do not know what I will be doing for the next few years, but whatever it is I expect that I will be dealing with grown-ups. I am sure that it will be more useful than this past seven years that I have spent in this rubber-stamp parliament. I shall not look back."

Morrison, a self-described redneck, was an idealist among a horde of professional politicians increasingly motivated by the need to get re-elected rather than a desire to change the world.

When the game is politics, the only thing that matters is getting, and keeping, power. No wonder so many Canadians are disgusted with politicians. Perhaps it's a good thing that tighter budgets, international trade agreements and global financial markets mean there are fewer meaningful decisions for our politicians to make.

It wasn't always that way. In my father's generation— Trudeau's generation—people often established themselves in law or business or some other line of work and then ran for office out of a sense of civic duty. (That's why my Tory father distrusted Trudeau so much: not only was he a "draft dodger," my dad insisted, he'd never had a real job.) Fifteen years ago, I had friends who I was sure would end up in politics. Some of them even worked as political aides. But now we all view traditional politics as a geekfest—the only people interested are strivers, the hopelessly naive and the devoutly religious. (It makes perfect sense that the latter group still have faith in institutional politics: they already believe in an institution—the church—that most of us gave up on as soon as our parents stopped making us go.)

To be fair, a few politicians do manage to make a difference in spite of the system. Svend Robinson, for example, is an activist who also happens to be an NDP MP. Meanwhile, Liberal John Godfrey, though not even a cabinet minister, has earned praise for his work on children's issues. And back in Brian Mulroney's government, backbencher Patrick Boyer became an expert on referenda. But these are the exceptions, and it's hard to shake the feeling that most MPs are glorified pothole fillers.

Third-generation activist Bob Penner, who's my age, has been involved in advocacy—first in the peace movement, then with Greenpeace and now as the president of his own consulting firm—for two decades. His grandfather took part in the Winnipeg General Strike of 1919; met Penner's grandmother at a speech by

Emma Goldman, the famous radical; and helped found the Communist Party of Canada. Jacob Penner's political beliefs meant he had to spend over two years in a concentration camp during the Second World War, though that didn't prevent Winnipeggers from electing him to city council for more than thirty years, including during the cold-war 1950s.

"When I was younger," Bob Penner admitted to me, "I might have thought elected politics would be a good thing to do, but I definitely wouldn't be interested now—unless someone assured me I'd be prime minister one day. I have more influence than an NDP backbencher somewhere, so I'd much rather be doing what I'm doing."

John Willis works with Penner and sees his point. "Given the option between party politics and activist politics, more people become activists," said the 39-year-old, "probably because the system is sclerotic with old white guys, representing old coalitions that don't even really exist any more, and, moreover, government seems so slow and powerless."

If my generation soured on politics, those who came after us never had any taste for it. Often called Generation X (or the Nexus Generation), these people learned early on not to trust institutions: their parents' marriages ended in divorce, their parents' jobs were lost in a frenzy of corporate downsizing and their parents' governments racked up huge deficits, while being completely powerless to ease the pain of two deep recessions in ten years. Now grown up, they are entrepreneurial, flexible and fixed on short-term goals. And as much as they believe their parents sold out, they do want to change the world.

Lyndsay Poaps certainly does. The 22-year-old is the co-director of Check Your Head, a group that gives workshops on globalization in high schools and universities. She says young people don't like the bureaucracy of traditional political parties, nor do they like the way they are treated by their elders in those organizations. "When you join a party or get involved in municipal politics, you have to go through so much bureaucracy," she said. "And there's always the possibility you'll just be used as a prop to get young votes for the party." She's found a world of difference in the anti-globalization movement. "You're involved and your opinion is totally valid, and your energy and ideas are needed and you are respected."

This baby-bust generation was the subject of much hand-wringing by politicos from both sides of the border at a conference I attended in August 2000. It's one of several sponsored every year across North America by the American trade magazine *Campaigns & Elections*. The three-day political-training conference promised to increase the professionalism of the politicians, campaign managers, consultants and, increasingly, activists who attended. The people who packed the Pavilion Ballroom of the Sheraton Wall Centre Hotel in downtown Vancouver were, for the most part, casually dressed. But there was an air of seriousness in the room that not even the frequent ringing of cellphones could shatter.

With a federal election just a few months away, everyone heard the bad news early. In the first session of the conference, Bani Dheer, an associate with The Strategic Counsel, a Toronto consulting and research company, told the crowd that the eight million people between the ages of 18 and 34 will make up 40 percent of eligible voters in the upcoming election and that two million Canadians—most of them young people—will be able to vote for the first time. Representatives from the Liberal Party might have taken comfort when Dheer explained that 65 percent of these people characterize themselves as liberals, but the Grits knew it wouldn't mean much if this crew didn't get to the polling stations. Indeed, a recurring theme throughout the conference was what to do about a generation that has little interest in voting and even less in working for political parties. South of the border, the Democrats and Republicans face the same problem. "Kids are not voting not because they're apathetic, as they were in my day," Democratic Party consultant Cathy Allen suggested on the second day of the conference, "but because they think they can make a difference in other ways."

Poaps does vote and doesn't rule out politics in the future, but she has already turned down an offer to run in a municipal election. And she understands why many of her generation prefer activism to politics. "A lot of young people feel they have an ability to make more of an impact outside the traditional political system because they feel completely alienated from that system," she said, dragging out "completely" and "alienated" for emphasis. "You can vote when you're 18, but when you're that young, politicians are just trying to get your vote. They don't really care what you have to say. They're just vying for your vote so they can win." (I didn't tell her that politicians don't treat older people any differently.)

On the third day of the conference, I met Rob Sinclair. After fifteen years as a staffer with the Ontario Conservatives, he went to work for the International Fund for Animal Welfare, a group dedicated to improving the lot of wild and domestic animals. His biggest triumph was the campaign that forced the Ontario government to ban the spring bear hunt in 1999. I asked him about the difference between party politics and activism. "There's no difference," he said. "But advocacy is more fun."

In the days after Trudeau died, everyone agreed we won't see his like again. And it's true: if another Canadian with the intellect, charisma and vision of Trudeau comes along, he or she will be an entrepreneur, a filmmaker or an activist—anything but a politician.

WALTER ROBINSON is no Pierre Trudeau, but he's no slouch either. He speaks well and forcefully, in both official languages, about his favourite causes; he's good with the media and has a talent for, in his words, "framing the debate." His impressive resumé is full of professional successes and extracurricular activities—he did stints on the boards of the Ottawa Hospital and the Ottawa Board of Trade, for example—even though he's just 35. And while his colleagues have nicknamed him Cocaine, because of his energy level, he's squeaky clean. He even looks like Dudley Do-Right, though that doesn't mean he's about to back down from a fight. In short, he's a dream political candidate.

But Walter Robinson is idealistic and intelligent. He knows Trudeau was wrong when he said backbench MPs were nobodies fifty feet from Parliament Hill; what Trudeau couldn't say was that they're nobodies even when they're in the House of Commons. More and more of the power in this country is shifting away from elected politicians, and Robinson knows it.

"There's no doubt that the rise of interest groups and advocacy organizations is directly proportional to the dysfunction we have in our elected representative system and the fact that political parties are seen by many young, idealistic people—including me—to stifle debate and ingenuity and creativity," he said. "I see it in friends still working for various parties: people are saying, 'Why am I doing this? I'm not making an impact.'"

So Robinson swallowed his aspirations for elected office and now works for the Canadian Taxpayers Federation (CTF). The scrappy, unabashedly in-your-face citizen watchdog group regularly infuriates tax-and-spend liberals as well as its natural allies. Meanwhile, the organization's issues—most notably, taxation and government spending—currently dominate the political discussion. And Robinson meets with the finance minister before budgets, works with the auditor general and enjoys regular (and usually fawning) media coverage.

Despite all his interviews with reporters, sessions on talk radio and appearances on television—3,500 of them in his first three and a half years on the job, by his count—Robinson remains far from a household name in this country. Precious few activists are well known. Maude Barlow, head of the Council of Canadians, can claim a national profile, but even David Suzuki may be better known as host of *The Nature of Things*, his long-running TV show, than for his environmental work. Although some activists do have regional reputations, most operate in relative obscurity. And it's not a nefarious attempt to fly under the public's radar; in fact, most activists are publicity hounds. (Barlow, who is the author of several books, was the only activist who declined my request for an interview. Her assistant said she was too busy, but Barlow appears in the media all the time.)

As much as journalists rely on activists to provide confrontation and juicy quotes, the media rarely go deeper to explain the influence of these rabble-rousers. During my career as a magazine writer, I've been fortunate to do a handful of profiles of activists—I say fortunate because such story ideas usually generate yawns from editors. When I started working on this book, my boss at Ryerson University's School of Journalism joked that I should call it *In Dubious Battle*, after my least-favourite John Steinbeck novel.

As the butt of yawns and jokes from the media, and perhaps because of them, activists don't get the credit they deserve. With some exceptions—feminist Marilou McPhedran and peace activist Douglas Roche, for example—the prestigious Order of Canada has been a no-go zone for the people who increasingly shape our society. So while the heads of tobacco companies can proudly wear the honour, Garfield Mahood, the executive director of the Toronto-based Non-Smokers' Rights Association, and the man most responsible for changing Canadian society's attitude to cigarettes, remains excluded.

Short-sighted journalists and politically motivated award panels aside, many activists do make a difference. And that power is only going to increase as our traditional political system rots from the inside out. After Robinson first got the job as the CTF's Ottawa-based federal director in the spring of 1997, he and Andy Crooks, the group's chairman, and their wives had dinner in the Panorama Room, the revolving restaurant atop the Calgary Tower. As Robinson enjoyed a good Alberta filet mignon and a nice Merlot, he asked, "What sort of influence can I have?"

"On certain issues, you can meet with cabinet ministers," Crooks explained bluntly. "You can have the profile of a mid-level cabinet minister. Whether you are a provincial director or a federal director of this organization, you can have that level of influence."

LONG AGO, GAR MAHOOD realized that elected politics was no place for anyone with a desire to change the world. "I represent a lot of people and organizations who have accomplished stuff that no cabinet minister would ever accomplish on his own," he said. "A cabinet minister might be in the public eye for a period of time, but the track record is simply not going to be there without leadership. So if you want to effect change, I think you can do so much more rapidly being on the outside, playing a leadership role in the advocacy community."

That wasn't a popular notion back in the 1970s, when Mahood started, but it's gaining acceptance now. According to *Strengthening Canadian Democracy: The Views of Canadians*, a study by Paul Howe and David Northrup for the Institute for Research on Public Policy, Canadians who believe interest groups are a more

effective way to work for change outnumber those who believe
political parties are by three to one.

We tend to view activists as people who aren't out for personal
gain the way politicians, corporate executives and union leaders
are. And while the not-in-my-backyard ethic does drive some
activists, many others are out saving whales or whatever just
because they feel they ought to. As "experts," politicians and
establishment leaders lose standing with the public, and those
who were once seen as outsiders seem more and more convincing. "What used to be fringe groups now have a credibility that
those in the mainstream can't approach, because people are a
little more cynical not only about what the mainstream groups
are saying but who is paying them to say it," said Craig Jones,
president of the British Columbia Civil Liberties Association.
"Activist groups have that extra added credibility of being able to
say, 'This is what I believe and no one's paying me to say it.'"

While many people associate activists with the political left,
advocates work on many issues and from a variety of perspectives.
Yes, people who work for anti-poverty groups tend to be on the
left (though it's not as though most people on the right are in
favour of poverty), but the Canadian Taxpayers Federation is
decidedly on the right. On some issues—abortion, for example—activist groups fight it out from the two extremes, while governments try to find a compromise. And, of course, many activists
don't fit any neat political label, much to the chagrin of their opponents. Smoking cuts across political lines, and Mahood has
worked with—and against—three different parties at the provincial level alone. Meanwhile, the gun-control debate pits rural
Canadians against urbanites, regardless of political orientation.

The hoary left-versus-right political spectrum is giving way
to one with elitism at one end and populism at the other. And
as Canadians continue to lose respect for elites and

experts—including Big Government, Big Business and Big Labour—they are just as likely to trust activists as much as anyone. Inevitably, some politicians have gone out of their way to tout their refusal to be held hostage to "special interest groups." Of course, that's just doublespeak, intended to hide the fact that they are listening to different interests. Any organization a government agrees with is a "grassroots movement," while any group it wants to marginalize is a "special interest group." (This is eerily reminiscent of the early '80s, when Americans considered the Contras, the anti-Sandinista guerrillas in Nicaragua, "freedom fighters," while the guerrillas struggling against the U.S.-backed government of El Salvador were "terrorists.") Wendy Cukier, president of the Coalition for Gun Control, believes advocacy groups are "public interest groups," while industry associations and other self-serving lobbies are the real "special interest groups." In some ways, in fact, the rise of activism is a response to the growing influence of "special interests," such as the Ontario Medical Association, the Canadian Federation of Independent Business and the mob of corporate lobbyists.

Cutbacks to the civil service have also opened the door for activists. Mahood, for example, watched in dismay as Health Canada staff dwindled and funding for tobacco control disappeared. "The issues are so complicated now. So where is the policy advice coming from? It's coming from the outside. With the complexity of issues, it's the specialty groups that have the expertise." Perhaps that's not such a bad thing: no one in Canada knows as much about tobacco control as Mahood.

The politicians can posture all they want, but activists play a useful role for them. Not only do they generate policy ideas, they save politicians from making huge blunders. In 1971, for example, Jane Jacobs and other Toronto citizens stopped the construction of the Spadina Expressway through the heart of the city. By bringing the provincial government to its senses, they saved the neighbourhoods, which everyone agrees are the city's strength. Activists also help our elected officials by moving public opinion so government can act.

"It's not always comfortable for governments to be seen to be too far out in front of public opinion," said Mahood. "We can create the public opinion that allows the good health policy to come forward." Or as American President Franklin Delano Roosevelt once told a delegation: "Okay, you've convinced me. Now go out there and bring pressure on me." Finally, once the politicians are ready to introduce legislation, activists can help sell it. The Coalition for Gun Control, for example, played an essential role in selling the gun-control legislation to the public as well as to reluctant backbench MPs and senators.

When people first asked me if activists were watchdogs or gadflies, I'd joke that they all see themselves as watchdogs, while their opponents all dismiss them as gadflies. But I soon realized that the most effective activists are both: they do the unglamorous research, organizing and other spade work, but they're not afraid to be provocative. Robinson sees his work as a three-step process. In the first, proactive stage, the CTF "adopts an issue" it believes needs to be addressed. Second, the group tries to "frame the debate" by using what Robinson calls, "the 'air wars' of media—print, talk radio, the Internet and speeches—to get the issue onto the public-policy radar screen." Finally, it "drives the agenda" by securing victory in the legislative arena.

Other activists may use different terminology and not all of them seek legislative change, but most of the successful ones use some variation of Robinson's approach. And there are triumphant activists working on just about every important issue facing Canadians. Malkin Dare, a Waterloo, Ontario, mother who launched the Organization for Quality Education, helped force grammar and basic reading skills back into the provincial curriculum. Martha Kostuch, an Alberta veterinarian, won an environmental assessment case in the Supreme Court of Canada. Jim Green, a Vancouver anti-poverty organizer, built places for people to live in Canada's poorest neighbourhood—and arranged free opera performances for them. John Fisher, of the Ottawa-based Equality for Gays and Lesbians Everywhere, shepherded changes to the Human Rights Act.

With or without legislative, judicial or other victories, advocates help change attitudes. When Mahood started his anti-tobacco crusade in 1974, smokers smoked and non-smokers kept their mouths shut. Today, lighting up has all the cachet of spitting on the sidewalk. Mahood didn't do this alone, of course, but he led the fight for workplace smoking bans, pushed for an end to tobacco advertising and helped create the graphic warnings that now grace every cigarette package—warnings that are being copied in countries around the world. Although he's never been elected to office, Mahood has influenced legislation at all three levels of government. More importantly, he's helped erode public acceptance of smoking.

We are not witnessing a bloodless coup d'état. And the end of politics as we know it does not, of course, mean extinction for politicians or governments. Activists can't replace government, but they can help set the political agenda, they can educate, motivate and mobilize the public, and they can pressure politicians to pass or abandon legislation. In other words, they get to do all the fun and creative stuff, leaving the rest of the job for bureaucrats and political dullards. In his book, *The Decline of Deference*, University of Toronto professor Neil Nevitte says the falling public confidence in institutions and the weakening attachments to traditional political parties does not mean that democracy is in crisis. Rather, he believes, it's just in transition.

"All that is in crisis," he wrote, "is 'old politics'—the traditional notion that democracies work best when publics are passive, disengaged, and relatively uninformed." And those who cling to the old notion are in for interesting times ahead, as more and more citizens become informed, engaged and active.

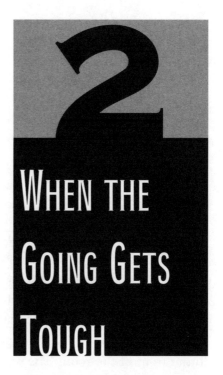

2

WHEN THE GOING GETS TOUGH

ACTIVISTS TURN PRO

IN THE SUMMER OF 1990, Ontario Premier David Peterson and his Liberals were riding high in the polls. Sensing a recession on the way, he called an election just three years into his mandate, but his best-laid plans were soon sabotaged. Just a few seconds into his opening statement, at the press conference Peterson had called to start his campaign, a man carrying a steel case handcuffed to his wrist jumped out of his seat and bounded to the front of the room. His scraggly beard, his shorts and the glare in his eyes made him look like a terrorist, and he had several people in the room convinced they were about to witness an assassination.

But Gord Perks, a pulp-and-paper campaigner with Greenpeace, had no weapons, and the case contained a tape recorder, not a bomb. He plopped it on the table in front of the premier, and the machine played a message from Greenpeace attacking the government's environmental record. When the tape ended, Perks continued badgering Peterson as television cameramen moved in to catch the premier face to face with the protester. Eventually, Perks stood down, and Peterson, stunned and sweating, finished his press conference. But he was off his game and in no shape to effectively explain his rationale for calling an early election—his intended message, and one that was crucial to the success of the campaign. That night on television and the next morning in the papers, the story was the confrontation between Perks and Peterson.

Incumbents have come to expect a few protesters during re-election campaigns, but after the success of the Greenpeace intervention, other activists and union members piled on, hounding the Liberal leader at every stop. And the media couldn't get enough of the ready-made conflict. Thirty-seven days later, the New Democratic Party became the government in Ontario for the first time. In their 1991 book, *Not Without Cause: David Peterson's Fall from Grace*, Dan Rath and Georgette Gagnon described what Greenpeace did at the opening press conference as the turning point in the election. A decade later, Rath, who'd since become a consultant, also saw it as symbolic of the new-found power of activists. "It was a very graphic embodiment of something that was taking place everywhere in subtle ways," he said. "And Perks nailed it."

For a long time, politicians ignored activists, considering them marginal, unrepresentative of where their votes came from and with very little serious, substantive thinking to offer. To politicians and middle-class voters alike, activists were the lunatic fringe. "The government had no interest in listening to even its most credible of critics," said Rath, "even guys like Norm Rubin of Energy Probe, who was a straightlaced guy in a suit and wasn't averse to dipping into inflammatory language once in a while but still was solid, approachable and more civilized-looking than the hairier breed of activist likely to be on the street in front of Ontario Hydro."

Attitudes toward activists started to change in the mid-1980s. For one thing, governments changed. In Ottawa, the Conservatives won a massive majority after more than two decades of almost uninterrupted Liberal rule, and in Ontario, the electorate booted the provincial Tories out of office after forty-two years.

The new crop of politicians were, initially anyway, less arrogant and more willing to listen to new ideas—even when it came to the budget-making process. Canada had always followed the British tradition of budget secrecy, and that meant if any details got out before the tabling of the budget, the finance minister was duty-bound to resign. From time to time, there were leaks of one kind or another, though ministers rarely stepped down. (So much for duty in politics.)

One of the more bizarre episodes occurred in 1983 when federal finance minister Marc Lalonde playfully showed off a copy of his about-to-be-tabled budget for the assembled media during a photo op. One television cameraman caught enough of it to make out a number. In the ensuing controversy, Lalonde avoided resignation by changing the amount of the expenditure, a bit of finesse that cost the taxpayers $200 million. But that flap, and others like it, further showed how ludicrous it was to create budgets under the cone of silence. Michael Wilson in Ottawa, as well as provincial finance ministers, began opening up the process, and by 1997 Paul Martin called budget secrecy "an archaic notion." The end of the old traditions allowed governments to float budget measures in the press ahead of time; it also meant finance departments could listen not only to business lobbyists but also selected advocacy organizations. In the weeks before the Liberal's pre-budget mini-budget in the fall of 2000, for example, Walter Robinson, federal director of the Canadian Taxpayers Federation, twice met with Martin to press for further tax relief and debt reduction. (In the end, Robinson had to settle for plenty of the former and not so much of the latter.)

As this new consultative approach spread to other ministries, some activists began to think more strategically and work at winning a few small battles instead of gambling with their credibility by trying to get everything they wanted in one fell swoop.

This new approach went hand in hand with the adoption of more professional techniques, and it helped lead the public—and, hence, the politicians—to see activists as increasingly credible. "They were no longer viewed as those shrill little voices whining in the wilderness," said Rath, who worked as a reporter, a political aide and a pollster before starting Ideation, a Toronto consulting firm. He believes many activists started to become calmer, more serious-minded, more focused and more skilful than ever before. "They seemed to be more relevant, more realistic and more understanding of the way that small changes can actually make a difference."

THE RISE IN PROFESSIONALISM among activists extends to everything from fundraising to media training to sophisticated research. Universities now offer courses in activism; Wendy Cukier, president of the Canadian Coalition for Gun Control, for example, now teaches a Web-based course on advocacy at Ryerson University in Toronto. Consulting firms such as Strategic Communications and Manifest Communications now count many activists among their clients. And when Dan Rath decided to hold the second Canadian Campaigns & Elections conference in Vancouver in August 2000, he made close to half of the breakout sessions about issue advocacy because of the growing number of activists attending the conference.

The day after Campaigns & Elections ended, I headed down to the Gastown offices of Strategic Communications. As I waited for founder and president Bob Penner to appear, I noticed a couple of dozen people working the phones. While about 60 percent of the work Stratcom does is fundraising through direct-mail or phone campaigns, it also helps groups with such increasingly popular techniques as polling, focus groups, media training and strategy development. "Some groups, like the Sierra Legal Defence Fund and Greenpeace, are really making use of what's out there," he said, "but most groups are not. So, most of the time, we're persuading them to use the service, not necessarily to choose us over our competitors." Canadian activists still trail their American counterparts in fundraising and other techniques (which usually require fundraising because they're expensive), but by the summer of 2000 the 43-year-old Penner had attracted enough clients to generate $3 million in annual sales and hire 110 employees, 35 of them full-time. As well as helping the NDP and other politicians, charities and unions, Stratcom has worked with dozens of advocacy organizations. Many are well-known groups—the David Suzuki Foundation, Women's Legal Education & Action Fund and Amnesty International, for example— while others are smaller.

Rath followed Penner's move to consulting with particular interest. In the early 1980s, Rath was a Toronto-based reporter for CHCH, a Hamilton television station, and Penner worked for the Toronto Disarmament Network. At the time, Rath viewed Penner and other activists such as Dan McDermott, then with Greenpeace and now with the Sierra Club of Canada, as a ragtag bunch that was shrill and largely ineffective. "They were really voices in the wilderness that were unrealistic and out of step with the mainstream," Rath told me. "They weren't very credible but they sure made good TV—I could stick a mike in their faces and they would make the most outrageous statements in a colourful way. And, bingo, I'd have my story done."

In other words, they gave good quote. So while most of the media, especially the national reporters, treated the rabble-rousers with disdain, Rath was only too happy to take advantage of their entertainment value. Nearly twenty years later, both Penner and Rath offer media training to activists. I joined them for a drink at the Steamworks, a brew-pub near Penner's office, and soon they were chuckling about the good old days over a beer.

"I used to dine out on you guys," Rath laughed.

"No," Penner corrected him. "We used to dine out on you."

Like many of the media's relationships, the one between reporters and activists is both symbiotic and complicated. In the early 1970s, Greenpeace demonstrated how people with no money—but lots of courage and imagination—could generate enough media attention to sell their message. Many reporters never really felt comfortable about elevating activists to star status—in fact, there remains a sneering tone to much of the coverage—but the explosion of media outlets forced even the more reluctant ones to rely on activists for material. When Rath started as a reporter in the late 1970s, he could watch maybe a dozen stations on his television; now his satellite dish brings in 200 channels. Torontonians, for example, can choose from three Canadian around-the-clock news stations—CBC Newsworld, CTV Newsnet and CablePulse24, a local all-news channel—as well as a couple of hours of news and information programming each day from most other broadcasters. In addition, the city has four daily newspapers, as well as all-news and all-talk radio. "There is just a voracious media appetite for content," according to Rath, "and activists provide unlimited content."

The media also crave conflict, and all but the most inept activists can provide that. A small protest march will often be rewarded with a few seconds on the local news, but that doesn't mean it's doing anything to get the protesters' message out to the public. In June 2000, I travelled to Calgary for the protest against the World Petroleum Congress. Despite the blanket media coverage, precious little of it was about the issues. Later that week, a Queen's Park demonstration organized by the Ontario Coalition Against Poverty turned violent. (Like a conflict-craving reporter,

I grumbled about travelling all the way to Calgary looking for some action and it turned out there was a riot a mile from my home.) The next morning, I turned on the TV; Newsworld led with a story about the riot and followed it up with a piece about homelessness in Toronto. Perhaps there's hope for the media after all, I began to think. But by the time I returned home a few days later, all the media coverage was about the violence and city councillor Olivia Chow's forced resignation from the Police Services Board.

The street protesters who've made so much news in the past few years tend to be the media's most suspicious viewers. At the headquarters for the WPC protest in Calgary, for example, reporters from mainstream newspapers and televisions had to wear "Corporate Media" badges and be accompanied by an escort at all times. I was luckier: I got to sport an "Alternative Media" badge and walk around freely.

Among anti-globalization activists, there's considerable debate about what, if any, engagement strategy they should take with the media. One faction wants to operate its own news-gathering service; in Seattle and other protest sites, they've set up their own independent media outlets on the Internet. Garth Mullins, who first came to prominence during the controversy surrounding the APEC Summit protests in Vancouver, supports such alternative media. But while he believes activists should never determine what they do or say based on how their actions will look in the media, he also works with traditional media to help them to communicate to a wider audience. "We can't control what the media does, but we can certainly try to use it to get our messages across. It's such a media-driven society, and in the last few years protests have become a really interesting item for the media, with lots of visuals and things," said Mullins, who admitted he's been both smeared by some reporters and denounced as a "media whore" by some hardliners in the movement. "Someone who is not initiated into the activist world will be sitting at home watching the news and will get your message in between two other stories, and I think that's a great 'in.' Even though we have to get through a serious corporate bottleneck, it's worth trying to shove it through."

Like Mullins, most activists know they need the media. Sometimes it's the only weapon they have. Jim Green, a long-time Vancouver anti-poverty worker, found that out in 1983 when he began fighting on behalf of tenants being evicted to make room for Vancouver's Expo 86. Initially, BCTV said it wouldn't cover the issue until Green could prove people would be evicted. Two days later, the evictions began. Suddenly media reaction changed, and soon it was such a big story that even the American networks came to cover it. "The media was the only tool we had," said Green. "We didn't have a pickup truck to relocate people. We got our photocopier that year, but we certainly didn't have a fax machine. We had no tools except for the media. We had the community and our ability to organize and research and to deal with the media."

But it is getting harder and harder to get the media tool out of the toolbox: while journalists will initially lap up colourful and creative messages, they quickly get jaded. Worse, there's a disturbing shortage of investigative reporting. Too many newspapers have slashed their environmental beats, for example, and education coverage usually amounts to little more than reports of teacher strikes and violence in schools. Aside from less in-depth and well-informed coverage, it also means activists must spend more time helping reporters, many of whom are new to the issues, get up to speed.

Poverty is a perfect example of an overlooked beat. So when Michael Shapcott was the public face of Bread Not Circuses, a Toronto group that played a crucial role in ensuring that city didn't get the 1996 Olympics, he helped create the Real Toronto Tour as a way to show poverty in the city. Originally offered to journalists covering the 1988 Economic Summit, the bus tour visited both the wealthy neighbourhoods and the sections of town that the city's PR machine pretended didn't exist. When the city was bidding for the 1996 Olympics, Shapcott revived the tour as a two-hour walk past the housing projects, hostels and boarded-up rooming houses of Regent Park and Cabbagetown. This came with a running monologue from Shapcott that mixed civic history, social planning theory (including examples of how the design and structure of a housing project—such as the absence of garbage cans—undermine the residents' self-esteem) and stories about police brutality, the evictions of roomers and the deaths of homeless people.

The Real Toronto Tour was not just an attempt to get media coverage, it also educated reporters. However, although an activist may spend an hour briefing a journalist, the only result the public will see may be a ten-second clip in a TV item or one quote in a newspaper piece. What the viewers and readers don't know is that the source helped shape the piece with patient explanations, copies of reports and other background information.

Activists are also growing more careful about how they pitch their message. Save Our Seas and Shores, a coalition fighting oil production in the Gulf of the St. Lawrence and nearby waters, decided to focus its public-information campaign on what people had to lose in financial terms, rather than talking about global climate change. "We saw that as the way to get more grassroots concern," said Irene Novaczek, a PEI scientist and member of the coalition. "When you beat people over the head with big issues, they get overwhelmed and blank out on you."

Meanwhile, the Canadian Taxpayers Federation likes to use many of the creative media tactics that have long been the stock-in-trade of underfunded social and environmental activists who have trouble attracting media attention. Though he's not about to do anything life-threatening, Walter Robinson, the public face of the anti-tax group, says he and his colleagues marvel at Greenpeace's masterful, and often dangerous, tactics. "With all the competing messages out there, you need to differentiate yourself," he said, pointing out that he is up against the National Citizens' Coalition, the Canadian Federation of Independent Business and myriad other groups of various political persuasions. "Whether you have a budget of $10 million or $50,000, you need to deliver—especially in the TV age—a visual to capture attention, sound bites that resonate with people to get on radio and analytical reports for newspapers. It's marketing in a public policy environment."

Such sophisticated targeting may separate the serious activists from the pretenders, but Green warned that people who think colourful quotes and outrageous media events are all they need for success are doomed to failure. "Organizing is not about being a talking head for fifteen seconds on the news," he said. "That's a way to promote what you're doing, but that's not organizing. A lot of people don't get that. It's the stuff the media never sees that makes the difference." He pointed out that if an activist promises five things in his fifteen seconds of air time but those five things never get done, there'll be a major credibility problem for that issue, that activist and that organization. "There's a ton of work that has to be done at a whole different level. Some people do that and some people don't."

AS ACTIVISTS SHED their image as troublesome fanatics, they discovered an even greater challenge. John Willis and David Kraft are both senior consultants with the Toronto office of Penner's Strategic Communications. But in 1990 they were senior people in Greenpeace and they helped plan the dramatic intervention at the David Peterson press conference. At the time, the Liberals seemed unbeatable, so booting Peterson and Jim Bradley, who'd actually been a far more effective environment minister than most, out of office was not what Greenpeace was trying to do. The polls, though, showed that the environment was a huge concern for the people of Ontario, even though none of the three main political parties had any interest in making it an election issue. The Greenpeace organizers figured if they jumped in front of the cameras, they could alter the agenda. And, by that measure, the plan worked like a charm.

But when I sat down with the pair in Willis's cramped office and asked about the famous Greenpeace campaign—which had one newspaper calling the group Ontario's "fourth political party"—I discovered it was a bittersweet memory. They'd come to believe they ultimately failed. "We achieved so much," said Willis, "and yet achieved so little, because afterwards we didn't have the chops to push and push." In a way, they had been too successful too quickly, and then found themselves unprepared to take advantage of their good fortune. Willis, who went on to work for Greenpeace in Amsterdam and Japan, compared the situation to an army that advances so far into enemy territory that it soon finds its supply lines cut off. "Once the NDP won, Greenpeace didn't have a robust political campaign to jam in the policy gains that it had won."

"Absolutely," agreed Kraft, who was campaign director for Greenpeace at the time. "That was the biggest thing I learned. We were totally incapable of carrying the line into the legislature. We could have walked into the new NDP government and said, 'You're in power because of us. Let's get to work.'" Instead, Greenpeace activists sat around and waited, or went to work for the government and soon found themselves buried inside the bureaucracy. When the environmentalists did do something radical, their former allies denounced them. And then the economy tumbled into recession, taking the public's interest in the environment with it. But to Willis, that was further proof that they weren't going about things the right way. "If your issues only go anywhere when the economy is good, then, almost by definition, you aren't taking account of the way society works. There are cycles, and there are going to be recessions," he said. "It illustrated the thinness of the environmental movement when the economy went south in Ontario, and we didn't know what to do."

What disappoints Willis is that he hasn't seen much improvement over the years; activists still aren't good at locking in their gains at the legislative level. And now the jumping-in-front-of-the-camera tactics don't work as well. The media's attitude is "been there, done that," and the political handlers are smarter about keeping their puppets out of the kind of situation David Peterson found himself in. "Stuff used to work and now it doesn't," said Kraft. "We tried when Mulroney was in power, and they just dragged us out of the room. Nobody covered it—nobody, nothing."

And Willis worries that the trend for activists to go after business, instead of government, isn't going to help. A global economy and the proliferation of international agreements mean politicians have a lot less room to manoeuvre, so more and more activists now set their sights on changing business and industry rather than governments—and they've racked up enough victories to whet their appetite for more. The fight against genetically modified foods, for example, is mostly a battle against corporations. Similarly, Greenpeace eased off on its attempts to get B.C.'s government to protect the Great Bear Rainforest, and started trying to convince retailers to stop selling products made with old-growth wood. But Willis believes that even in a climate of corporate globalization, the need for government hasn't disappeared. "The loop has to be closed," he said. "You have to come back to political organizing at some stage."

Although he is the chair of the board of Greenpeace USA, he cited the organization's old-growth forest markets campaign as an example. Despite the success of the campaign—even giants such as Ikea and Home Depot came on board—the B.C. government would not budge. "So the danger in B.C. is the market will be wrecked, the jobs will be lost, the communities will be destroyed, and while the trees will be saved in the short run, eventually we'll cut down all those trees because people will need the income so desperately," said Willis in the fall of 2000. "You need government to step in with transition programs and subsidies and move the thing along to the next stage. As activists, we often focus on just our part of the equation, which is causing pressure, but not enough on taking responsibility for the overall, final outcome, which usually has to include action by government."

Six months later, in April 2001, the B.C. government announced a deal between environmentalists, native groups, logging companies and the province to protect a big chunk of coastal rainforest. So I gave Willis a chance to take back his words. Instead, he e-mailed me this response: "Yesterday's announcement simply confirms my point that some kind of social consensus ultimately has to underpin the campaign victories of activists. And governments—love 'em or hate 'em—are the most important mechanism for achieving that."

This, said Willis, is especially true when it comes to global trade agreements. Through street protests and other methods, activists have enough power now that they must figure out what the "end game" should look like. "What deal are we trying to cut? Who has to be inside the tent? What role can we expect from government? What role can *we* hope for? What would a 'good' trade regime look like? It's not for moral reasons that we have to do this, it's for political ones," he said. "As we get closer to winning, society at large has a right to ask, 'So how come we should go along with you?' Activists have to be able to honestly make the case for how different interests within our society can be accommodated. That's government's job, but activists cannot ignore it if they hope to win."

Willis's take represents just the type of good political judgment that too few activists have shown, according to Lorraine Fry. Now the general manager for the Non-Smokers' Rights Association, Fry first became active during a twenty-five-year battle to save the homes on Toronto Island. When the leases expired on the land, the city's old Metro government wanted to get rid of the homes and the people who lived in them. After an extended series of legal battles, the Islanders won the right to own their homes and hold ninety-nine-year leases on their lots. Fry has also worked as a political aide—first at the municipal level and then as chief of staff to two ministers in Ontario's NDP government, from 1990 to 1995. When she was on the government side, she saw many advocates win over a minister, but then fail to get what they were seeking because they didn't help sell their positions to the bureaucrats and other ministers. "One of the things I tell activists, and they don't believe me, is that really only 40 percent of the solution is on the outside," she said. "The toughest activism is on the inside. It's one thing to get the government to say yes to legislation; getting the damn thing actually passed is a huge, much tougher fight."

When Bob Rae's NDP government introduced new employment-equity rules, it was the most progressive such legislation in North America, if not the world. But it wasn't enough for the Alliance for Employment Equity. (This provincial group wants to see the workplace become more representative of the community through the hiring of more racial minorities, aboriginals, people with disabilities and women.) The activists attacked the government because they didn't get everything they wanted. "They dumped on us at the press conference because they only got 90 percent instead of 100 percent," she said. "Dumped all over us." The incident was typical of what she calls the shoot-yourself-in-the-foot tactics that she witnessed far too often. "It's particularly common with left-of-centre activists," she said, "because, quite frankly, I think they're even less clued in to how government works."

WHEN GARFIELD MAHOOD and Rosalee Berlin started the Non-Smokers' Rights Association in 1974, Mahood insisted on professionalism. The group could be run from Berlin's house, but it couldn't look like a kitchen-table organization. So despite a shoestring budget, he made sure all correspondence was type-written and on letterhead. That seems obvious today, but it wasn't back then.

When Bob Penner was in the peace movement and organizing a lot of demonstrations for the Toronto Disarmament Network almost two decades ago, professionalism was far from common in the activist community. Penner usually had a tiny budget to organize protests, but as he started to think more strategically, he realized they needed a lot more money to be successful. So in 1983, while planning a Toronto demo and coordinating organizers in other Canadian cities as part of an international day of protest against Cruise and Pershing missiles, he proposed a $50,000 budget. "People just freaked out," he remembered. "They said, 'We've been doing these for years and have spent a few hundred dollars, maybe a thousand. Where are we going to get all this money?' It was a big controversy, but it typified the difference between where I—and other people—wanted to go and where the peace movement had been before."

In the end, Penner and his supporters won the day: they raised and borrowed $45,000, and the Toronto protest was a huge success, attracting 25,000 people. The experience confirmed his instincts about the need for more professionalism in activism. "I was interested in developing a stronger, more effective, more sophisticated movement," said Penner, who worked for the Canadian Peace Alliance and then Greenpeace after leaving the Toronto Disarmament Network. "That's what I was doing within those groups, and I saw the need to do it in other groups as well." And so, in 1991, Penner started Strategic Communications. Even he wondered if there would be enough work beyond fundraising, which other companies were already doing. But, in many ways, the timing couldn't have been better, because the 1990s were a difficult decade for many activists.

On the one hand, cheap, new technology made life easier. Computers, laser printers, fax machines, cellphones and slick Web sites allowed even the smallest organizations to project a professional sheen. More than any other technology, though, the Internet changed the way activists operate. Organizations can send press releases, alert other groups and keep supporters better informed, all while saving money on stamps. "The Internet is revolutionizing activism," said Craig Jones. Now the president of the B.C. Civil Liberties Association, he first made a name for himself in 1997, when he was a law student protesting the government's attack on free speech during the APEC Summit in Vancouver.

"Traditionally, activists had to go with word-of-mouth or posters or whatever to communicate with their own supporters, so just getting your ducks in a row was 70 percent of your effort. And you only had 30 percent left to project your message outside. Now, with the Internet, you can have listservs, notification chains and all kinds of things. In the aftermath of APEC, we were able to communicate very effectively amongst ourselves and with the media. We could let a select two hundred people know of a piece of news or ask them a question, and within minutes, or hours at the most, get an answer back. So that becomes 10 percent of your time, and 90 percent of your focus can be outside. Look at what happened with the WTO in Seattle: I think that would have been impossible before e-mail and the Internet."

For months, activists from all over the continent used the Internet to organize the Battle in Seattle. Sarah Kerr, a Calgary anti-poverty advocate, heard about the planned protests a few days before the WTO meetings and decided she wanted to go. She got on the Internet, and within an hour she had maps of march routes, schedules for workshops and seminars and information on the different organizations involved. And after sending a few e-mails, she had three offers of places to stay.

Meanwhile, John Fisher, executive director of the Ottawa-based Equality for Gays and Lesbians Everywhere, said the Internet is invaluable, especially since the gay community is so far-flung. If people in one city have created homophobia workshops for schools, for example, they can share the information with a group in another area, reducing the need to reinvent the wheel. The Canadian Taxpayers Federation's Walter Robinson likes the way the Internet helps keep an issue alive, and his group now tries to integrate the Web into campaigns such as Gas Tax Honesty Day. And during the 2000 federal election, the David Suzuki Foundation created a Web site called *clickforcleanair.org* that sent faxes to the prime minister.

While technology made things easier for activists, external forces were making things tougher. Just as advocacy organizations were gaining some much-needed credibility, the sand began to shift under their feet. Some groups had enjoyed government funding, but a new era of fiscal restraint meant an end to that. And when the political consensus shifted to the right, it left many groups—even those groups that didn't look to government for handouts—dazed and confused.

"For over twenty or thirty years, people have pounded away at the doors of power and made some progress—you can now sit down with a minister in a way that was reserved strictly for the wealthiest, most powerful business people," said Stratcom's Willis. "Now, because we have citizen politics on a much more organized footing, it is possible to do that." But he worried that as governments try to do less and less, corporations wield more and more power, and as international trade agreements handcuff politicians, activists may be gaining access to an increasingly impotent system."

It's not going to get easier for activists, especially on the left. While most politicians now accept that they will, from time to time, consult with advocacy groups—and use them to help sell their messages when it suits their purposes—governments still like control. And even activists who are allies are too unpredictable for politicians to really feel comfortable. Despite court challenges, the federal government keeps re-introducing gag laws designed to prevent anyone (other than registered parties or candidates) from spending more than $3,000 per riding or $150,000 nationally during an election campaign. And Revenue Canada's rules on charitable status can seem arbitrary and unfair when some groups get the right to give tax receipts and others don't. Worse, Willis feared, government no longer reacts to public opinion the way it once did. Ten or twenty years ago, the issues and the politicians were close enough together that activists could make government feel the heat of public opinion directly.

"We practically beat the crap out of David Peterson during that election campaign by just making environmental issues higher-profile," said Willis. "These days you watch [federal environment minister] David Anderson traipse across the country saying, 'I don't care what you have to say. I know you're all professional activists, I know you all disagree with each other and I know that I have more money to spend on advertising, so I'll do what I want with endangered species.' Which is what he's done and why we have a bad piece of legislation. The problem for activists is there is so little real experience with how politics works, and I think it's a bad situation now because government just walks away from the table."

And that's made it essential for advocacy organizations to mobilize their supporters, something many of them are not good at. Back when Willis and Kraft worked for Greenpeace, for example, they didn't do anything to reach out to their members or to organize their supporters, aside from publishing a newsletter. "Basically we saw the news media as a route to our membership," said Willis, "and I don't think that's satisfactory any more." Successful Canadian activists are now learning from the Americans about professional organizing. As a consultant, Willis has used direct mail and telemarketing to help groups take advantage of their supporters. Fundraising is a big part of it, of course, but good campaigns go further. "You can just ask people to give you money and they will give it to you," said Willis, "but they'll give you a lot more money and a lot more clout if you design activities for the average member that are easy to do and have some demonstrable impact."

Strategic Communications has used call-linking technology to help the Council of Canadians on issues such as water exports and bank mergers. It works this way: a Stratcom staffer calls a council member who has, for example, donated money to fight water exports, and then links the supporter to the office of a cabinet minister—but not before suggesting what needs to be said to the politician. "Building your organization is about building the relationship you have with the people that support you," said Kraft. "It's about understanding who you are and then telling the people most likely to care who you are, what you'll give them and what you need from them. And I think we can help them a great deal with that, but it's a tough slog, because you can't decide when movements are going to happen, they just happen. In that sense, organizations are professionalizing because they have to."

For some groups, a more-professional approach has made all the difference. Penner points to the Council of Canadians as a client that transformed itself. When Stratcom started working with the council in 1993, the organization had 12,000 members and raised about $200,000 a year; by 2000 it had 100,000 members and brought in well over $2 million annually. "We raise lots of money," added Penner, "but we also get lots of petitions signed." More important than the swelling coffers has been the change in the group's reputation. Penner sat in on a strategy meeting in 1993 and heard some of the senior people floating the idea of winding up the organization. After all, they argued, they didn't have much money, nor did they have many victories to their credit.

The council did have a couple of things going for it, though. Maude Barlow, the national volunteer chairperson, was an effective speaker and public face for the group, and Peter Bleyer was a strong executive director. And the organization really started to grow through the 1990s. "It is a good example of how activist work does take time," said Penner. "They were really considered losers for a long time, even by a lot of people within the council. Their big thing was stopping free trade, and they didn't do it. And then it was stopping NAFTA, and they didn't do that. They didn't have many victories, but they just kept working at it." While Stratcom helped the organization raise money and build its membership, public opinion also caught up. And then the council started notching victories: it helped block the bank mergers, forced the government to backpedal on its changes to pensions and played a leading role in the 1998 defeat of the Multilateral Agreement on Investment. "Now," said Penner, "the reputation of the council is exactly the opposite—it's seen as a really effective group that can make things happen."

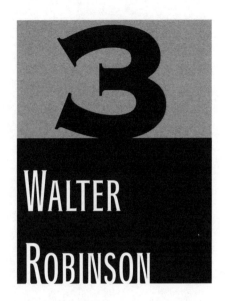

WALTER ROBINSON

AND THE RISE OF CONSERVATIVE ACTIVISM

WALTER ROBINSON walked into his office grumbling about the traffic. "Come on, people, it's just rain," he implored his fellow Ottawa commuters. "Leave a little more space to stop and keep driving." But not even his late arrival and the miserable weather could dampen his spirit—or his energy. Robinson was, as usual, pumped. He laughed and cracked a joke about running for the Liberals as he showed colleague Bruce Winchester a copy of his local MP's mailing to constituents. It featured Robinson's praise for the 2000 federal budget. Then he mockingly boasted about his "strategic decision" to hold his Gas Tax Honesty Day press conference inside.

With his goofy, clean-cut sense of humour, Robinson seems like nothing so much as a grown-up version of Opie Taylor, Ron Howard's character from *The Andy Griffith Show*, the old chestnut from the days of black-and-white television. But Canada's top tax fighter has a passion and an intensity that would have gotten Opie thrown out of Mayberry. However, it's working in Ottawa, and in May 2000 Robinson was on a roll. The federal director of the Canadian Taxpayers Federation was claiming victory for three of his pet projects in six months: the Ontario government's introduction of balanced-budget legislation, federal Industry Minister John Manley's flip-flop on subsidies to pro hockey teams and Finance Minister Paul Martin's decision to end the bracket creep in the tax system.

In early May, Robinson's report on the Atlantic Canada Opportunities Agency—which showed that most of the financial assistance doled out in the last ten years went to big business, big labour and big governments—generated plenty of media coverage and embarrassment for the Liberals during question period. But on the Thursday before the first long weekend of summer, he had something else up his sleeve. And even though his attempts to put on a little outdoor razzle-dazzle for the media fell apart, the rain, fog and cool temperatures made him look good once again. The CTF's campaign to lower federal and provincial taxes on gasoline got off to a rocky start the year before, but Robinson and his colleagues were sure they had a winner on their hands. So they were determined to do it right this time— and given that the price at the pumps had gone up 20 cents in the past year, the timing couldn't have been better.

Victor Vrsnik, the CTF's Manitoba director, first suggested Gas Tax Honesty Day to his colleagues during a meeting in the fall of 1998. Robinson and the provincial directors hashed out the idea, did research for a report and finally decided to launch the campaign in Manitoba, Alberta and Ontario. The media response was strong in Manitoba, fair in Alberta and poor in Ontario. "It was a disaster," Robinson admitted matter-of-factly. Hoping to generate national coverage, he'd arranged a media event at a Pioneer station in Burlington, near Hamilton. On a beautiful, warm Thursday in May 1999, he filled up his Dodge Caravan and calculated how much he had to pay in taxes. As part of the show, the gas station posted the pre-tax price of 26.0 cents. Needless to say, excited motorists pulled in to the station in droves.

Although he'd managed to snarl traffic at a major intersection, Robinson had overplayed his hand. It didn't help that a provincial election was underway, but the CTF wasn't a known media commodity in the Golden Horseshoe, and Robinson didn't have the personal relationship with reporters that he enjoyed in Ottawa.

The turnout wasn't that bad—two television crews, a couple of radio reporters, a pair of photographers and four or five newspaper journalists showed up—but Robinson had hoped for better play and a more positive spin. In particular, he wasn't happy with suggestions that he was a pawn of Big Oil. Part of the problem with the gas-tax campaign, he knew, was that it challenged conventional wisdom. Canadians do rant and rave about high gas prices, but either they tend to blame greedy oil companies or they aren't sure where to direct their anger—at Big Oil, OPEC or government. "Gas taxes are an issue," he said, "and people get upset about them, but it's kind of like the weather—they feel they're powerless on this file." Robinson knows a campaign has a greater chance of success if there's one identifiable demon, just as there was with the hockey subsidies or when the cable companies enraged customers with negative-option billing. On this campaign, he wanted that villain to be the taxman.

While the first Gas Tax Honesty Day had been a disappointment, Robinson learned a lot. More importantly, he was taking a long-term view. A big believer in annual campaigns that give an organization authority, he cites Tax Freedom Day from the Fraser Institute, a Vancouver-based, right-wing think-tank, and the Alternative Budget from the Canadian Centre for Policy Alternatives, an Ottawa-based, left-wing think-tank, as successful role models for regular CTF offerings. These include its reports on corporate welfare; the Teddies, the group's tongue-in-cheek awards for government waste; and Gas Tax Honesty Day.

The CTF directors hold a one-and-a-half- to two-hour conference call the first Wednesday of each month, as well as regular and occasionally vicious e-mail debates on policy. When they did a post-mortem after the first gas-tax protest, they all committed to doing it again. The next year, they decided they should prepare a better research report with more data to accompany the press conference, take advantage of the organization's Web site and work at countering the perception that they were doing Big Oil's dirty work. Initially, the group wanted to hold six or seven press conferences at gas stations across the country, but the oil companies didn't want to be seen to be rocking the boat. (They wouldn't even give the CTF an old pump to use as a prop for a press conference on the lawn in front of the Parliament building.) As it happened, the bad weather turned that setback into Robinson's "strategic decision" to hold his press conference inside. The regional directors would back it up with local radio interviews.

On the morning of the press conference, Robinson sat at his desk with a phone headset on and did a series of radio interviews. Gas Tax Honesty Day is an ideal campaign for generating radio coverage, because people listen to the radio in their cars and that's when they're thinking about gas prices. (By contrast, the CTF's reports on corporate welfare—necessarily dense, number-laden documents—make good newspaper copy, and the Teddies—when Robinson puts on a tuxedo and has a Vanna White–like model help him award little golden sow statues—are perfect eye-candy for television.) The fax machine beside Robinson's desk churned out petitions from angry taxpayers. "Our fax machine has been going for three days straight," he told Roy Green from Hamilton's CHML enthusiastically. "I've never seen a response to a campaign like this."

At a little after 10:00, Robinson and Winchester left for the Hill. Robinson wore grey flannels and a blue jacket over a green polo shirt. In the elevator, he admitted he didn't have time to do any ironing, but he hoped the golf shirt would look right for the long weekend and give him more of an average-guy appearance. Once in the press theatre, he joshed with a cameraman wearing shorts. The press conference was routine fare: for visuals, Robinson held up a copy of the report (entitled "Canada's Gas Taxes =

Highway Robbery") and a bumper sticker ("Cut Gas Taxes Now!"). But he got his message out—and during the Q&A session, he insisted, "I'm no fan of Big Oil." He also reminded the reporters about the CTF's victories on bracket creep and hockey subsidies.

As he and Winchester walked back to the office, Robinson was clearly happy. The press conference, he was sure, went well, and his morning nervousness had given way to a quiet elation. He even allowed himself to think about the possibility of taking a week off—a holiday when he could actually turn his cellphone off. That would be a change for a guy who banks holiday time and regularly checks in with the office when he does take a vacation. "It's not a job for me," he said. "It's a passion."

And that didn't sound like a line.

SEVERAL YEARS AGO, a tall, attractive woman asked me to dance at a party. Although I was pleasantly surprised, I declined. "No, thanks," I said, "I can't stand Madonna."

"Oh? Why not?"

"She's the triumph of marketing over music."

"Are you a socialist?" she asked, a bit wide-eyed.

I am, in fact, a capitalist, though judging by my annual income not a terribly good one. Yet, in our conformist society, anyone who questions the way things are must be a deluded lefty. One friend of mine, the owner of a small business, dismisses all activists simply as "freaks." But Walter Robinson is neither a lefty nor a freak. Rather, he represents a growing trend by conservatives to push their agendas by adopting—sometimes with great gusto—techniques long associated with the left. And few do it better. Soon after he opened the Ottawa office in 1997, the CTF became Canada's leading conservative advocacy group. "In 1992, we were kooky right-wingers for pushing for balanced budgets," said Troy Lanigan, the CTF's Regina-based national communications director. "But the organization has become a player and not just a voice in the wilderness. Walter has really topped that off."

Traditionally, we've viewed activists as people not just outside the political process, but also beyond the political mainstream. That has so often meant just people on the left that, even today, some activists don't like the term because they think it carries too much ideological baggage. Although more activist groups do hail from the left end of the political spectrum, there's no shortage of conservatives. Regardless of their bent, all activists are out to do the same thing: change the system from the outside. And if there is a difference between activists on the left and those on the right, it may be in their trust of traditional politics. Those on the left are more likely to say they have no interest in elected office. There are plenty of exceptions, of course: many activists have carried the NDP or Liberal banner in elections. But few have risen to prominent cabinet positions, although Gerard Kennedy went from operating food banks, first in Edmonton and then in Toronto, to nearly winning the leadership of the Ontario Liberals.

Conservative activists, on the other hand, tend to have less antipathy for electoral politics. Priscilla de Villiers, the founder of CAVEAT, a victims' rights group, ran unsuccessfully for the Ontario Conservatives in a 2000 by-election; and in the last federal election, Peter Stock of the Canada Family Action Coalition stood for the Alliance, just as Joe Wamback, another victims' rights advocate, and Rose Dyson of Canadians Concerned About Violence in Entertainment ran for the Tories. More successful examples include Chuck Cadman, a victims' rights advocate who is now an Alliance MP, and Jason Kenney, the young Canadian Alliance finance critic who was president of the CTF before he won a seat in Parliament.

Whether the leaders see it as a stepping stone to traditional politics or not, many single-issue groups with a right-wing perspective are now pushing their point of view. Social conservatism, for example, has spawned organizations such as the Campaign Life Coalition, an anti-abortion group; and the Canada Family Action Coalition, which champions its version of traditional values. And conservatives are involved in many other issues, including gun control, victims' rights, education reform and even, in some cases, unlikely causes such as the environment. For many years, though, the National Citizens' Coalition, with a mantra of "more freedom through less government," was the leading conservative advocacy group.

In 1967, Colin M. Brown, a London, Ontario, insurance man, placed a full-page, anti-medicare ad in the *Globe and Mail*. The response was so positive that he eventually created the NCC to fight for free markets, individual freedom and responsibility, limited government and a strong defence. By the 1980s, the group had hit its stride, lobbying for the inclusion of property-rights protection in the Charter of Rights and Freedoms, attacking the National Energy Program and going to court to overturn legislation outlawing advertising by third parties during elections. But some of the group's positions were bigoted (NCC favoured an all-white immigration policy) or overly hawkish (it wanted the Canadian government to get involved in Ronald Reagan's Star Wars project). After Brown died in 1987, David Somerville took over as president. He maintained a high profile in campaigns on a variety of issues, including several that are also on Robinson's hit list: taxes, MPs' pensions and government spending. And the NCC continued to delight in brash ads aimed at individual politicians such as Ed Broadbent and Sheila Copps. (While Robinson relishes any opportunity to anoint politicians with mocking monikers, he has always avoided personal attacks. "It's not the style of the organization," he said, "and it's never been my personal style.")

Stephen Harper, a one-time Reform MP, became NCC president at the beginning of 1998. Some political observers tout Harper as the ideal leader for the Alliance; he's a westerner who appeals to central Canadians because he's thoughtful and well spoken and without the stigma of fundamentalism that dogs Stockwell Day. Under Harper, the NCC has 45,000 supporters and continues its work on primarily western issues such as abolition of the Canadian Wheat Board. Early in 2001, Harper and five other prominent conservative thinkers, including CTF chairman Andrew Crooks, called for Alberta to create an economic firewall around itself and reduce ties with the feds by collecting its own taxes, withdrawing from the Canada Pension Plan and creating its own provincial police force.

The NCC's increasing western preoccupation, which actually started when David Somerville moved from Toronto to Calgary, has left the group less visible in national debates—except when it comes to Canada's gag law, legislation limiting the amount third parties can spend during elections to $150,000, or not more than $3,000 in a single riding. Early in the 2000 federal election, a Calgary court ruled the law unconstitutional and several activist groups, from pro-gun groups to environmentalists, began preparing advertising campaigns. But before the election was over, the Supreme Court of Canada overturned the decision.

Despite its leadership in the gag-law debate, the NCC lost media time to the CTF, because Harper doesn't share Robinson's taste for colourful and creative tactics; instead, he continues to rely on targeted advertising and direct-mail campaigns. And unlike Somerville, Harper is more a pundit—albeit a good one—than an activist. So the NCC lost both influence and visibility at the national level, leaving Robinson to happily scoop them up for the CTF.

WHEN I FIRST HEARD about the Canadian Taxpayers Federation, I assumed it must be a bunch of old curmudgeons, or a front for what was then the Reform Party. Neither turned out to be true. First of all, Robinson was a fiscal conservative and a liberal on social issues such as abortion and gay rights. (Oddly, all of the CTF's spokesmen graduated from high school in 1985. If the Canadian Alliance, the Fraser Institute and the editorial board of the *National Post* are anything to go by, conservatives have done a great job of finding, nurturing and promoting fresh talent. The left, on the other hand, has not, and that's one reason why the young people marching against globalization in the streets of Seattle and Quebec City have little or no interest in the NDP.)

Second, although even Robinson thought the CTF was in Reform's hip pocket before a headhunter called him about the position, nobody pulls the CTF's strings. True, many of the group's supporters are also Alliance supporters, but board members and staffers may not be members of political parties. In fact, many joined the group after disillusioning experiences in politics and government. And while the CTF is not much loved by the Liberals, or tax-and-spend liberals of any stripe, it also angers people on the right. Back in 1995, when Kenney was in charge, the group stuck more than two hundred pink pigs in the lawns of Parliament Hill to embarrass then-Reform MPs for refusing to opt out of the parliamentary pension plan and not insisting on a recorded vote on a pay increase for themselves. In 1998, the CTF hammered MPs who wouldn't answer its survey about whether they intended to opt back into the generous pension plan. Some Reformers weren't happy about that: Jim Hart denounced the group as "Brownshirts," and Randy White, the party's House Leader at the time, crabbed, "It's unfortunate the federation is so narrow-minded."

More recently, when Alliance MP Deborah Grey bought back into the pension plan early in 2001, Robinson declared she'd been

"Ottawashed," and suggested she had come to change the system and ended up being changed by it. Given that the pensions of parliamentarians account for just $23 million of the government's annual expenditures of $175 billion, Robinson realizes the issue is a lot more symbolic than expensive. But he also knows it's a winner. "When we slam the Alliance, or question its integrity on an issue, some of our supporters say, 'Lay off,'" said Robinson. "Not on this file. We haven't had one single call to any of our offices." Meanwhile, the Ontario Liberals quoted the CTF in television ads during the 1999 provincial election. And when he was premier of Saskatchewan, Grant Devine called the CTF the research arm of the NDP. "I used to get invited to a lot more cocktail parties," Robinson told an *Ottawa Citizen* reporter in 1999. "Those have dried right up. I take that as a sign of effectiveness."

Created in 1990, the CTF had its roots in two western anti-tax groups: the Saskatchewan Taxpayers Federation and the Alberta-based Resolution One. By 2001, it had 83,000 supporters, mostly individuals and small businesses, and a budget of $3.2 million, though half of that is earmarked for fundraising. As a western grassroots group, the CTF agonized over the decision to open an office in Ottawa. Given that he was born and raised in Toronto, then went to Ottawa for university and never left, Robinson might have been an unlikely choice as the first federal director. But he impressed the hiring committee by bringing up the concern first. Once he got the job, he quickly earned the respect of his colleagues with his commitment to the issues and his understanding of western concerns. "I grew up in Toronto and moved to Ottawa," he jokingly told them, "so I know everything."

Robinson soon became the federal face of the CTF, galling the provincial spokesmen more than once by getting the bulk of the coverage, even when they'd held simultaneous press conferences. Robinson attributes his success to being in Ottawa. "You could have put Bozo the Clown here and got more media," he said. But Bozo would not have been as eager for the attention. When Paul Martin brought down his 1998 budget, Robinson sent out a press release telling reporters they could find him by looking for the guy with the ball cap that read, "Tax me, I'm Canadian." He didn't need the hat the next year, because he'd already developed a cozy relationship with many members of the media; they soon realized they could always count on him for a good quote. "The Fraser Institute is a think-tank," said Robinson, in an example of true words spoken in jest. "We're an ink-tank." When a TV reporter wanted to interview him about an expensive tunnel being built between the House of Commons and East Block, Robinson showed up at Parliament Hill in a winter coat. Even though it was a hot summer day, he pretended to shiver. "It's c-c-cold out here," he mugged for the camera. "We need a t-t-tunnel."

While Robinson has a knack for getting attention, he isn't the only person at the CTF with one. British Columbia director Mark Milke, for example, came up with the idea for the Teddies. Named for a senior civil servant who lost his job for expense-account abuse, the Ted Weatherill Awards recognize egregious government waste and taxation. In 1999, the inaugural year, the lifetime achievement award went to former Finance Minister Michael Wilson for de-indexing the income tax system. That choice was part of the CTF's campaign to put an end to bracket creep. Like Gas Tax Honesty Day and the pink pig stunt, the Teddy Awards represent standard operating procedure for the CTF.

But even some of Robinson's friends admit it can be a risky game. Jim Facette, of the Canadian Construction Association, has known Robinson for over a decade, since they both worked for the federal Progressive Conservative Party. Both want the government to dedicate gas taxes to maintaining Canada's highways, which need $17.4 billion worth of improvements. But he admits there's concern within his organization about working with the CTF. "We exchange information with them," he said. "But we don't publicly go out arm in arm with them." That's the price of not being afraid to rub people the wrong way.

Claude Bennett, a prominent Ontario cabinet minister during the Bill Davis era and one of Robinson's mentors, sees a more serious downside to the CTF's approach. "If you pull a prank once or twice, that might be okay, but there comes a time when people wonder if you are serious. Look at the Conference Board of Canada, which I take to be an icon in the world of politics, I don't recall it pulling screwball stuff," he said. "You want to be very careful you don't lose your credibility over some move that people think is childish."

Robinson counters that the credibility is in the numbers. And there is usually substance, and a good deal of research, behind CTF campaigns. Although he launched his battle against government loans and grants to industry with a press release that had a typically cheeky headline—"Welfare Bums Wear Armani Suits"—it was no cheap stunt. When he met with the CTF hiring committee in the spring of 1997, he had already prepared "Robinson: 100 Days of Action," an outline of what he intended to do if he got the job. It included nuts and bolts—establishing an office and building relationships with members of the press gallery, for example—and a couple of issues he wanted to tackle. One was corporate welfare.

Although then NDP leader David Lewis coined the term in 1972, Robinson delighted in the opportunity to resurrect it. He had been particularly disturbed by the shift in terminology from "loans and grants" to "investment." After he joined the CTF in the summer of 1997, it took six months to get the data he needed through the access-to-information process. In late January the next year, a computer disk arrived at his office. It contained 32,697 items on a spreadsheet: company names, amounts, dates and so on. Over the next three months, he scoured and massaged the data to build a damning case against Industry Canada.

Released in April 1998, the CTF's 141-page study, *Corporate Welfare: A Report on Sixteen Years of Industry Canada Financial Assistance*, indicted the government department for doling out $11 billion in grants, loans, loan guarantees and conditionally repayable loans. (The last, which are only repaid if certain royalty or sales targets are met, accounted for $3.2 billion of the government largesse. By the time of Robinson's study, however, Industry Canada had seen only 15 percent come back to its coffers.) Half the money went to seventy-five companies, many of them household names such as General Motors of Canada, Domtar and accounting giant KPMG. The Canadian aerospace industry is particularly fond of government generosity; Pratt and Whitney, for example, sucked up various "investments" worth nearly $1 billion.

The numbers earned the CTF plenty of news coverage, except, notably, on the CBC. As the first big project of his tenure as federal director, the campaign helped Robinson define himself to his colleagues, the media and CTF supporters. Unfortunately, the Hepatitis C scandal broke at the same time, so corporate welfare did not become a defining issue with the public. Still, the editorials and the letters to the editor—both for and against—were heartening. "That's when you know you're framing the debate," he said.

If that meant angering people in high places, well, that was just another part of the job. "A lot of innovation policy is, frankly, more complex than he portrays it," said John Banigan, assistant deputy minister at Industry Canada, noting that capital is mobile, and the government had to keep an eye on what other countries do. In addition, he argued, the effectiveness of a program shouldn't be measured solely on repayment but on the broader benefits to the economy, such as advances in technology. "I find his point of view is often not very worldly and not very knowledgeable about how high-tech businesses work today," said Banigan. "Just focusing on repayment is a very simplistic approach to things."

Bureaucrats are one thing, but the CTF also alienated members of Corporate Canada. "We are totally against subsidies and handouts," insisted Peter R. Smith, president and CEO of the Ottawa-based Aerospace Industries Association of Canada. "We're not looking for handouts, but he keeps referring to the Technology Partnerships Canada program and the Defence Industry Productivity Program as outright subsidies, which is not the case at all." Smith also complained that Robinson used a distorted, two-year-old snapshot of repayment rates, without admitting the loans will continue to be repaid over the next twenty years or longer.

Meanwhile, the CTF lost a potential partner in the tax battle. "It's ironic that we're on the same wavelength about the high tax rates," said Smith. "But we don't agree that the reason taxes are so high is because government is providing assistance to business."

A few lost allies don't bother Robinson. He knows his actions may limit future coalitions, but if he worried about that, he wouldn't be effective. And the corporate welfare campaign did have the desired effect: in the 1999 federal budget, Industry Canada got just half the $100 million it was seeking for Technology Partnerships Canada. "That's $50 million too much," said Robinson, who plans to make his attacks on corporate welfare an annual treat for the government, as long as he can get the necessary data through the access-to-information process. "But we think the visibility we brought to the issue was partly responsible for Minister Manley losing that battle." Manley, who has since left Industry for Foreign Affairs, was also a CTF victim in January 2000. Three days after offering to give up to $20 million to the National Hockey League's six Canadian franchises—and one day after the CTF announced its Great Canadian Puck-Off, which would have seen the prime minister's office deluged with pucks—Manley cancelled the bailout.

A bigger victory, though, came later the next month, when Finance Minister Paul Martin put an end to bracket creep with his 2000 budget. Until 1986, the tax system didn't penalize Canadians who received raises to keep up with inflation. But after the Conservatives partially de-indexed the system, such raises meant taxpayers would creep into a higher tax bracket without ever really making any more money. The Tories had created a silent annual tax increase, one that netted the government $90 billion over fourteen years. While the CTF wasn't the only organization fighting bracket creep—the measure certainly wasn't popular with the left either—the anti-tax group was the most aggressive. And its campaign turned out to be a textbook example of Robinson's three-pronged strategy for activists: adopt the issue, frame the debate, drive the agenda.

In 1997, the CTF adopted the issue. Since income de-indexation is a complicated concept, and Canadians could hardly be expected to respond emotionally, the group started popularizing the term "bracket creep" by using it as much as possible when dealing with the media and speaking in front of legislative committees. That done, the CTF directors framed the debate. Instead of just mentioning bracket creep, they devoted op-ed pieces, speeches and interviews to the subject. And they tried to push buttons by using words like "silent," "hidden" and "taxation without representation." When the finance department failed to wipe out the measure in the 1999 budget, the CTF began to drive the agenda by increasing their media appearances and upping the pressure.

By the time Martin killed bracket creep, Robinson and his colleagues had done over seven hundred media interviews on the subject, written seventy-six "Let's Talk Taxes" commentaries, issued forty-eight press releases, seen twenty-three of their op-ed pieces published, made twelve legislative submissions, compiled two reports and held one news conference. When it was all over, communications director Lanigan called the campaign "the most significant public policy victory for the CTF in its ten-year history."

THE ENDURING IMAGE I have of the first day I spent with Walter Robinson is trying to keep up with him as he rushed to make it to Ottawa radio station CFRA. His friends and colleagues had warned me about the pace he set. Ken Azzopardi, the CTF's Regina-based chief operating officer, for example, told me about sharing a hotel room with Robinson only to see the guy working on his laptop until 2:30 in the morning, then up again doing jumping jacks at 6:30. But what I'd witnessed of Robinson seemed more hyper-normal than hyperactive.

By mid-afternoon on an unseasonably cool mid-June day, though, he was running late. Suddenly, Robinson seemed to switch into another gear in order to make a 3:00 appearance on CFRA's "Franklin and Co.," a local drive-home show. Fortunately, by the time he reached his van, I hadn't fallen too far behind, and he didn't take off without me. As we sped along Highway 417, Robinson told me that host Geoff Franklin wasn't afraid to challenge guests, so I expected some sparks. Instead, I saw a one-hour, unpaid infomercial. Franklin decided against opening the phone lines in favour of lobbing questions—on topics Robinson had suggested to him in an e-mail. He let his guest sell his messages about tax rates, the brain drain and the gag law, and after the show, the tax fighter taped a promo spot for the radio station.

Talk radio is the perfect vehicle for Robinson. Yes, the hosts and most of the listeners are usually sympathetic to his politics, but more importantly, he's always loved to talk about policy. "He was a very unusual commerce student," said Ian Lee, a professor at Carleton University's School of Business and a mentor to Robinson. "There were lots of Alex Keatons in the program, people who just wanted to get a job, but Walter had a very acute interest in policy issues such as free trade and taxation." That interest, combined with a quick and analytical mind, made him an ideal CTF spokesman because of his ability to take advantage of like-minded radio hosts and hold his own in hostile debates. Opponents regularly portrayed the CTF as narrow-minded, short-sighted and unable to get past black-and-white thinking. "In arriving at our policy decisions," he countered, "we've sifted through the shades of grey."

Robinson is too thoughtful to be dismissed as just another knee-jerk conservative, and he has too much respect for people with opposing views, especially the smart ones; he loved debating left-wing author Linda McQuaig on television, for example. And he is more than willing to work with people on the left on issues such as electoral reform. After a failed attempt to start a coalition with Duff Conacher, the coordinator of the citizen-watchdog group Democracy Watch, Robinson teamed up with Judy Rebick, the former head of the National Action Committee on the Status of Women. (Rebick described Bob Rae's term as NDP premier of Ontario as "pallid centre-right politics with a shrug" in her book *Imagine Democracy*.)

"I have a lot of time for a Judy Rebick or a Duff Conacher because they're pure and committed to their ideas," he told me. "I think they're wrong most of the time, and I'm sure they think the same of me, but we can have a great debate about finding common ground."

Of course, it's always more fun to be on the winning side in the political debate, and Robinson has had the luxury of watching rank-and-file Canadians fall in behind the CTF. In the early 1990s, Canadians finally rallied around the idea that deficit financing had to stop; by the end of that decade, with the taming of the red ink, the clamour for lower taxes drowned out calls for the status quo. But once the federal and provincial governments started cutting taxes, the CTF's job became more difficult. After all, who doesn't want a cut in taxes? But when it comes to cutting government spending, consensus is harder to come by. It's easy to get people upset about subsidies to millionaire hockey players and their billionaire owners—especially when so many Canadians feel the NHL has forsaken them and the game they love— but other cuts may be far more contentious. Take, for example, government money for arts and culture, something Robinson called "an abuse of our money." When it comes to spending from the public purse, he sees no difference between a power forward with a multimillion-dollar contract and a $20,000-a-year second violinist. But if he tries to turn funding for the arts into a high-profile campaign—and he might—he may find most Canadians don't mind a little government support for the local symphony.

We talked about this as he drove to Toronto after his visit to CFRA. I expected we'd make the journey in record time because I assumed he'd be a speed demon on the road. But we kept getting deep into one discussion or another, and his right foot got lighter and lighter. Periodically, he'd look down at the dash, realize what was happening and stomp on the gas again.

"In a world of limited taxpayers' dollars—and this is the debate we haven't had in Canada—what is the role of government?" he asked rhetorically. "What do we want to do and do exceptionally well, instead of this hodgepodge of government we've created?"

"If we have that debate, are you going to say we can't give any money to the arts or to culture?" I wondered. "At what point do you say, 'Okay, we can afford to support culture.'"

"I don't think we'll reach that point."

That position, though, may say more about the man than the nation's finances. He has no art on the wall of his office, nothing on the wall of the living room in his middle-class townhouse in suburban Orleans and just one lonely painting in the dining room. His idea of a good read is *The Spin Wars*, by Bill Fox, former aide to Brian Mulroney.

And yet, it wouldn't be fair to write him off as a cultureless policy wonk. There's something likable about the guy. He can drive from Ottawa to Toronto without ever cussing at another driver. In fact, I never heard him swear once. More importantly, while he's definitely not averse to sarcasm (he can be quite caustic), I've never heard him say anything cruel, bigoted or vindictive about anyone, not even his political opponents.

Even his two heroes attest to his choirboy qualities. One is Martin Anderson, a friend from university who, despite cerebral palsy, became a lawyer. Robinson sees him as a living example of "Destiny is what you do with it." His other hero is his late father, who was a security guard. Like many kids, Robinson often bridled at his strict upbringing. As a teenager, he'd want to hang out with friends, but his dad would make him spend time with his family. He later realized his father was right. "I've already given the most important speech of my life," he said of the eulogy he gave at his father's funeral. "Anything that I accomplish professionally or personally, anything I say, will never have the same resonance or meaning or impact for me."

But there's more than good old-fashioned values at work here—there's also Robinson's uncommon passion and drive. His friend Glen Nelson told me a story about when they went to

Burnhamthorpe Collegiate Institute together. The school, located in a working-class area of Etobicoke, a Toronto suburb, didn't have a football team or even a hockey team. It was a basketball power. Robinson, who was a little chubby before he started running five miles a day, tried out for the team in grade 10. He didn't make the cut, but that only made him more determined. He stayed on as manager and went to basketball camp in the summer. The next year, he made the team, and by grade 13 was co-captain and helped the school win the city finals. At Carleton, the self-described "nasty" player made the Ravens. "When he gets determined," said Nelson, "nothing is going to stop him."

Robinson applied the same principles at work. Soon after he joined the CTF, he realized his writing was weak. He wanted to be a catchy and focused writer, but he was, by his own admission, "abysmal." Not for long. He asked for samples of writing by CTF national communications director Troy Lanigan, and worked hard at improving. Today, Robinson is a frequent contributor to the op-ed pages of major papers and does a weekly column on local tax and policy issues for the *Ottawa Sun*. This drive can worry his colleagues, but in a CTF employee evaluation in 2000, Ken Azzopardi—who described Robinson as a thoroughbred—wrote, "Walter is still intense and preoccupied with his work, but my concern for his personal health and welfare have eased since my last evaluation. He seems to have struck a balance between work and personal activity, and I am pleased to announce he has actually taken a vacation without his computer and his pager."

IN FEBRUARY 2001, I got together with Robinson for a third time. We met for lunch in his hotel after he finished some meetings in Toronto. He was, as always, in a buoyant mood and eager to talk politics. His colourful opinions have made him popular with the television and radio producers who book guests for political panels. When I wondered if he worried about blurring the line between punditry and activism, he admitted that all CTF directors were wary about it. Such appearances can be an opportunity to get the group's message out, but they turn down more offers than they accept. "We can't be experts on everything and we can't comment on everything because that's demagoguery. That's not our job," he said. "Taxation is everything, but we self-limit because if you're out there on everything then you're just a clanging cymbal."

That doesn't mean Robinson won't continue to expand his repertoire. Some issues—MPs' pensions, for example—grow stale; others, such as personal taxation, become mainstream; and some, like bracket creep, end in victory. So he's always on the lookout for the next issue to adopt; for example, he's determined to play a role in the debate over the future of health care. Meanwhile, he plans to continue hammering away at corporate welfare and gas taxes. By early October 2000, the CTF had collected 50,000 names for its Gas Tax Honesty Day petition, and Robinson delivered three boxes of petition sheets and coupons to the office of Finance Minister Paul Martin. He'd hoped for more names, but 50,000 was still respectable, and he was confident he'd helped put gas taxes on the agenda. However, the volatility of oil prices—some cities saw the pump price spike eight or ten cents in a day—derailed the group's message a bit. Mixed results aside, the CTF will continue with its annual Gas Tax Honesty Day campaign.

And Robinson plans to boost his commitment to electoral reform. That, he realized, requires a bipartisan push, so he and Duff Conacher of Democracy Watch looked at creating a voting reform coalition dedicated to changing the way Canada elects its politicians. The current first-past-the-post system means candidates need only a plurality, rather than a majority, to get into the House of Commons, and parties can win comfortable majorities even though only 40 percent of the electorate support them. Aside from these inequities and distortions, many activists are convinced that another voting system—some variation on proportional representation is the most commonly touted alternative—would help decentralize power and give other ideas and points of view a fighting chance.

Just because groups on the left and right share this conviction doesn't mean all of them are willing to put aside their ideological differences and past battles to join forces. When Robinson and Conacher tried to put together a bipartisan coalition, they quickly discovered too many groups on the left didn't want to work with the CTF—and too many on the right didn't want anything to do with an alliance that included unions. Undaunted, Robinson carries on. He and Rebick wrote a provocative op-ed piece on electoral reform that ran in the *Globe and Mail* a few days after the 2000 election. And he has great hope for Fair Vote Canada, a nascent group dedicated to the issue. "In the end, it may work counter to activist organizations," said Robinson, who believes activists now function as a much-needed check and balance. "It may refocus people's belief in the institution of Parliament. If that happens, so be it."

By then, he might be sitting there anyway. For all his disillusionment with the system, Robinson—who has registered *www.vote4walter.com*—will likely run for office. It wouldn't be the first time: he tried to win a seat on the Ottawa school board in 1991. At the time, he was unmarried, had no kids, didn't own a home and was just 25. Not surprisingly, some people were skeptical of his motives. "You're just using this as a stepping stone," they'd say to him. "You want to build a political career."

Robinson, who has an answer for everything, had an answer. "Yes, absolutely, I have some political ambitions, and the only way I can use this position as a stepping stone is to effectively serve you," he told them. "If I don't, I'm not stepping anywhere; you're stepping on me come next election."

He ran for trustee again in 1994, and lost again, and then put his political ambitions on hold. Now, with a young family, the time isn't right. "The more I think about it, the further away it is," he said early in 2001, noting how much fun he has with his three-year-old son. Nor would he rule out another stint in the private sector before taking the leap, especially since his salary is just $66,300—with no pension plan. That's great money for an activist, but nowhere near what he could make in business. In the meantime, he'll continue working at changing Parliament before he even gets there. "If we're successful in voting reform, the role of a backbencher will have increased," he said. Of course, he has a bigger goal for himself. "When I do seek office, I'll be confident I can be more than a backbencher."

4

EDUCATION

ACTIVISTS

WILL HAPPEN

MALKIN DARE KNEW her son Laurie was not the academic star of his grade 2 class. But the school didn't seem worried, and his glowing spring report card made it easy for her to maintain what she now thinks of as "a willing suspension of disbelief." The day after she read the report card, however, the school summoned Dare to an interview. That's when she learned Laurie couldn't read, and it was small consolation that the school officials thought he'd probably pass his year. A shocked Dare, who had briefly been a teacher, found a phonics workbook at a bookstore and began working with her son. Within six weeks, he was reading at a grade 2 level.

As Dare wondered why it had been so easy for her to teach him how to read, she heard that many of her Waterloo, Ontario, neighbours had kids who were also struggling. So she did some research and was appalled at what she discovered about the "child-centered learning" that was all the rage in schools. The theories, she was convinced, were just junk. She volunteered in Laurie's classroom to see how the ideas translated into practice. Some kids, it was true, were thriving under the system; but others, mostly boys, weren't even surviving. And the widening gap between the brainiacs and the stragglers made life more difficult for the teacher.

In the autumn, Dare trooped off to the school board to reveal what she had learned. In her political naïveté, she was sure the trustees would be delighted to hear from her. After listening to Dare for ten minutes, the chair of the school board—who was Elizabeth Witmer, now Ontario's environment minister—scheduled another meeting to discuss the issue further. But rather than getting to the heart of the matter, the second meeting was only an opportunity for an education consultant to sing the praises of "child-centered learning." When the consultant finished her presentation, the board turned to Dare and said, "Thank you very much." And that was that.

Dare called the local paper. The education reporter who interviewed her in December seemed unenthusiastic, and the story didn't run until the following June. When it finally appeared, the piece generated twenty phone calls. Several of the callers met in Dare's living room and decided to form a group called Parents for Learning, which would lobby the school board for change. But the group's presentations earned even brusquer brush-offs than Dare had earlier. Then, in 1991, Dare saw something on television about a group called Concerned Parents of Etobicoke. Together, they created the Organization for Quality Education.

Dare's son is now in university, and her daughter is a high-school student at the same private Mennonite school that Laurie had ended up attending. Although Dare had never had any particular interest in politics—still doesn't, she says—she is a passionate and tireless leader in the battle to reform Ontario's schools. It wasn't anything she planned or hoped to do, but learning that her son couldn't read galvanized her. "I am surprised I became an activist," she said. "It was so gradual. I didn't sit down and say I'm going to change the world. I started out trying to fix things for my son."

If Malkin Dare is an accidental activist, Annie Kidder was an activist waiting to happen. When she was growing up, family dinners were invariably political screaming matches. Her father, a mining engineer who moved around the country, was an active and committed Conservative and a master of inventing statistics to bolster his side; her mother was a teacher and a Liberal who occasionally voted NDP. With the five kids full of 1960s idealism and rebellion, the family's raucous battles taught Kidder that politics are personal.

She marched against the Vietnam War as a high-school student in Vancouver. (Kidder also spent a year—grade 10—at Havergal College, an exclusive girls school in Toronto, but she was, in the delicate parlance of private schools, "asked not to come back.") After university, where she studied theatre, she worked as an actor and dramaturge and fought cuts to the arts. But she didn't become a full-time activist until she had become a mother.

Today, Kidder is the spokesperson and public face of People for Education (P4E), a group that got its start when the principal at Toronto's Palmerston Avenue Public School asked the Home and School Association to raise $6,000 for math textbooks. The association agreed, but it also decided to take political action, and P4E now fights to preserve public education in Ontario. Kidder, who got involved after showing up at the first meeting of Palmerston's social action committee, is an eloquent, high-profile and effective advocate. She also believes she can make a difference. Recently, her 7-year-old daughter asked, "Do you think you can change the world?"

Without missing a beat, Kidder answered: "Absolutely."

ALL ACTIVISTS WANT to change the world—or some little piece of it. Dare and Kidder may have taken different routes to advocacy, but both women started trying to improve the Ontario education system because they were dissatisfied with their children's experiences in school. But self-interest isn't their only motivation. Dare, after all, continued to work for better education long after she took her kids out of the public system—and she was no less committed because her family wouldn't benefit directly. Similarly, if Kidder cared only about her daughters, she could spend her time raising money for their school or simply find a way to pay for private school.

It's the same with most activists. Walter Robinson of Canadian Taxpayers Federation, for example, isn't devoting his life to fighting taxes and government waste for the few extra bucks he finds in his pocket whenever a government lowers the tax rate. If money were all he cared about, he'd have no trouble making serious coin in the private sector. As one former gay advocate told me, "There are two things to remember about being an activist— you don't get paid and you don't get laid." Still, when activists invest their time and energy, become more knowledgeable and perhaps even notch up some victories, they develop a passion for their pet issues. If politics is personal, activism is intimate.

Like Annie Kidder, I come from a family of five kids. But by the time we were old enough to talk politics seriously, much of the idealism of the 1960s had proven to be illusory. We still had some good battles, though, and still do. At Easter dinner, I innocently mentioned I'd be driving out to Waterloo to interview the founder of the Organization for Quality Education (OQE). To my surprise, this news sent my youngest sister, a textbook editor, into a lather. With four mouthy older siblings, she's usually the quiet one—we know she has strongly held opinions, but we rarely hear them. "OQE?" she growled, not biting her tongue this time. Like politicians, my sister and her colleagues were convinced they were doing a good job and didn't appreciate being pressured by outsiders. She ended her rant by saying, "It pisses me off that they have so much influence."

I was glad to hear OQE has some influence. One of the group's main goals remains an improved curriculum, and, as a part-time journalism instructor at Ryerson University, I often wonder what, if anything, schools are teaching these days. Most of my students have no sense of history or current events and few read newspapers or magazines, let alone books, even as they profess to want careers in journalism. When I teach second-year students, I must spend the first few minutes of each class going over basic rules of grammar. But I can't blame my students; usually only one or two in a class of twenty-five have had any grammatical training. Under "child-centered learning," teachers don't worry about grammar or spelling, they just want the kids to "express themselves."

Fortunately, grammar is starting to make a quiet comeback in Ontario—though it will be years before I see the results in a university classroom—and some of the credit has to go to people like Malkin Dare. So, despite my sister's warning, I headed to Kitchener-Waterloo, the twin cities famous for Octoberfest, a fall festival of beer drinking, and the burgeoning high-tech industry that has sprouted around Waterloo University's renowned engineering and computer programs.

The Dares live in a standard, middle-class suburban home: reddish brick on the main floor, brown siding on the second, lots of lawn, a low basketball net in the driveway and a two-car garage. After telling me the living room is the most comfortable room in the house, she led me into a room that looked, well, lived in. A home office (computer, fax, etc.) took up one corner. Books, mostly non-fiction, filled the built-in shelves. The piano had three music books on it: one was open to something from *Cats*, while the others—Scott Joplin and the Beatles—were closed. On the other side of the front window, there was a stereo and a couple of shelves of classical CDs. There was a fireplace, but no television.

I expected someone crustier. For one thing, OQE board member Mark Holmes told me that after reading the first draft of her book, *How to Get the Right Education for Your Child*, he'd suggested she not be so hard on teachers. So I came prepared for some discomforting diatribes, but though she makes the odd cranky remark, she never rants. Passionate, but also quiet and self-effacing, she hates doing radio and television interviews—in fact, after she self-published her book, she wouldn't promote it. (Needless to say, this hurt sales. Despite a favourable review in *Western Report* magazine, it sold just 500 copies beyond the 1,100 that went into libraries.) "She stays very focused," said OQE vice-president Nancy Wagner, "and she leaves the PR and the schmoozing to everyone else."

Although Dare took on the role of president when Parents for Learning first became OQE, she didn't enjoy it and gave it up after two years. She's still a crucial member of the group, though, and she devotes one or two hours a day to education reform during slow times and four or five hours a day when it's busier. "She's the backbone of the organization and our resource centre," according to current president John Bachmann, a former high-school teacher and a professional engineer, who said he's president mostly because he runs tight meetings. Dare, meanwhile, produces the group's quarterly newsletter, develops position papers and reads every book on education she can get her hands on. "Like a lot of activists," said Bill Robson, director of research at the C. D. Howe Institute and a OQE board member, "she's tireless."

When I had first called her, she'd groaned when I said I was writing about the growing influence of activists. The sad reality, she said, was that OQE wasn't all that influential. Dare has survived eight ministers of education from three different political parties, and she's seen more frustration than success. But other OQE board members were more positive about the group's impact. "We have managed to become one of the stakeholders in the system," Bachmann said, pointing out that the Education

Improvement Commission, the Ontario College of Teachers and the Ministry of Education all regularly consult OQE. And it's no easy task to reach that status. "You build up that credibility by doing instead of just talking." Members of OQE were involved in revising the elementary curriculum and, more recently, the secondary curriculum. The group also meets with new ministers. "Depending on who the minister is, we're either taken fairly seriously or just treated courteously," admitted Bachmann, adding that, when it serves their purpose, ministers are all too happy to quote a group with close to a thousand members. "When our agendas coincide, they'll use us to their advantage; when we're not onside, we don't get mentioned. But that's the nature of politics."

Education is one of the toughest issues for activists who want to make their voices heard. It's a huge, expensive and complex program for governments to manage, and because it embodies issues that can get normally docile voters up in arms, politicians lack the necessary fervour to really change things. So OQE has tried to address the problem locally, by encouraging and helping like-minded people run in school-board elections. But the group has never have been able to get a majority on a board. Meanwhile, the teacher unions are powerful, entrenched and not open to change. And since reform is a threat, the unions eagerly dismiss groups like OQE as back-to-basics dinosaurs. "It's just an easy label," said Dare as she curled up in her chair and stroked her gold-and-white cat. Then she tried to remember a quote from Machiavelli's *The Prince:*

> There is nothing more difficult and dangerous, or more doubtful of success, than an attempt to introduce a new order of things in any state. For the innovator has for enemies all those who derived advantages from the old order of things, whilst those who expect to be benefited by the new institutions will be but lukewarm defenders.

Her inability to convert the majority of Ontario parents into anything more than lukewarm defenders of education reform frustrates Dare. And the government's intransigence baffles her.

"She's like an engineer who sees things as black and white: this works, that doesn't, why are we doing what doesn't?" said Dare's friend Nancy Wagner, who joined Parents for Learning, as it was known then, after discovering her son couldn't read in grade 3. "It makes no sense to her." Despite her own stage fright, Dare admitted she and the group could be better at packaging and positioning. "Maybe we should be more wily, instead of serious, boring do-gooders," she said, while marvelling at Annie Kidder's ease with the media. "We probably haven't celebrated enough. We're far too serious, dour people."

Causes for OQE celebration include improvements to the curriculum and the introduction of standardized testing, but the champagne remains corked on the struggle to push the power down to the local level. The group wants a bottom-up approach that would see school boards replaced by more-effective school councils and allow for a more diverse system, including charter schools and partial government support for religious and independent schools. Dare has never bought the argument that such changes would weaken the public system. Instead, she paints another scenario: a critical mass of parents—about 15 percent— ship their children out of the public system, which then begins to feel its monopoly threatened and shapes up.

Despite OQE's high hopes for the Conservative government, however, centralization has actually increased in recent years. This has been demoralizing for the members. "As in any activist group, these are people who are committed and think the issue is enormously important, and many of them aren't all that psychologically well disposed to dealing with that kind of frustration," said Bill Robson. "But one of the things that makes OQE fairly effective as an advocacy group is there's a lot of level-headedness among many of the members. So while there is frustration, there's also a realization that this is a game where you measure progress in very small increments."

Such level-headedness may be why OQE has survived, while Dare watched about a dozen similar groups come and go over the years. "It's a lot harder than I thought it would be. Probably if I'd known then what I know now—well, it's hard to say. Would I have done it? In some ways it has been an adventure," she said, noting she has learned a lot, become familiar with the Internet, written a book and made many friends. "I enjoy aspects of it. But also it's the calls that I get from parents." When Ontario teachers went on strike in 1996, Dare offered her home for tutoring. OQE let a radio station know, and within an hour forty parents had signed up their children. She gave them an hour of reading and an hour of math three afternoons a week. Once the strike was over, some of the parents wanted to keep sending their kids to the tutoring sessions, even if it meant missing some school. Dare, who had turned her house upside down to accommodate the students and refused to take any money, explained that the sessions ended when the strike did. But she did keep working with two young boys who were really struggling.

"I don't even know if she sees herself as an activist necessarily," said Wagner. "She is one of those people who sees a need and is hell-bent that she has to do something about it. It's not a political agenda for her, as it is for some; it's about the kids. She sees it as neglect for anybody to see this and not do something about it."

CRITICS SOMETIMES dismiss OQE as a bunch of religious fanatics, though Dare says it's an unfounded charge. "I'm an atheist," she told me matter-of-factly. But religion does play a

crucial role in the growth of home schooling—or home education, as it's increasingly known. And Alberta, not surprisingly,
leads the movement. In fact, about seven thousand children are
being educated at home in that province. But parents didn't get
the right to do it themselves without a fight. One of the long-time
leaders of the movement is Ray Strom, former president and
now vice-president of the Alberta Home Education Association.

I've heard the stories and jabs about Bible-thumping home-
schoolers, and religion has always made me nervous. (My father
was a Presbyterian elder, but I became an atheist in the spring of
1971. When Ken Dryden, then an unknown rookie goaltender
for the Montreal Canadiens, stoned my beloved Big, Bad Boston
Bruins—a team with seven of the top-eleven scorers during the
regular season, including the incomparable Bobby Orr and
the prolific Phil Esposito—in the Stanley Cup playoffs, I knew
there could be no God.) Still, I resolved to keep an open mind.

Ray Strom turned out to be a friendly, soft-spoken and polite
man. A couple of things kept me off balance, though. First, he sat
behind his computer on a cluttered desk, and when we talked, he
frequently stared at the screen, instead of looking at me. That was
disquieting, especially since I had no idea what he was looking
at. Second, sometimes when I'd ask a question—particularly a
potentially contentious one—he'd give me a weird little smile (or
was it a wince?) and look at me for a long time through the silver-
rimmed glasses that sat partway down his nose. Then he'd answer.

Strom is an evangelical Christian whose education battles
started in 1984 when his eldest daughter was still in the public-
school system. He'd become concerned that what she was learning in school was at odds with the values that reigned at home. In
particular, he didn't want his daughter exposed to liberal ideas
about homosexuality and abortion. He asked for course outlines
and was alarmed to learn that the school's definition of family

included, "two males, with or without children, and two females, with or without children." He set about trying to get help from provincial politicians, but found they had no idea what the schools were teaching. And even after he let them know, they had no stomach to take on the school boards. But Strom didn't give up. "I will attempt to change something before I jump ship," he said, though he admitted he started to think about private schools or moving to another school board. (Alberta did not yet have charter schools.) "It doesn't matter what level you deal with," he told me. "People are reluctant or fearful to change the system radically." It's a refrain I hear a lot from reformers.

Then one day in the fall of 1987, his daughter came home and asked her parents if they would home-school her. A social kid in grade 8, she was disturbed about the sex and drugs around her. So a surprised Ray and Lois Strom spent a few months looking into home education. Their first two questions were the same as everyone else's: is it legal? and what about socialization? Satisfied with the answers, they began home educating their two daughters (the youngest was in grade 4) the following February. And Strom, who likes to get involved—in the church, in political parties—joined the Alberta Home Education Association.

If the teachers' unions and school boards weren't so threatened by home education, that might have been the end of the story. But the struggle for acceptance of home education lasted for several years, and in that time Strom rose to the presidency of the AHEA (he's now vice-president even though both his daughters are adults). In the late 1980s, the AHEA fought to get school boards to accept home education, all the while putting up with what the parents considered intimidation tactics, including frequent visits to families educating their kids at home. The turning point came in 1991 when the Assumption school board agreed to act as a "non-resident board." That meant parents who wanted to educate their children at home could be part of that board no matter where they lived in the province. Soon, other boards followed suit, but some—Calgary's board, for example— remain hostile.

As president of the group from 1991 to 1994, Strom believed the courts were a last resort. Instead, he worked with school boards and, whenever that proved fruitless, he went to the province—and used phone and mail campaigns to get his point across to MLAs and the minister of education. "It got to the point where we would tie up the phone lines for two or three days," he remembered, adding that home educators who weren't AHEA members joined the campaigns. Although the group had over a thousand members by 2000, it had just three hundred when Strom was president. "Home educators are a very independent lot," he admitted.

Many parents want to teach their own kids for religious rea- sons—the AHEA counts as members not just evangelical Chris- tians but people of many faiths, including Catholics, Sikhs and Mormons. But as home educating grows in popularity in Alberta and elsewhere in Canada, it's also catching on with secular par- ents. This doesn't bother Strom, who is for diversity in education. "We don't walk into the minister's office or the minister's advisory committee with our Bibles," he said. "That's not why we're there. We're representing home educators and the view that parents are responsible for the education of their children."

THE WOMEN SITTING around Annie Kidder's dining-room table, amidst a growing pandemonium, share that sense of responsibility. They just have different ideas than Dare or Strom. These parents are working to save public education in Ontario from neglect, budget cuts and a hostile government. As they planned a symposium on the role of school boards, small children ran around and clamoured for snacks; Kidder's bird chirped away; and her dog slobbered and wrestled with Valerie McDonald's dog under the table. And then the phone rang. It was a typical People for Education meeting.

Kidder lives in Toronto's Annex, a gentrified area known as a hotbed of artists, university professors and CBC types. And while it's actually a diverse neighbourhood, the stereotype—usually delivered with a sneer by outsiders—has just enough truth behind it to stick. (Needless to say, Kidder and her husband, Eric Peterson, an actor best known for the CBC series *Street Legal* and the play *Billy Bishop Goes to War*, don't do much to kill the cliché.) The area was the perfect breeding ground for a group like P4E. While parents in more affluent neighbourhoods simply respond to a disintegrating education system by sending their kids to private schools or raising huge amounts of money at fun fairs, Annex parents are the kind who'll fight back.

The twelve mothers who make up P4E have no titles, and everyone helps out with grunt work such as photocopying and stuffing envelopes (one reason the few men who have been part of it didn't last). Although they say they are all equals, Kidder is the best-known member of the group, because she's the one most likely to appear on television and be quoted in newspapers. Not everyone buys the idea that P4E is leaderless, though. "That's a nice euphemism, but it glosses over the reality," said Kathleen Wynne, the founder of a Toronto advocacy group called the Metro Parent Network and, since 2000, a school-board trustee. "She holds a lot of sway."

Whether the group works as a collective or not, Kidder's prominence is a sore subject in P4E. After all, it can't be easy to work just as hard as Kidder and have people say, "Oh, you're in Annie Kidder's group." But I spoke to several P4E members and got the impression that while they resented the public giving all the credit to Kidder, the media had burned most of them at one time or another, so they were happy someone else took the flak. Besides, she's good at it. "Annie has been good at branding People for Education," said Wynne. "She's great with the media." Even her rivals at OQE agreed. "I like her," said Robson, who once debated Kidder on television. "Annie is very effective, personable and reasonable. And she's politically astute." Malkin Dare told me she'd love to see Kidder join OQE—if Kidder accepted the OQE philosophy.

Aside from an ability to go on television and make her point without sounding strident or wacky, Kidder has a strong sense of what makes good TV. "Annie really likes rallies," said Valerie McDonald, who called the first meeting of the Palmerston Avenue Public School social-action committee that eventually became P4E. The group's first big splash (even before it was known as P4E) was Elves Against the Cuts. Late in 1995, the parents collected a sack of letters from children at several downtown schools. The letters, addressed to then Education Minister John Snobelen, were wish lists for the kids' schools. With Matthew Behrens, a veteran anti-poverty activist, dressed up as Santa Claus, Eric Peterson playing Scrooge and some grades 5 and 6 students on a field trip to learn about democracy, the group took the subway to Queen's Park. After a press conference where Kidder spoke, the children tried—unsuccessfully—to deliver the letters. The media loved it.

More protests followed, and journalists soon learned they could count on P4E for colourful material. "Our rallies were fun, short and had lots of entertainment," said Kidder. After Premier Mike Harris claimed he was listening to parents, P4E and its supporters donned Mr. Spock ears and Dumbo ears. When Snobelen announced Bill 104 would cut the number of trustees in the province, they wore gags and rang school bells outside the Enoch Turner Schoolhouse. As a former actor, Kidder isn't shy about such stunts, but it's not always so easy for others. "It can be very humiliating," said Kathryn Blackett, another long-time member of P4E. "My mother can tell you how horrified she was to see a picture of me with a gag in my mouth. And it can be embarrassing for my kids. It's not easy to do these things when you're middle-aged. But if it can get in the press, then it's a good thing."

Eventually, though, the group began taking a more "respectable" approach, including spreading the message through speaking engagements at parent councils and school-board meetings. That work involves more research than drama. "We actually do a lot of really hard, boring work. We've evolved from a protest group to one trying to influence people with facts and information," Kidder said. "It became serious and we felt we had a responsibility. When you give information to other people, you have a responsibility that it be correct and not be hysterically one-sided." She pointed to the tracking survey P4E does with the help of the Metro Parent Network. It monitors the effects of policy and funding changes on the province's schools, something nobody—not even the government—does. "We used to do more fun, silly things," said Kidder, "but the press gets jaded." The other problem, as McDonald pointed out, is that the stunts too often become the focus of the coverage. "The media like visuals and one-liners, but sometimes they broadcast the visuals but not the story behind them."

At the symposium on school boards, Kidder had promised to call me. But it took her forty-eight hours to get back to me. She apologized, explaining that after the symposium the organizers had gone out drinking beer until 2:30, and the next day had been marred by a hangover. "Our theory about People for Education and why we've stayed together," she explained, "is we drink together and we laugh together. We have a sense of humour."

At her Annex home, Kidder picked pieces of spilled cereal from a cloth placemat as she cleared a space for us to sit. My first question was about something from one of her speeches. "Anger and an ability to laugh are the two most important prerequisites for the life of an advocate," Kidder said when giving the Margot McGrath Memorial Lecture in the spring of 1999. She'd gone on to explain, "Laughter is the fuel you need to keep going when you feel as if you're banging your head against the wall."

But I knew about her sense of humour. I was more interested in the anger, so I asked her when she first got angry. "Here's a government that comes in and appoints an education minister who hasn't graduated from high school, who makes incredible comments about education, that denigrates the importance of education, that talks about it as a business and looks at it as of it were just a really big pile of money the government could be spending on something else or using to fund tax cuts. Maybe it's more self-righteous than angry," she said and then let out a big, enthusiastic laugh. "But it has more to do with saying, 'This is wrong. This goes against everything I was brought up to believe in and it goes against what I know.' What helps keep all the people in People for Education from giving up—and maybe all activists—is a sense of being right. So you go, 'We're right and they're wrong.'"

Lots of people, of course, believe they are right and the government is wrong. But most people are far too cynical about the intelligence, motives and abilities of politicians to do anything about it. So it also takes a certain naïveté to be an activist. "All of us in People for Education have this belief that if we just say these things . . ." Kidder didn't finish her sentence, but she added, "It's very naive."

As she talked, the phone rang every few minutes, but she didn't answer. And it didn't seem to faze her. In the early days of P4E, the group used Kidder's phone number and address. "It drove my family nuts," she said. As she sat on a stool on the other side of the counter, I could see the resemblance to her sister Margot, the Hollywood actress best known for playing Lois Lane, dating Pierre Trudeau and her own human rights, anti-nuke and mental health activism.

Kidder, who frequently flipped her red hair back with her hands, struck me as animated, enthusiastic and passionate. She is also, by her own admission, indiscreet. In July of 1999, for example, she said a little more than she should have to *Toronto Star* columnist Jim Coyle. The Conservatives had just won re-election in the province and Premier Mike Harris named Janet Ecker as the new minister of education. Ecker had phoned Kidder, but Molly Kidder, then 12 years old, was talking to a friend on the other line and told Ecker to call back later. That would have been just a cute little story about kids and phones, but in the meantime, Kidder had told Coyle what another reporter had told her: Ecker got the job because she was weak and the premier's office would be able to stay in control of education.

This was not the best way to start a new relationship, especially with someone who appeared to be reaching out to her. Nor was it a good way to dispel the perception of P4E as Harris-bashers. Like most advocacy organizations, P4E bills itself as non-partisan, but that's done nothing to soften its reputation as an anti-government, pro-union, left-wing group. Kidder rejected this characterization. "It's a Canadian issue, not a left-right issue," she argued. "It's a 'we forgot' issue. We have forgotten why we have public education and that you actually have to pay for it and why you have to pay for it. We have forgotten what governments are supposed to do. If the Liberals had gotten in, we'd still be here, and a lot of the things these guys are doing came from the NDP." She pointed out that P4E agrees with the government's decision to centralize school funding, acknowledges that class sizes have gone down slightly, and didn't fight standardized tests or curriculum changes, only the way they were introduced. At the same time, P4E refuses to take union money, disagrees with the unions over teacher strikes and vehemently opposes any attempt by the unions to organize parents.

From the beginning, the group, whose members support different parties, wanted to appeal to all voters, including Conservatives, and be different from the existing education activist organizations. They wanted to tell the story that got left out in the polarized fights between the boards and the province or teachers and the province. "There was a hole in the activism roster for the regular, everyday, middle-of-the-road, middle-of-the-political spectrum, concerned citizen. We were conscious quite early on about the importance of not aligning ourselves with a political party or a union, but also that we not make our focus narrow. We've gotten shit for it sometimes, because we've been very generic. It wasn't for a bunch of lefty Annex-living yuppies, it was the people in Thunder Bay or in Exeter that we cared about. We had to tell those people what was going on," said Kidder. "This is not a special interest. What they say now is that we aren't real parents, that we're 'professional parents.' They say they talk to 'real parents.' Even if we all get really, really good at talking on TV or if we have lots of facts, I am a fucking real parent and I fight with my children about practising the piano, and I take them to school."

While Kidder rejects any suggestion she isn't a real parent, she never pretended P4E is democratic. The group hasn't tried to attract supporting members or to grow beyond its current twelve women. And when people in Windsor wanted to start another chapter of P4E, the Toronto group asked them not to use the name. For one thing, the Windsor parents took union money. But Kidder and her colleagues also had no interest in growing into an organization with far-flung branches—that would mean having a structure and telling people what to do and think. "We don't want to run anything," she said. "We aren't democratic, we're not representative, we're not elected. It leaves us completely free, but it means we're horrible to work with because we never consult. We could never be part of a coalition. All we can do is say, 'We are who we are and we've really looked at this stuff and we really believe it's true,' and be the most plausible, most clean, most together group in the world and try not to say, 'Parents think . . .' Janet Ecker says, 'Parents think . . .' Anybody can say, 'Parents think . . .' We've just tried to say, 'Here's the information; you do something with it.'"

Kidder started unloading her dishwasher. Other P4E members were coming for lunch, and Kidder had been talking for two hours instead of preparing for her guests. But I had to ask one more question before I was willing to take the hint and go. A friend of mine, a disgruntled Toronto high-school teacher, insisted P4E's only accomplishment has been to attract television coverage through stunts such as getting thrown out of the public gallery of the Ontario legislature for wearing gags. So I wanted to know about the group's victories.

"It's hard to know, because the government is never going to say, 'This is because of People for Education,'" she laughed. "I think more money would have been cut. By encouraging other parents to get up and scream and yell, fewer schools have closed, more money hasn't been cut." She pointed out that under the province's funding formula, 53 percent of schools wouldn't have principals. But because P4E hammered away at the issue, the government backed off and agreed all schools should have principals. "We've been successful because we've kept it all out in the open. It's like being a watchdog. They can't sneak anything by, they've had to be honest. We've just called them on everything, so I think they don't feel quite so easy about saying, 'Oh well, we'll just do this now and nobody will notice.'"

CANADIANS, BELIEVES OQE's Mark Holmes, are giving up on institutions and starting to look after themselves. In the 1980s, Holmes, then a renegade professor at the Ontario Institute for Studies in Education because of his back-to-basics views, addressed many parent groups. "Start with your classroom teacher," he told them, "and see if you can get the teacher to understand the problems. Very likely that won't work, so talk to the principal and then go through the ranks: go to the super-intendent, go to the director, go to the school board. And at the same time, perhaps as a group, you can lobby the provincial politicians." But he eventually stopped giving that advice. "Look after your own kid," he started saying. "You're not going to change the system."

That, said Kidder, just plays into the government's divide-and-conquer strategy. "What we've tried to do with parents—and it's really hard when schools are closing—is to say, 'Do both things at the same time. Save your kid or your school, but try to remember that this is happening to all of the kids in Ontario and the whole public-education system.'"

While OQE trashes P4E for being too cozy with the unions, and P4E resents OQE for being being tight with the Conservative government—both groups deny the charges—there's more common ground between the two groups than they like to admit. Neither OQE nor P4E likes the government's plan to test teachers, for example, and while both agree the centralization of funding is a good thing, they hate the way the government is centralizing control over education policy. More importantly, both groups want children to learn to read and spell and multiply.

Education activists of all stripes fight for a better education for their kids; they just can't agree on the best way to get it. OQE wants to get rid of school boards and push the power right down to individual schools. On the other hand, P4E wants to keep school boards. OQE believes that more choice for parents, including charter schools, is the best way to make the public-education system thrive, while P4E sees charter schools as a threat to that system. Perhaps the biggest difference between the two groups, though, is the way they attack the problems. OQE works hard to improve the curriculum, while P4E doesn't get involved in the nitty-gritty of what gets taught in the classroom. "It's not about fighting for one issue. It's not about fighting for phonics or charter schools," said Kidder. "Maybe it's wimpy of us, but we just go, 'There is public education. It's really, really, really important. And it's really important that it has money and that you're careful about how you change it.'"

Despite their differences, both groups play a vital role in the education debate. Politicians and bureaucrats know parents will, from time to time, get worked up, but the education establishment counts on them losing the fire in the belly as soon as their kids move on. Ontario's education system is better for having consistent, well-informed critics. OQE, despite many disappointments, has shown it has some staying power, but the long-term survival of P4E, for all its current energy, remains uncertain. "It will be interesting to see what happens," admitted Kidder. "But the thing about us is that it isn't just about education. None of us are obsessed education people, none of us was very involved before. For us, it's much more about citizenship."

GLOBALIZATION

THE YOUNG
AND THE
IDEALISTIC

FOR MOST CANADIANS, it began with a cop right out of central casting. Burly, mustachioed and mean-looking, Staff-Sergeant Hugh Stewart of the Royal Canadian Mounted Police carried a canister of pepper spray in his right hand as he led a phalanx of cops up to a group of young people sitting in the middle of a road on the University of British Columbia campus. The protesters, many of whom were UBC students, hoped to stop a motorcade carrying the eighteen world leaders attending the November 1997 Asia Pacific Economic Co-operation Summit. "I am clearing this roadway," barked the grim-faced Stewart, a few minutes ahead of the dignitaries' cars. "I am going to use force, whatever force I deem necessary. I do not intend to fool around, I intend to clear this road and I intend to clear it now."

Knowing that protesters had faced pepper spray the day before, when police arrested forty people, the students started rising to their feet. Some moved off the road to Stewart's right. "Put the dogs on the side," he told his colleagues. To the students, he pointed to his left and ordered, "You are going that way." The words were barely out of his mouth before he raised the canister and unleashed a torrent of pepper spray at the students, some of whom were clearly trying to follow his orders. Then he went after a CBC cameraman, spraying him in the face at close range. Even as the protesters walk away, Stewart continued his attack.

The media played up the dramatic TV footage, but spent little time or effort trying to explain what the protests were about. When reporters asked Prime Minister Jean Chrétien about the actions of the police, he sputtered with typical aplomb, "For me, pepper, I put it on my plate." The one-liner—followed by the hearty laughter of the press corps in the background—quickly became a fun little clip on the news.

Within a few weeks, Terry Milewski, a Vancouver-based CBC television reporter, got his hands on letters that showed the government had reneged on its agreement with UBC to allow peaceful protests in view of the leaders. Milewski alleged that in an apparent effort to appease Suharto, the Indonesian dictator, the government pressured the RCMP to create what some law professors called a "Charter-free zone." The following September, Milewski came up with smoking-gun documents that suggested the intimate involvement of the Prime Minister's Office in the affair. The stink began to stick, and soon Peppergate, as it was inevitably called, centred on heavy-handed and undemocratic behaviour by Chrétien and his aides. But the protesters hadn't set out to reveal Chrétien's true colours, and as welcome as that outcome was, it also meant the real purpose of the APEC demonstrations was lost on most Canadians.

If we had been paying more attention to what was really going on in Vancouver, we wouldn't have been so surprised when 50,000 people showed up to protest the World Trade Organization meetings in Seattle two years later. While some of the students who protested during the APEC Summit were against the Suharto regime, and some were unhappy about the presence of police on campus, others were part of a nascent movement against globalization.

"The media really played up the anti-Suharto and the human rights and the police aspects," admitted Garth Mullins, one of the protesters, "because there was no context to talk about glob-alization." Even on the eve of the Seattle protests, the media remained clued out, as Mullins discovered when he appeared on a Canadian TV morning show.

"What are you doing down there?" asked the host. "Isn't the WTO an eye-glazer?"

"That's funny," Mullins replied, "because someone said the exact same thing to me before APEC."

THE SUMMER I TURNED 14, I spent a month in England with my family. I was at an age when it embarrassed me terribly to be seen with my oh-so-square parents. In retrospect, I realize they must have been cringing just as much to be with their sullen teenage son. I insisted on wearing a jean jacket with a Canadian flag sewn on the back and, on the front, a Committee for an Inde-pendent Canada pin that read "Keep it Canadian." It was 1972, and a lot of people were worried about American takeovers.

For some, of course, that sentiment never really went away, as we found out during the bitter debate over free trade in 1988. But people my age and older make a huge mistake when we con-fuse the protectionist nationalism of the past with the current anti-globalization movement. As I was growing up, my mother often reminded me that generals always re-fight their last war. The thought never meant much to me until I saw conservative commentators committing the same gaffe when they tried to counter the street protesters by citing the benefits of trade to countries such as Japan, which rebuilt itself after the Second World War as a trading nation. Globalization activists are not against international trade—in fact, it's perfectly natural to them. But they aren't happy when secretive and undemocratic interna-tional decision-making bodies, such as the WTO, the International Monetary Fund and the World Bank, write the rules for the benefit of a few at the expense of everybody else.

Those who want to understand what globalization protest is really about could do worse than watch the brilliant boardroom scene in the 1976 movie *Network*. As he confronts Howard Beale (the news anchor turned mad prophet of the airwaves played by Peter Finch), the corporate chairman, Arthur Jensen (played by Ned Beatty) does a masterful job of explaining corporate globalization. Jensen dims the lights (for dramatic effect) and begins to thunder his message down an impossibly long conference table at an awestruck Beale: "You are an old man who thinks in terms of nations and peoples. There are no nations, there are no peoples," the executive bellows. Eventually, he lowers his voice and explains calmly, but firmly: "There is no America. There is no democracy. There is only IBM and ITT and AT&T and Dupont, Dow, Union Carbide and Exxon. Those are the nations of the world today." It's a testament to screenwriter Paddy Chayefsky that the film captured so perfectly what so many believe twenty-five years later.

For young people today, nation-states have about as much relevance as black-and-white television. They have internalized the idea of a global community; they take it for granted and see themselves as citizens of the world. While their parents back-packed around the great cities of Europe, many of today's protesters have travelled more widely. They've been to places like Suharto's Indonesia. But more than the travel, technology really has, as the cliché goes, made the world a smaller place. And in a global village, Indonesia might as well be part of North America.

"This generation intuitively sees one side of their identity as global," said Bani Dheer, an associate with The Strategic Counsel, a Toronto consulting and research company. "For them, tapping into a value system that touches all of these issues—

environment, labour issues, human rights—seems to be a natural step." After studying people born between the mid-1960s and the early 1980s, Dheer came to the conclusion they are a lot more entrepreneurial, flexible and self-reliant than those who came before them. They're also more interested in issues than ideologies, and they have a different approach to changing the world. "In the '60s, people were rebelling against something that was very tangible and finite and saying, 'That's not the answer, this is the answer,'" she explained over a cup of tea. "Today's group doesn't have the answer in tangible terms. Their answer is, 'We need to figure it out and you've got to give us room to do that. We need corporations to back off, we need the environment to stand still, while we figure out the answers.'"

This is the new generation gap and it threatens to make the 1960s-era rift between parents and kids seem like a love-in. It is such a significant shift in thinking from one generation to the next that most middle-aged media types still don't understand what's been going on in Seattle, Quebec City and the other places that have hosted anti-globalization protests. Columnists and commentators, for example, sneer at the range of interests represented at these demonstrations. Jeffrey Simpson, Ottawa columnist for the *Globe and Mail*, spoke for many of the old and out-of-touch in a June 2000 column after the protests against the Organization of American States meetings in Windsor. Unlike the anti-war and civil-rights marchers in the 1960s, he carped, these new protesters don't seem to have a focus. "Some get exercised about human-rights abuses, some can't abide free trade, others dislike multinational corporations, still others favour variations on Marxism, while others are worked up about the environment."

Simpson and his generation may see support for human rights and concern for the environment as mutually exclusive, but the activists do not. "The mainstream media don't get it," said

Lyndsay Poaps, the twenty-something co-director of the Vancouver group Check Your Head. "More and more, people are starting to see the connection between corporations and the destruction of the environment, between corporations and the destruction of national sovereignty and between corporations and the lack of human rights. People who are on the streets understand that globalization affects everything."

Most of those who march at international trade meetings are not against globalization, they're against the current model of globalization. They don't want protectionist policies, but rather than free trade, they want fair trade. Instead of a global economy without any labour, environmental and human-rights standards—which, they insist with an already-overused expression, only leads to "a race to the bottom"—they want progressive labour laws, strict environmental standards and unimpeachable human-rights practices. And they want powerful global organizations to be open and democratic. They are, as all activists are, idealistic.

AS A TEENAGER, Garth Mullins took part in anti-free-trade protests in the run-up to the 1988 federal election. He was amazed to see people standing around a flagpole singing "O Canada." "It was all about protecting *our* jobs from *them*," he said. Much to his relief, the movement has developed a lot since then, and while some—notably union leaders—can't let go of the old thinking, most people have moved well beyond it.

"I'm opposed to protectionism and economic nationalism—all this stuff about Canadian sovereignty and the idea that we can put up giant tariff walls so we can all just be victimized by our own corporate bosses instead of by an international cartel of corporate bosses. I'm not up for that," he said. "I think we should trade resources, ideas and services around the world. There's nothing wrong with doing that. It's not that these things are traded around the world, it's by whom and for whose benefit."

While Mullins believes globalization really started with the end of feudalism, he sees the anti-free-trade debate—even if it did miss the point—as the beginning of the current anti-globalization movement, at least in Canada. The late 1980s and early 1990s were not good years for anti-free-traders in Canada. In 1988, Brain Mulroney's Conservatives won re-election—despite considerable efforts by the Council of Canadians, the unions and others to defeat the government—and signed the Free Trade Agreement with the United States. In 1993, Jean Chrétien's Liberals came to power and quickly reneged on their promise to reconsider the deal. They soon signed the North America Free Trade Agreement, bringing Mexico into the arrangement.

Many of the people opposed to free trade began to realize they had to change their target. Instead of lobbying the government with national, state-focused protests, some adopted a more internationalist focus. And by the mid-1990s, we began to see unions bringing Mexican speakers to Canada to explain the Zapatista uprising (in the southern part of that country) or to talk about the working conditions in the *maquiladoras* (along their northern border). At the same time, resentment toward corporations began to boil over.

In 1997, Canadian-born writer Malcolm Gladwell wrote a now-famous piece called "The Coolhunt" for the *New Yorker*, where he's a staff writer. Writing with nerdish reverence, he explained how coolhunters make big money sniffing out what's cool for their corporate clients. Mullins, however, saw a more insidious side to the phenomenon than Gladwell. "As soon as rave culture gets from Britain to North America, it gets marketed. So before most youth even get to a rave, it's already being sold to them through their TV sets," he said. "People can't get involved in a culture as a participant, only as a consumer or a spectator. I think that's helped to build this anti-corporate sentiment that exists now."

Despite the growing backlash, companies continued their attempts to sell shrink-wrapped youth culture. But people grew increasingly appalled by the widespread use of sweatshops by Nike and others. And on several university campuses, students rejected the rampant corporatization of education by fighting sponsorship deals with the likes of Pepsi and Coca-Cola. The protests at the APEC Summit may have been just a little too far ahead of the wave for most people to make the connection, but they may also have helped push the wave. And then in 1998, the movement had its first victory when the Organization for Economic Development abandoned its plans for a Multilateral Agreement on Investment. The about-face came after activists— led by Maude Barlow of the Council of Canadians—did such an effective job publicizing the dangers of the proposal, which would have given multinational companies the right to sue countries that introduced legislation limiting the corporations' ability to make a profit. "All these different things came together to create the circumstances where this movement could explode onto the scene in Seattle," said Mullins. "The time was right."

DAYS AFTER THE SEATTLE demonstrations, the cover of *Time* magazine featured a picture of a protester, apparently shrieking in pain as two policemen held him down by twisting his arms. That protester, it turns out, lives in the woods on Prince Edward Island, about half an hour or so east of Charlottetown. And while the Seattle photograph catapulted Aaron Koleszar to local-celebrity status, he already had a solid reputation as an activist. A member of Earth Action, a controversial environmental group on the island, he's often at the centre of PEI protests. In 1988, as part of IRATE (Island Residents Against Toxic Environments), he burned Ronald McDonald in effigy outside the opening of a new McDonald's restaurant in Charlottetown. "The reason McDonald's food is cheap," argued Koleszar, whose main issues are international trade and genetic engineering, "is because the true costs are borne by their workers, the environment, animals, and the health of the children and others who consume their food." Later, in August 2000, he was part of the PEI Pie Brigade, the group responsible for throwing a whipped-cream pie at Prime Minister Jean Chrétien. While Koleszar didn't toss the ersatz pastry, he handled the media interviews afterward.

When he's not travelling, the 27-year-old lives with his mother, a potter, on a bucolic piece of property with an organic vegetable garden. He has a long beard, long light-brown hair, and on the day I dropped by, he was wearing a T-shirt that read: "Stop Global Piracy." We sat at a red table; he fiddled with two blue pens while we talked; outside, a rooster crowed. He explained that he ended up in Seattle because of his work on a campaign about genetic engineering and the WTO for the Sierra Youth Coalition, a branch of the Sierra Club of Canada. One of his tasks was to organize young people to go to Seattle. Koleszar and about twenty others—from PEI and Toronto and points in-between—took the train across the country, stopping in various cities to make their presence known. In Montreal, they held a teach-in; in Ottawa, they demoed at Parliament Hill; in Toronto, they went to Bay Street with banners and sang songs about globalization and genetic engineering. As the train continued on, they stopped in prairie cities, and when they got to Vancouver, they found TV cameras waiting for them. From there, they took a bus to Seattle.

During the first day of the protest, Koleszar performed scouting and support duties and later ended up on the receiving end of a blast of pepper spray while sitting in a blockade line. On the second day, he got arrested while marching. The police boxed the protesters into a plaza and then told them to leave. As people left, the cops arrested them. Koleszar was one of a group of protesters kept on a bus for fifteen hours despite their demands to see a lawyer.

"Then they came on the bus and pepper-sprayed us and dragged us off," said Koleszar. Charged with resisting arrest, he spent three days in jail, but when his case finally made it to court, the judge let him go. Despite the arrest, the pepper spray and the jail time, Seattle was an exhilarating experience. "Being on the street with all these people making a statement is so empowering," he said. "People go back to their communities and spread the word and lead trainings and teach-ins and do media work of their own. The magnification power of it is just amazing."

He bristled a bit when I asked him about protectionism, free trade and fair trade. Admitting there are protectionist elements within the movement, Koleszar blamed the media for playing them up and distorting what the movement is really about. (He blames the media for a lot.) For him, the movement of capital is a bigger concern than the movement of goods, and he even sold fair-trade coffee for a while. (Fair-trade coffee comes from growers who get a reasonable price for their produce, don't exploit their workers and don't harm the environment.) But he was importing so little of it—and without a car, deliveries were a hassle—that the business never really went anywhere. Besides, he worried people would say, "I buy fair-trade coffee, so I've done my part." And that made him less keen on the idea. "I used to really push fair trade," he admitted. "Now I think it's like saying that the way to solve the problem is through our elite consumption. It's not challenging the system. Fair trade is not a bad thing, but I don't think it's The Answer."

Nor does he have much faith in traditional lobbying. A letter-writer, he argued, doesn't stand a chance against a well-funded, well-connected corporate lobbyist. "I won't say it's totally pointless," he said, "but it's almost pointless to try to influence government through writing letters or petitions or whatever. For specific laws, for specific issues, yes, that can be really good, but what I think we need to do is to change the system."

Campaigns against genetic engineering have had a lot more success going after corporations than governments. Because of pressure from activists and the fears of consumers, McCain's, for example, stopped using genetically modified potatoes even as the federal government continued promoting the high-tech Franken-foods. "Not many people are trying to target governments about genetic engineering," said Koleszar, "because it's hopeless."

This attitude doesn't surprise consultant and researcher Bani Dheer, who believes the twenty-four-hour news cycle and constant real-time access to the Internet have reduced young people's patience with traditional tactics. "Lobbying takes too long," she said. "When you're trying to figure out the best way to lobby for change, you figure out the institutions that are most receptive. This generation has figured out that for governments to change policy takes much longer than a corporation that's responsive to its customers. Companies have lots to lose."

By the same token, Koleszar suggested that while simple protests can play an effective role in a campaign, especially locally, big international meetings demand something more militant. "I think the movement could really benefit by looking at other tactics, such as civil disobedience and other things that might force the issue a little more. Because it's really urgent, and we need to force these issues sooner rather than later," he said. "We can't just talk about them for another generation, we need to start challenging the inherent beliefs of our society."

Changing society is, of course, a tall order. But Koleszar remains hopeful, pointing to the defeat of the MAI and the success of the Seattle protests. "There's this constant pressure now and they have to be careful about what they do, whereas before they used to do it totally in secret," he said. "So that's a victory. We have slowed them down and stopped things. That's a really good sign for hope."

IN AN EFFORT to get a better handle on the anti-globalization movement, I went to a teach-in a few weeks before the June 2000 protest against the Organization of American States in Windsor, Ontario. An alliance of countries from North, Central and South America, the OAS plans to negotiate the kind of hemispheric trade agreement that anti-globalization activists fear. At the teach-in, thirty-odd people sat in chairs arranged in a circle in a basement classroom of the University of Toronto's Ontario Institute for Studies in Education. It was a surprisingly clean-cut crew; there was a range of ages and looks—some piercings, some ponytails, some grey hair—but I couldn't see anyone who resembled the media caricature of the wild-eyed radical. The morning began with a couple of speakers, including a political-science professor from York University, talking about the OAS and its proposed trade deal, the Free Trade Area of the Americas. When the audience had a chance to ask questions and make comments, a debate erupted about whether reform of institutions such as the OAS is possible, and if it was a good idea to work with those who believe in reform. The inevitable speechifying began, and while one middle-aged man droned on, the white-haired fellow beside him fell asleep. Still, the session suggested that those who denounce anti-globalization activists as uninformed partiers aren't terribly informed themselves.

After a short break, and when we were just about to learn how to resist, a reporter from the *Windsor Star* showed up. A long debate ensued about whether or not to let her attend the teach-in. Many argued for openness with the media, figuring the Windsor paper's coverage of the planned protest couldn't get any less sympathetic. A few people disagreed, and when one man said he'd leave if she stayed, that was it. She had to wait outside and interview participants later.

With that administrative hassle out of the way, we discussed the difference between a demonstration and direct action. The former includes marching, placard-waving and chanting; the latter usually involves some level of civil disobedience—people taking over an intersection to prevent delegates from getting to a convention centre, for example, or lockdowns, in which protesters lock themselves to something like a fence, or to each other, to make it more difficult for police to remove them—or even violence. We also talked about affinity groups. Usually consisting of between three to twenty people with a common goal, an affinity group should include a medical person (someone with first-aid training who will avoid arrest in order to assist the injured), a legal person (who will avoid being arrested in order to help the incarcerated) and a communications person (who will act as a liaison with organizers).

Once we knew the terminology, and before we were to break into mock-affinity groups of four or five, we played Lifeboat. It seemed a little silly at first, but it eventually became clear that the game was designed to help us figure out our moral limits. The leaders—Justin, a tall, thin, blond guy with face piercings, and Tim, a short, wiry guy in shorts that went halfway down his calves—asked questions such as, "Would you defend yourself against police brutality?" If our answer was yes, we went to the side of the room designated "the lifeboat"; if no, we went to the other side. Then we talked about why we were standing where we were. It started off a little slowly, but by the time Justin and Tim asked if we would join in if we saw someone trashing a Starbucks, we seemed to have caught the hang of the exercise. And we knew where we stood: most of us wouldn't join in, but one guy said he would because he'd see it as a worthwhile expression of the rage that has been building within him his whole life.

RAGE AGAINST GLOBALIZATION is not a given throughout today's youth, of course. We romanticize the 1960s and imagine everyone was marching against injustice—while enjoying lots of free love and cheap drugs—but the truth is most young people back then wore skinny ties and wanted jobs in plastics. It's the same today; some young people take to the streets, but most prefer the comfort of their brand-riddled lives. Although my nephew is a little young to be part of the anti-globalization movement, I don't see him ever having to worry about how to get the pepper spray out of his eyes. When he turned 12, his parents gave him a ticket to New York, so he could spend a few days in Manhattan with his aunt. I asked him what he wanted to do there. "Go to Niketown," he said. It was a dispiriting answer for an uncle to hear, and so, when he turned 13 in 2001, I gave him a copy of J. D. Salinger's *The Catcher in the Rye.* Perhaps Holden Caulfield can straighten him out, and the next time he's in New York, he'll be more interested in looking for the lagoon in Central Park where the ducks go. But I'm not holding my breath.

Lyndsay Poaps was not surprised to hear about my nephew. The co-director of Check Your Head frequently hears some variation of it when she visits high schools and universities to talk about globalization. She's given workshops to 12-year-old boys who say, "Yeah, but if I don't buy Nike I won't have a lot of friends." Or, "I know it's crap and it's bad, but if I don't buy it, nobody will think I'm cool." Many older kids, though, know what globalization is, even if they don't call it that. "They're totally aware of being assaulted by brands," she said. "They're aware of what corporations are doing."

Tall and thin, with short, pixieish strawberry-blond hair, and just a few years out of high school herself, Poaps sat in a chair by her desk, pulled her knees up to her chin and explained that, initially, she became active in environmental issues. At 16, she got involved with the Canadian Environmental Network youth caucus, and that shed light on national issues for her. She left her hometown of Ottawa for Vancouver before the APEC protests, and quickly became interested in how trade issues affected the environment. And then in March of 1999, she helped launch Check Your Head. Poaps and her co-director, Kevin Millsip, run the group from an office on the edge of Vancouver's Downtown Eastside in the Dominion Building—or the Save the World Building, as they call it, because of the number of advocacy organizations that have offices there. It's a beautiful old edifice, but it's in considerable disrepair, so the rent for their office is just $350 a month. Check Your Head, which takes its name from a Beastie Boys album, raises its annual budget of $45,000 from unions and foundations and special fundraising events such as the launch of *No Logo: Taking Aim at the Brand Bullies*, Naomi Klein's influential book on brands and globalization.

The group's workshop leaders go from classroom to classroom—often at the invitation of teachers who are concerned their students are becoming billboards for corporations—to talk about globalization and related issues. The workshops, with titles such as Globalization 101 and Media Awareness and Commercialization of Education, vary, depending on the interests and age of the class. Younger students, for example, might get the Sweatshops session as a way of introducing the concept of globalization. But Poaps and the other leaders insist they don't preach and they aren't trying to brainwash anybody. "We're just there to facilitate an open discussion," she said, "and get them thinking critically about choices they make in their lives and how those choices have ramifications internationally."

When Poaps leads a workshop—as she does about fifty times a year—she might start by writing "globalization" on a blackboard and inviting the students to discuss what the word means to them. After the brainstorming session, she'll often break the class into groups of four or five for a game such as Funky Shoes. Each group acts as a country trying to woo Funky Shoes Ltd., the imaginary manufacturer of the popular Groovin' Sneaker. But the students must set labour, environmental and human-rights standards, as well as tax rates for their countries. Most of the students set high standards, but there's always one group—usually boys—that says, "No, we'll just have the lowest standards, and we'll have a lot of guns, and the government will be fine and we'll get the contracts." That's disheartening for Poaps, but it does give the class something to discuss.

Along with the workshops, Check Your Head also organizes conferences. In November 1999, the group, in conjunction with others, held a day-long forum on the WTO at UBC. Set up by and for young people—so they could learn about trade issues without feeling embarrassed or intimidated about asking questions—it attracted 250 people to a 200-seat room. At the end of the day, many of them signed up to travel to the Seattle protests at the end of the month.

While Poaps takes part in street protests such as the one in Seattle, she separates that activism from the workshops she does in high schools. She doesn't believe institutions like the WTO can be reformed, for example, but she realizes it's not her place to impose her beliefs on students. "If I'm talking to a 15-year-old who thinks it can be reformed, I'm not going to shut that 15-year-old down by saying what I think is right." And while some activists may think Check Your Head's school workshops aren't radical enough, she sees the value of both pushing and pulling at the issue of globalization. "We're talking about very radical things, but we're not lifestyle fascists," she said. "We're not going to high schools and telling students that what they're wearing is bad and the way they live their lives is pathetic and they have to get out on the streets right now because if they aren't, they just don't understand what's going on. We're not trying to stuff these ideas down the throats of young people; we're trying to encourage them to think about these issues themselves."

Some students are more receptive to the workshops than others, of course, but Poaps believes young people are increasingly active. She sees a wave of generational insecurity caused by unprecedented downward mobility and diminished expectations. "You either buy into the insecurity and start to look out for yourself, or you say, 'Things look bleak so I might as well work for change,'" said Poaps, who describes herself as an optimistic cynic. "When I go into a high school, I'm optimistic because I know that if we don't encourage young people to talk about these issues, to become active on these issues, to really think about their lifestyle choices, then there is no hope. Especially in North America, we use more than we can afford to use and we have this completely unsustainable lifestyle—and we are driving this force known as globalization. So if I wasn't optimistic about young people being able to change society, I would have to stop now."

IN 1991, GARTH MULLINS marched with thousands of striking public servants in Ottawa. He was right at the front of the protesters as they threw down the barricades and stormed the Parliament Buildings. "It was fantastic," he told me. "That's what everybody who wants to change things dreams of doing, storming Parliament."

Such comments may make Mullins sound like a dangerous radical, but he's bright, articulate and thoughtful. The 30-year-old has a masters in political sociology from the London School of Economics, and when I met him in August 2000, he was a doctoral student in sociology at UBC. His East Vancouver apartment was small, messy and musty-smelling—a typical student dwelling. There was a pile of junk on the coffee table, and his bookshelves were mostly filled with academic and political books; the only one I immediately recognized was Naomi Klein's *No Logo*.

A tall, thin albino with a hoop earring in his left ear, a piercing in his right eyebrow and a two-stranded choker around his neck, Mullins developed a bit of a national profile in the aftermath of the APEC protests. As part of Democracy Street, a group of activists who got together to sue the federal government and the RCMP, he wanted to educate Canadians about globalization and how it has an anti-democratic effect on government. APEC was a perfect example. When the government created a Public Complaints Commission inquiry into the RCMP's actions, it ignited a debate among anti-globalization activists about whether they should boycott or cooperate. Initially, Mullins was one of the loudest voices calling for a boycott; he knew the feds were only launching the inquiry to contain anger and criticism, and the participation of activists would only legitimize the cover-up attempt.

Before the inquiry could even begin, the heat started to grow on the government, and Mullins changed his mind. "As we were able to produce documents," he said, "we were able to really raise the temperature on the government and create an outrage across the country and also an interest in what APEC was and what globalization is about." He went on a speaking tour of Ontario and Quebec and took part in a demonstration outside 24 Sussex. When the prime minister showed up in Vancouver a year after the APEC protests, Mullins helped organize the Jean Chrétien Welcoming Committee—or, as the media dubbed the event after police beat the protesters with batons, the Riot at the Hyatt.

Today, Mullins has no regrets about taking part in the inquiry. Unlike some in the movement, he argued engaging in the system can be useful—when activists are clear what their goals are. "I saw that if we went into the APEC Inquiry hoping to use it to get justice, we would be very much disappointed," he said. "But if we could use the inquiry process to build a movement, to agitate, to talk to the communities we're involved in, we could use it as a platform. It gave us an audience, an opportunity to spark a national discussion about police and the government, about corporate globalization. And I think it was really valuable."

Democracy Street is typical of the groups in the anti-globalization movement. It has twenty-seven members plus other supporters, but no formal hierarchy, no staff and, needless to say, no interest in *Robert's Rules of Order*. This organizational model baffles many oldsters who grew up on the autocratic military model and keep waiting for a leader to emerge. But technology and a different attitude toward leadership make that unlikely. Since the movement is really a web of groups that communicate and organize through the Internet, there's no need or desire for a top-down structure. Besides, the insistence on consensus and democracy within the groups would make them difficult to rule with any real authority.

Mullins is one of two spokespeople for Democracy Street, not because he necessarily holds more sway than the other members, but because they realize they need to present a consistent face to the media. Nevertheless, engagement with the media is controversial within the movement. While most anti-globalization activists see the mainstream media as part of the problem, Mullins also sees opportunities. "A lot of people think the corporate media distort your messages—and certainly they do and I understand that media concentration is quite problematic—and they take the position that you shouldn't engage the media for that reason," he said. "We decided we wanted to use the media because they complemented the Public Complaints Commission. That was a media circus, so not to take advantage of them would be crazy."

He takes a similar broad-minded approach to tactics. Mullins, who has been arrested more than a half-dozen times but never charged, went to Seattle and took part in a direct action to prevent delegates from getting into the convention centre. While he sat cross-legged with other protesters trying to block an intersection, the police began using tear gas liberally. Unable to get out of the tear-gas cloud fast enough, he threw up and passed out. Mullins was willing to pay the price—not simply to stop the WTO from meeting, but to build a movement. "My politics are that the project of emancipation and freedom from oppression and exploitation is something that is taken on by individuals themselves," he said. "It's a project of self-emancipation. It's not a group of students who have the ability to travel around the country and get to these things or a small segment of society that should do it for everybody else. We should use those events to mobilize other people and bring them into the movement."

"So will the tactics have to change?" I asked.

He wouldn't say. While he refused to condemn property damage—or even violence in certain circumstances—he suggested that people should think strategically about their actions. "People who break the Starbucks windows in Seattle, for example, should ask themselves if they're doing that to declare war on a corporation and just damage the corporation somehow, because breaking a window certainly isn't doing much damage to a corporation. Or are they breaking windows as a symbolic act, to send a message to somebody else? And if they're doing that—and if we're all doing that by virtue of a demonstration—they should always be asking, 'Does this actually empower and mobilize other people?'"

Unfortunately, he admitted, too many people are debating logistics instead of objectives. Some activists aren't even convinced the movement should be larger, believing that most of the population have been bought off by corporate culture and can't be radicalized. But Mullins pointed out that no one is going to stop globalization with an affinity group. Still, that doesn't necessarily mean the movement will adopt more traditional tactics. "There's always been this instinct to lobby the state first, or write letters or whatever it is, on the way to being radical. People can go right past that now," he said, because the state and the people who run it can't be reformed. When he demonstrates outside 24 Sussex or at a hotel hosting the prime minister, he's not so much lobbying as he is trying to put a face on what's going on. "When we have a demonstration against Chrétien, it's not that we think he's going to change or that we want to change people's minds about him as an individual. Chrétien is shorthand for a whole bunch of things. He's almost like the Nike swoosh for globalization in Canada—or we're trying to brand him as that."

Hoping to spur others to join the fight may seem hopelessly idealistic, but Mullins can imagine a world full of active citizens. "I want people to become engaged in our society, for us to rise out of the positions we're put in as producers or consumers or spectators—and become agents and activists," he said. "It doesn't mean you have to do what I do; it just means taking an active interest in what's going on with your society. If a lot of people do that, they're going to very quickly realize they don't like what they see and will be moved to do something about it. And what comes out of that I don't know, but it will be massively democratic."

ENVIRONMENT

TOOLS FOR

RADICALS

WHEN BLAKE O'BRIEN, a friend since high school, picked me up at the Calgary Airport, I wondered if he'd turned paranoid since I had last seen him. It was a few days before the June 2000 World Petroleum Congress, and the city, he warned me, was in a state of high anxiety. Since the WPC is an international forum for oil executives, technicians and government officials, activists concerned about the industry's environmental and human-rights records had planned a street protest. "The hippies won in Seattle and the police won in Washington," a cop told one of Blake's friends. "Calgary will be the grudge match."

My friend's apartment is the penthouse atop the eleven-storey, art-deco office building he owns in downtown Calgary. (This sounds grander than it is. In a turn of events similar to the episode of *The Simpsons* in which Bart buys a dilapidated warehouse for a dollar, Blake snapped up the Barron Building at a bankruptcy auction during the depths of the recession in the early 1990s.) It is just four blocks from the section of the city the police closed to protect the 2,500 people attending the WPC. Some nearby buildings planned to board up windows, and Blake's ground-level retail tenants asked him if they should do the same. Despite the public sabre-rattling, the cops weren't much help when he called to ask what to do, so he suggested his tenants put up signs offering 10 percent discount to all protesters. ("Just show your Birkenstocks," he joked.)

Since it was a Thursday night, our first order of business was bar hopping. That's when I realized Blake wasn't pulling my leg about the town's jitters. A charter school in the Telus Convention Centre, I soon heard, was moving to the suburbs for the week. And the police had visited local high schools to scare teenagers off talking to the "dangerous radicals." One woman, who worked in a bar six blocks from the no-go zone, told me she had a note from her employer in case the police stopped her to ask why she was downtown. Another claimed an American protester had been turned away at the border because he had 10,000 feminine napkins, which double as first-aid supplies, in his car. Everyone was talking about the protest.

We awoke the next morning to hangovers and a *Calgary Herald* headline that read: "City battens down hatches for WPC" above a picture of police in riot gear. Even as the protest organizers tried to lower expectations, the police and the media were busy whipping Calgarians into a lather. More than a month before the conference, Paul Jackson wrote a column in the *Calgary Sun* asking who was "covertly financing and directing" the protests. He then gave his readers a multiple-choice offering of potential answers: Moammar Gadhafi, Saddam Hussein or Osama bin Laden. But finances and direction seemed to be two things in short supply at the End of Oil Action Coalition's headquarters—or convergence space, as the protesters called it—in a dingy storefront not far from downtown. Outside, under the bright Alberta sunshine, a swarm of testosterone-riddled cops periodically made a big show of coming into the muddy parking lot, walking around looking tough and filming everything with their fancy digital Handycams. A police chopper buzzed ominously overhead.

I joined Josh Raisler Cohn as he scouted for a location to unfurl an anti-oil banner. A climbing trainer and logistics coordinator with the Ruckus Society, a California group that leads civil-disobedience training camps in the U.S. and Canada, he did-n't appear to be getting much money from international terrorists. His clothes—a green sleeveless T-shirt, dirty light brown pants and unhip running shoes—came from dollar stores, and he hadn't paid rent since December 1998. This direct-action consultant was soft-spoken and polite, almost deferential, when talking to people, even cops. Despite his best efforts, he'd been arrested four or five times, and after Seattle, he had noticed police forces ratcheting up the tension with expensive new equipment and intimidation tactics. "We're trying to do creative, colourful mes-sages," he said. "But the police spin it as confrontation."

Later, I joined thirty or so people sitting in a circle around legal workshop leader Alan Keane. An organizer of Co-Motion, a Calgary group that is part of the End of Oil Action Coalition, Keane explained people's rights, how they should handle con-frontations with the police and what they should do if arrested. As the workshop wound down and more protesters arrived at the parking lot under the watchful eye of the men in blue across the road, I met Plague, a large, red-haired man with several days' worth of stubble on his face, standing next to a large pot of licorice mint yurbawata tea by the soup kitchen set up at the side of an old, beat-up school bus. He let me have a sip from his cup—it tasted much better than it sounded—and told me about the Kevlar-knuckled gloves the cops were wearing. Meanwhile, over in the corner, the men and women of the Radikal Cheer-leaders, an Edmonton group that boasts it is "2% PROTEST, 98% FUNKY STUFF," changed into black skirts and red tops—or, in some cases, vice versa—and grabbed pompoms.

Eventually, everybody started walking to Eau Claire, Calgary's riverside market, where the peaceful Sunday afternoon march to a rally at Olympic Plaza would begin. Eau Claire was filled with regular folks, including union members, the curious and even a few families. There were plenty of signs with environmental and human-rights messages and demands to boycott the *Calgary Herald*, which was in the midst of a bitter strike, but no violent tension in the air. Following a police-approved route along near-deserted streets and past countless cops with digital Handycams, the marchers chanted, "Hey, ho, petroleum has got to go" and "Whose streets? Our Streets." The Radikal Cheerleaders did pat-a-cake skits and performed cheers such as, "To the left, to the left. Not to the right, to the left."

At Olympic Plaza, after a long wait for the solar-powered sound system to arrive, the speeches and the entertainment—provided by the Raging Grannies, a street-theatre group from Edmonton and local musicians—finally started. Given the relaxed atmosphere in the crowd—the next day, the *Calgary Herald* put the number at 700, the *Globe and Mail* estimated 2,000—there wasn't much for the hundreds of police officers to do.

At 6:15 the next morning, as the low sun bathed Fort Calgary Park in light and the mercury struggled to rise above freezing, a few dozen young people milled about while more arrived in groups. The police—and their chopper—made their presence felt, and the bleary-eyed greeted each other with hugs and pre-pared for the day's protest. Led by the Radikal Cheerleaders, the crowd of 150 or so began its march, passing bemused work-bound Calgarians on the way. At an LRT station, twelve cops formed a barrier with their bicycles while stunned transit-users watched.

"Look," yelled one protester, "we're human." Later, outside oil company office towers, the crowd chanted, "This is what democracy looks like; that is what a police state looks like," and "Ain't no power like the power of the people, because the power of the people won't stop." Though some car drivers were upset about being delayed, the march, which lasted until mid-afternoon, was peaceful and largely uneventful: there were chants, performances from the Radikal Cheerleaders, some street theatre and, in front of the Suncor building, six people mooned the crowd to reveal letters on their butts that spelled "Wind power now."

As we walked along, I chatted with an *Edmonton Sun* reporter in a black leather jacket. He was struck by both the police overkill and the lameness of the protest. More importantly, he was worried about what his editors were going to say. "I can only get so much colour," he fretted

"What do they want? Pepper spray?"

"Yep."

EVERYONE IN CALGARY knew about the WPC demonstrations, of course, but few people I talked to had any idea what they were all about. Some didn't care and just wished a few roughnecks from the oil rigs would give the punks what for; but others were genuinely interested. The media were no help—they covered everything but what the protesters believe in. But the demos were quixotic anyway: convincing the conservative and contented citizens of a city built on oil and gas that the environmental damage and human-rights abuses that go with petroleum aren't worth it would be a tough sell at the best of times. And with the media and the police doing everything in their power to sensationalize events and spread fear, the message never had a chance.

Whenever I voiced my doubts, though, the answer was invariably that such protests represented just one arrow in the quiver. ("The front is long" is a line I heard a lot. It's a quotation from Arne Naess, the Norwegian philosopher and father of "deep ecology.") A few days later, environmentalist Mike Sawyer admitted that the WPC protest wouldn't, by itself, change anything. "But as an element of an overall strategy, it was successful because to get 1,500 to 1,800 people out protesting the oil and gas industry in this town is remarkable," he argued. "I would rather have seen a more aggressive event, just by virtue of my nature, but I think there were some tactical benefits to the way it turned out, because absolutely none of the predictions from the media and the police about hooligans and violence came to pass."

Tactics are a matter of considerable debate in all areas of activism, but environmentalists use the greatest range of approaches—from education to eco-terrorism. While the movement is big enough, old enough and sufficiently well-funded by foundations to have spawned countless organizations, the activists haven't been able to come to any agreement on what works best or even what's acceptable. And they're not likely to do so anytime soon.

ALTHOUGH HE WASN'T one of the organizers of the WPC protests, Mike Sawyer was always a presence. At the Sunday afternoon rally, I watched him go up to the perimeter fence and photograph the cops on the other side, and he was the first person I saw running toward the police when they arrested a teenager dressed like a punk because his spikes and chains were, according to the police, weapons. The next morning at Fort Calgary Park, Sawyer overheard an undercover officer talking into a wire, and shadowed him until he left. And while Sawyer marched around the city with the protesters, he carried a drum and banged it with the hook where his left hand used to be.

We met a few days later at the Barron Building, where he once had an office. Even before I mentioned it, Sawyer said he enjoyed the irony of being an environmentalist who focuses on oil and gas issues and working out of that building. After the 1947 oil strike in Leduc, the logical place for the major oil companies to set up shop was nearby Edmonton, but there was little available office space. Jacob Barron, a Calgary lawyer and the owner of a chain of movie theatres, saw an opportunity and built an office tower. Calgary's "first skyscraper" opened in 1951, and Shell, Mobil and others moved in; the juniors soon followed, and the city became Canada's oil and gas headquarters. Barron lived out the last days of his life in the penthouse apartment. The suite had fallen into considerable disrepair, with wires hanging from the ceiling, but the wood paneling and the stone fireplace—and the 1950s-era furniture Blake collects at garage sales and government auctions—made the place look like something out of an old Rat Pack movie.

As Mike Sawyer, acting executive director of the Citizens' Oil and Gas Council, settled into a faux Le Corbusier chair, I wondered what Frank and Dino would have made of him. For a while, Sawyer's life was marked by a weird tension between paramilitary activities and a rebellious spirit. Active in the scouting movement until he left in anger at age 16, he went on to become a mountain guide (the hook on his left arm is the parting gift from a helicopter accident). After training NATO soldiers, he considered joining the British SAS. And he almost joined the Calgary police force, but backed off when it came time to sign on the dotted line. As much as he was attracted to that life and got along well with soldiers, he couldn't help but question authority. "When people say, 'You have to do this,' my first response is always, 'Who says?'"

At 41, he's just as much a renegade in the activist community. He argues that the "reason model" of decision-making—favoured by those who see advocacy as lobbying—is misguided. Most activists organize their ideas, collect facts to back up their point of view and then present their case. They're sure that if they're reasonable, those in power will say, "Okay, we agree with you and we'll do it that way." Sawyer saw this approach at work when he was a vice-president of the Alberta Wilderness Association in the early 1990s and he wasn't impressed. "The AWA has been around for thirty years and it really hasn't accomplished anything," he said. "There are very few protected areas because of them. It's the same with other groups."

Lobbying, he's convinced, plays into the hand of the Alberta government, which uses lengthy consultations to buy time while buoying the hopes and sucking the energy out of activists. "It allows government to play spin doctor and say, 'Well, we've been working with environmental groups for two and a half years in a cooperative way to resolve these issues,'" he said. "But in the meantime, on the ground, absolutely dick is happening." Rather than the "reason model," Sawyer prefers the "power model." It's not the people with the most reasoned argument who win the day, this line of thinking goes, it's those who have the most power— either money or the ability to offer benefit or inflict pain. "If you have power and the other side knows you're prepared to use it," he explained, "then you can sit down and negotiate."

The way activists view decision-making—reason model or power model—determines the tactics they'll use. And there's no shortage of people willing to go to extremes. Even though Greenpeace has grabbed power by creating in-your-face confrontations for the media since its start in Vancouver in 1971, the group tossed out co-founder Paul Watson for being too militant. Undaunted, the New Brunswick native launched the Sea Shepherd Society, an eco-terrorism group that uses dangerous but effective tactics to disrupt whale, seal and dolphin hunts. In the 1980s, for example, his group sank Icelandic whaling boats and vandalized miles of expensive fish nets. None of this has hurt Watson, who is now based in California and counts many Hollywood stars as supporters (several, including Martin Sheen and Pierce Brosnan, have accompanied him on his campaigns).

In Alberta, the most controversial use of the power model is the case of Weibo Ludwig. The national media portrayed him as a wacko and a vandal, so I was surprised to meet many people in the west—smart, thoughtful people—who supported him (or, at least, refused to condemn him). In April 2000, an Edmonton judge sentenced Ludwig to twenty-eight months in jail for five acts of oil-field vandalism. The farmer and former preacher defended his actions by pointing out that the people on his Trickle Creek Farm were suffering a rash of health problems, including several miscarriages and a stillbirth. The livestock weren't faring any better. He blamed the oil industry—specifically, he attributed the problems to the flaring (burning the excess gas from a well) of sour gas (which contains hydrogen sulfide). Sawyer, for one, is sympathetic: "What do you do when you know you're being poisoned? You know the companies aren't going to help you—you've asked and they've refused; the government regulators aren't going to help you—you've asked and they've refused; the government itself doesn't help you; the police don't help you. What do you do? It's a moral decision individuals have to make based on the circumstances."

While most Canadians deplore the violence, the Ludwig case did raise the profile of the sour-gas issue. "It helped the cause enormously," said Sawyer. "There was a twenty-fold increase in press coverage—regionally and nationally—of the public-health issues surrounding oil and gas. That press coverage would never have happened in the absence of conflict." And that's why some Alberta environmentalists are interested in creating more conflict. They want to emulate the activists who have transformed the British Columbia forestry industry with a mix of confrontational tactics, such as blockades, civil disobedience and campaigns that target retailers. But the more radical activists are frustrated that most of the province's advocacy groups remain afraid to be unreasonable, preferring to believe negotiations can still work. The debate has raged for several years in wild-rose country, but it's a common, perhaps inevitable, point of contention among activists across Canada. "If your objective is to be reasonable, you've already eliminated a lot of the potential advocacy tools that would generate power, and you end up dooming yourself to failure," said Sawyer, who looks for "soft underbellies" when searching for ways to gain power. "We need to look at a full range of tactics. Where I draw the line is where innocent people would be injured or killed. I wouldn't lose any sleep over damage against property if it's done strategically and it's justified."

THE DISAGREEMENT over tactics is not limited to Alberta, as I discovered on a trip to the Maritimes. Canada's smallest and least populated province, it turns out, offers a microcosmic view of the battle that pits environmentalist against environmentalist. And since Sharon Labchuk is at the centre of it, I went to see her first. She lives amid a stand of trees in rural Prince Edward Island, not too far from the home that inspired Lucy Maud Montgomery's Green Gables. I parked in her driveway and walked past her red Toyota Tercel, which was covered with pro-organic, anti-pesticide bumper stickers and the Island's famous red, red mud. We sat down at a table by the kitchen beside a large bowl of honeycomb and several just-filled jars of honey. And we talked about the weather.

Though it was mid-July, the weather was miserable, full of fog and wind and prodigious downpours. It wasn't a good day for tourists hoping to enjoy PEI's gorgeous sand beaches, but it had the potential to be a disastrous day for the province's rivers. Heavy rains a few days after the potato growers have sprayed their crops with pesticides can wash deadly chemicals into nearby rivers and leave them running red with mud and dead fish. Officially, nine such incidents—commonly known as "fish kills," though Labchuk prefers "river kills," because everything, including snakes, frogs and snails, dies—occurred in 1999. But many people suspect dozens more went unnoticed or unreported. "When it rains," she said, "I know things are dying."

An elfin woman with long, long dark hair, Labchuk is a self-described back-to-the-lander who home-schooled her kids. The 48-year-old university dropout built most of her solar home herself. When she returned to the Island from Alberta in 1988, there was no environmental group in the province, so she co-founded the Environmental Coalition of Prince Edward Island (ECO-PEI). Starting from ground zero was tough, especially since most of the residents cared little and knew less about the environment. "It was like the Dark Ages," she said. "Even now, it's shocking." Media coverage, however, was easy to get and she quickly earned a name for herself.

Initially, she devoted most of her energy to relatively safe issues such as garbage—fighting dumps and the Charlottetown incinerator and promoting recycling and composting—and didn't create too much of a stink. But in 1995, after receiving a lot of phone calls from people wanting her to do something about the spraying, she decided to tackle pesticides. Since a huge grant-driven expansion of the potato industry in 1988, there had been a massive increase in the use of chemical sprays by growers. After researching the subject, Labchuk, who wants to see the whole island go organic, tried to publicize the dangers of pesticides. It was not a popular message: agriculture and tourism dominate the Island economy, but the farmers have far more political clout. And the potato growers and politicians quickly dismissed her as a liar.

In August 1996, in an effort to pit tourism against agriculture and convince the tourism industry its interests were suffering because of pesticides, she handed out pamphlets to tourists waiting for the ferry to PEI. Entitled "How to Protect Your Family from Pesticide Poisoning While Visiting Prince Edward Island or What the PEI Government Won't Tell You in the Tourist Brochures," the leaflets included a map of the Island above the words "Toxic Playground?" Although tame by the standards of activism in other provinces, the move created a storm of controversy. Labchuk had called the media and was sure the stunt would generate coverage and upset some people, but even she was surprised at the reaction. "I knew they'd be pissed. I knew the politicians would be mad and the tourist industry would be mad and the potato growers would be mad. That's nothing new for me," she said. "But it just exploded."

While she was happy the issue was being discussed on the streets and in the letters pages of newspapers, she was also frightened by the anger it generated. Like a company town, PEI is filled with people who make their livelihood from the potato industry, or know someone who does. People accused her of driving tourists away and trying to wreck the economy. When she took her children to a fair, three potato growers surrounded her and threatened her. The backlash got so serious that she and her kids jumped in the car and fled to Nova Scotia for a few days. "Up to this point, I had been a local hero. I had a really good name with the public and I was seen as a good person fighting bad things like incinerators. All of sudden, there was raw hatred toward me. I'd been used to criticism, but not the feeling that someone could come to my house and do something to me," said Labchuk, who has since had her house vandalized twice. "So when I went to Nova Scotia, I had to make my mind up: either give up what I was doing or go back and tough it out."

IN NOVA SCOTIA, Labchuk stayed with David Orton. Until then, she only knew him through an e-mail relationship that began when he criticized her for taking a compromise position. That's typical of Orton. An influential philosopher among some environmentalists in Nova Scotia, he's a stubborn purist who doesn't believe in compromise. In fact, he's best known for his intemperate views on the positions of other environmentalists, including those he works with. Even a group he helped start, the North Shore Environmental Web, didn't last long. "It came undone mainly because of me," he admitted. "I'm fanatical."

A native of Portsmouth, England, he came to Canada in 1957 at age 23. A one-time academic (he was teaching at Montreal's Sir George Williams University during the infamous ten-day sit-in and computer riot in 1969) and a former vice-chairman of the Marxist-Leninist party, he started a research group called the Green Web in 1988. It's dedicated to what he calls the left bio-centricism, an offshoot of deep ecology. Based on the ideas of Norwegian philosopher Arne Naess, deep ecology is an influential school of thought among environmentalists. Believing all life on the planet is equal and interrelated, the movement questions the values and lifestyle of Western industrial society. Shallow ecology, on the other hand, refers to efforts to save a parcel of nature or clean up pollution, without challenging industrial society. While deep ecology adherents believe in more fundamental change, that doesn't mean they won't take part in shallow ecology. Orton does, too, but he can end up being a disruptive influence. "It's part of the responsibility of an activist to hold forth alternative visions," he said. "But when you're working just from a shallow point of view, alternative visions are considered counterproductive."

Orton lives with his wife, daughter and dog in the woods near Salt Springs (not far from New Glasgow). His green house has white trim and no indoor plumbing. He greeted me at his door in sandals, khaki shorts and a white shirt with red stripes. He wore unstylish glasses on his droopy face, and his hair was grey and mussed. As he welcomed me in, I noticed the posters promoting demonstrations and protests on the wall of his glassed-in porch. In the middle of the wall, Orton has placed a quote from Ed Abbey, an American novelist who wrote a book about environmental sabotage called *The Monkey Wrench Gang*: "Sentiment without action is the ruin of the soul."

I'd read some of Orton's own writing on the ferry from PEI to Nova Scotia, and I sensed he bristled at "the front is long," the popular Naess line. When I asked about it, he replied: "It's a mantra that usually means, 'Don't say anything negative because everyone does their own thing.' But sometimes when people do things, they have consequences for the rest of us." In 1988, for example, many Nova Scotia activists considered BTK, a biological spray used in forestry, a lesser evil. But it turned out the spray killed all the moths and butterflies. "So 'the front is long' means you have a lot of nonsense talk instead of a rigorous investigation. One of the things I've found—and that's why some people are quite negative about me—is it's very hard to have a critical discussion about things."

When it comes to tactics, Orton sides with those pushing for more aggressive action such as ecotage, or environmental sabotage. Although he realizes the importance of public support, his attitude is: you do what you have to do. "Deep ecology is a revolutionary movement, and people have to come to see the necessity of it. We're talking about a fundamental revolutionary change. I consider myself subversive or seditious because I want to replace the industrial paradigm. And I expect to be dealt with accordingly, as I have in the past," said Orton, who was arrested twice during his Marxist-Leninist days, and once spent forty days in jail.

"There's a whole intellectual discussion that you have to take part in, but look outside there." He pointed to his porch. "Those posters go back fifteen years. I've written many, many papers, taken part in many meetings and demonstrations and made pre-sentations. It doesn't change anything—they still clear-cut, they still spray. It won't change until people say, 'You're not going to do it anymore.'"

Orton's theoretical underpinnings and unyielding approach have made him enemies, but he made a big impression on Sharon Labchuk, who soon came to see him as a mentor. After she'd devoured his suggested readings about deep ecology, Orton asked her, "What do you think?"

"It's everything I've ever believed in," she replied, "but I never had the language before."

ARMED WITH NEW LANGUAGE and increased resolve, Labchuk returned to PEI. But she soon discovered her tactics had angered not just business and government but some of her allies, including Gary Schneider, the other co-coordinator of ECO-PEI. It didn't help when a Revenue Canada bureaucrat showed up to go over the group's books. What he really wanted to see was a copy of the pamphlet Labchuk had distributed to the tourists, because any registered charity risks losing its charitable status if it devotes more than 10 percent of its resources to polit-ical activity. And the taxman uses a broad definition of political activity. South of the border, all sorts of environmental organiza-tions get millions from American foundations, but in Canada activists can offer tax receipts and keep quiet or they can stay loud and poor.

Because ECO-PEI was the only such group on the island, it housed differing views and competing interests. There were committed activists such as Labchuk and well-meaning people who were happy just to attend meetings. "But then there was another contingent I have no respect for, who simply suck down at the government and corporate trough," said Labchuk. "Gary and I were the dominant personalities in the group. And Gary told me he didn't support activism and he didn't want the group to be an activist group." After the leaflet incident, the board introduced new policies to control the pesticide committee. All of a sudden, Labchuk couldn't issue a press release or write a letter to the editor without approval from the board.

The irreconcilable differences between the two co-coordinators came to a head at a meeting in early 1998. "It wasn't a meeting to say, 'This is the end, boys,' it was to talk about our differences and see what we could come up with," remembered Labchuk. "But all hell broke loose: there was swearing, yelling, the whole bit." She and the other self-described "shit disturbers" left to form a new group, Earth Action. While Schneider is tight-lipped about what led to Labchuk's departure, he's also philosophical about it. "I'm surprised any group stays together," he said, pointing out the need to find a fit between people that works. "We may differ on methodology, but she's brilliant on a lot of pesticide stuff."

Making no attempt to be another mainstream organization, Earth Action is based on the deep ecology philosophy. "Rather than just bringing in regulations," said Labchuk, "our overall objective is changing the consciousness of people in terms of their relationship to the planet and nature." While ECO-PEI had a traditional structure, with an executive, a board of directors and public memberships, Earth Action is a collective with no titles, no supporting members and few meetings. The four principals—

Labchuk; Irene Novaczek, a scientist; Aaron Koleszar, an anti-globalization activist; and Brad Duplisea, who moved to Ottawa to fight genetically modified foods with the Canadian Health Coalition—make most of their decisions by e-mail and phone. In other words, it's the kind of flat organization increasingly adopted by activists working on all kinds of issues.

No longer responsible to timid board members, Earth Action is free to push issues with more aggressive tactics. Along with organizing demonstrations and rallies, Labchuk writes as often as possible for environmental publications outside the province. "Small places are like a family where incest is going on: you don't talk about it, you keep it in the family," she said. "On the Island, we're not supposed to talk about bad things like pesticides. We're not supposed to destroy this myth of Prince Edward Island as this pristine, natural preserve. You don't do anything that's going to destroy that image, because if you do, you're going to have a lot of people mad at you." Still, she wants to have the right people angry at her, so she has to be careful not to lose supporters by going too far. "We're not averse to being publicly critical of anybody or anything or of saying exactly what we think and not sugar-coating it. But I never do anything without very carefully weighing the situation," said Labchuk, who knows she must operate within the practical limits of what's acceptable to PEI's citizens—as opposed to the politicians—and that's quite different from what activists in, say, British Columbia can get away with. "I think I'm a pretty good judge of what would be an appropriate action, of when to be as radical as I can be and when not to."

"GARY SCHNEIDER?" Sharon Labchuk sputtered contemptuously when I told her I planned to visit him. "He's not an activist." More than two years after the splintering of ECO-PEI, she was still bitter. He's a control freak, she assured me, and he's afraid to make waves for fear of losing government and corporate support. But I suspected that deep down she simply didn't respect his tactics.

When I'd first spoken to him on the phone, Schneider had said he didn't make a distinction between activism and education. And as we sat down in a renovated barn turned nature centre, he bristled at labels such as activist and environmentalist. "I think there are all kinds of people trying to change the world," he insisted. As we continued talking, though, Schneider revealed himself. "I do lots of education with kids; I also do tons of lobbying with adults," he said. "I just don't want to go into a room and have to yell at politicians any more. I've found it incredibly hard to change politicians, especially here in PEI. What I really work on is trying to get the public concerned, and for all of us to pressure the politicians."

While forestry is Schneider's pet issue, he is, in his own way, just as concerned about fish kills as Labchuk is. But it's certainly true the two have incompatible approaches to changing the world. The bearded, ponytailed 47-year-old runs the MacPhail Woods Ecological Forestry Project, about half an hour east of Charlottetown. Including a native-plant nursery, three nature trails and demonstrations of forest restoration, windbreaks and erosion control, the centre offers regular walks and workshops. The project relies on government and corporate money for survival, and ECO-PEI sells corporate memberships for $100. Schneider won't make apologies for that, though. Nor does he regret sitting on government-sponsored committees such as the Round Table on Resource Land Use and Stewardship. And he has no qualms about, for example, the joint workshops he gives with forestry department officials. "They know I don't have any use for how they do things," he said. "But I try not to make it personal. I don't have any grudges, I don't feel bitter and I don't feel they're evil people."

Instead of confrontation, Schneider is convinced that cooperation is the way to go. That's why ECO-PEI is part of a sustainable land-initiative coalition that includes eight groups, three of which are the International Farmers Union, Atlantic Salmon Federation and the Island Nature Trust. Together they went to see the agriculture minister. "It's very easy for governments to dismiss you if you don't have money, power or votes. I could have gone in and ranted and vented and probably made myself feel better, and he would have just ignored me," he said. "But the work we did organizing the other groups to finally get up to speed on these agriculture issues made a huge difference."

FACED WITH SCHNEIDER'S lobbying and the international scrutiny spurred by Labchuk, the PEI government introduced new rules—such as buffer zones around rivers and streams—for potato growers. The changes were far too little for Labchuk, but while Schneider knows the government needed to do more, he was happy about any progress. Though they may not like to admit it, both Earth Action's vinegar and ECO-PEI's honey were needed to force the politicians. "We need both," said Irene Novaczek, the one-time head of ECO-PEI's marine-issues committee. Now part of Earth Action—though she was working in Indonesia when the split took place—she's more forgiving than Labchuk about the environmental movement's wide range of approaches to changing government policies and people's attitudes. "We're all agents of change. Arne Naess says, 'The front is long.' And that's where I am—the front is very long, and as long as people are moving, I can disagree with their approach or strategy. But you won't find me calling down another activist or group."

Novaczek backs up that conciliatory talk by working in coalitions that include environmentalists and fishermen. A native of

Scotland, Novaczek now lives in a house with yellow siding near Breadlebane, PEI. She parts her thick shoulder-length dark hair in the middle, wears glasses and sports a T-shirt calling for the protection of old-growth forests. A working scientist with a doctorate in marine botany, she spends twenty-eight hours a week as a research coordinator in a lab. "I don't want to take on more paid work," she said, "because it interferes with my life." As we sat in her cramped office, she talked so passionately and forcefully—though not particularly loudly or quickly—that she often talked right through my questions. I didn't mind, though, because she usually had something thoughtful to say.

Of all the environmentalists I spoke to, Novaczek was the most pessimistic about the future of the planet, but she was also the most pragmatic—and the most distressed by the divisiveness and intolerance that run rampant in the ecology movement. When I wondered why there is such a range of tactics in the environmental movement, she initially made me realize what a naive question it was by asking, "Well, why are humans so different?" But after thinking about it, she continued: "I suppose it's because we are up against big money—government or corporations are always seeking to divide and conquer, co-opt and bribe and purchase, because that is the way they do their business. And they are only too willing to play us against one another and to provide incentives to collaborate and co-operate with them. The unfortunate part of the diversity is that the opposition can always find people who call themselves environmentalists who are willing to be purchased and co-opted or used, even if they don't recognize or admit it."

Novaczek has enjoyed good relations with the fishing community since she worked with fishing families in the 1970s as a summer student with the Department of Fisheries and Oceans. Since then, she joined the PEI Fishermen's Association and other groups in the fight against the building of the Confederation Bridge that now links the island province to the rest of Canada. And from 1993 to 1995, she lobbied the United Nations on the collapse of fish stocks. Because of various environmental campaigns—including the high-profile battle against the seal hunt—that alliance between fishermen and ecologists was not easy to forge. "It took a lot, a lot, a lot of energy, a lot of talking, a lot of meetings, a lot of flying around," she remembered. "But we put it together, and that coalition still exists." Later, she joined Save Our Seas and Shores, a coalition concerned with the effect of oil production on the fisheries in the Gulf of St. Lawrence and nearby waters. She acts as a technical advisor and, as a scientist with a Ph.D., she gives SOS[2] some credibility with bureaucrats. But she knows what really gives the alliance its sway is the inclusion of fishing organizations, aboriginal groups and tourism operators as well as disparate environmentalists, including David Orton. Novaczek is a lot more comfortable putting water in her wine than Orton is. "You need the David Ortons to lay down the philosophical framework and say these are the boundaries," she said. "Unfortunately, if you stay within the very strictest of those boundaries, you'll end up talking only to yourself, so at some point there are compromises that need to be made."

Activists of all stripes are increasingly using such alliances—the "unusual suspects," as Wendy Cukier of the Coalition for Gun Control calls them—to drive their agendas. Cukier's coalition is a perfect example. Because it represented dozens of organizations—including victims' rights groups, the Canadian Bar Association and the Canadian Association of Chiefs of Police—it was able to convince the federal government to introduce controversial gun-control legislation. Although such coalitions make it harder for governments to slag the people pushing for change as "special interest groups," they are difficult to create and maintain. The first meeting of Save Our Seas and Shores took place right after the Supreme Court had ruled on native fishing rights in the Donald Marshall case, so tensions were high between native and non-native fishers. At another meeting, Orton launched an attack on members who weren't prepared to call for an immediate ban on all petroleum production. But coalitions that include people with wildly different levels of environmental consciousness need to start with what everyone can agree on and build from there. So SOS[2] wants to stop all petroleum development along inshore fishing grounds, starting with the southern Gulf of St. Lawrence. As a first step, it is calling for a moratorium on Gulf exploration pending the outcome of environmental, social and economic impact studies. "As soon as you start coalition-building, you have to make compromises and you have to deal with your contradictions," said Novaczek, adding that it takes time and effort to build the necessary trust and to agree on what can be said publicly—and what can't—under the name of the coalition. "It's a very difficult process, and it can get you into all kinds of trouble because you can never control what's coming out of all ends of coalitions. And the more diverse you get, the more dangerous it becomes."

AS ACTIVISTS NAVIGATE the dangers of coalitions, they also seek to wield more power with governments—and, increasingly, corporations—through tactics such as legal challenges. While not new, the courts have, especially since the introduction of the Charter of Rights and Freedoms in 1982, become one of the most useful tools for people who want to change the world. Surprisingly, the best person to talk to about this subject is not a lawyer but a veterinarian in small-town Alberta. Rocky Mountain House is a two-and-a-half-hour drive from either Calgary or

Edmonton. Nestled on the edge of the Rockies, the town has a lovely setting, but is otherwise unremarkable. Just off a strip of fast-food joints and chain stores, a little way down a gravel road, is the Rocky Animal Hospital, a veterinary clinic in a house built in what may best be described as 1970s hippie style.

As I read the two Gandhi quotes on the wall of the clinic's lobby, Martha Kostuch came out, shook my hand and led me upstairs to her home. A small woman, she has long sandy hair with bangs, wire-rim glasses, freckles and pale blue eyes. After growing up on a farm in Minnesota, she became a vet and moved to Alberta in 1975 to be close to the mountains and the forests. Immediately, Kostuch, who had never been environmentally active, saw things she hadn't seen in Minnesota cattle herds: widespread postpartum uterine infections, long calving intervals and an unusually high number of miscarriages and stillbirths. She became convinced that sour-gas emissions were the culprit. Government and industry brushed off her concerns, so in 1977, she went public by speaking at meetings and conferences. She didn't know enough to call the media, but they soon called her.

Meanwhile, Kostuch joined a fight against a huge resort development planned for the Kootenay Plains, about eighty miles west of Rocky Mountain House. Environmentalism was far from a widespread movement at the time—even Greenpeace was just six years old—so the group, called the Alberta League for Environmentally Responsible Tourism (ALERT), learned from scratch, developing an action plan and paddling eight canoes from Rocky Mountain House to the legislature in Edmonton to deliver a petition. The media lapped it up; one reporter joined Kostuch in her canoe, and thirty-five more waited on the banks of the river in the provincial capital.

More importantly, ALERT took advantage of a sympathetic lawyer and donations from supporters to fight the $40-million project in court. It was not a common tactic at that time, but it worked. And Kostuch would use it again—and become something of a legend in environmental-law circles in the process. Most famously, Kostuch and a group called Friends of the Oldman River Society, with the help of the Sierra Legal Defence Fund, shepherded the Oldman River Dam environmental assessment case to victory in the Supreme Court of Canada in 1992. In a second case over the Oldman River Dam, she tried to prosecute the Alberta government for destroying fish habitats without approval. That case rose through the system until she was denied leave to appeal by the Supreme Court. In a third case, Kostuch and the Friends of the West Country battled to stop Sunpine Forest Products from building a logging road and two bridges without a proper environmental assessment. Again with the help of the Sierra Legal Defence Fund, Kostuch won in both Federal Court and the Federal Court of Appeal. But she is awaiting leave to appeal from the Supreme Court, because she was unhappy with some parts of the decision. She's now something of a lay expert on environmental law. "I've had many calls—today, for example—from people asking for advice, or help or direction," she said. "I'm not a lawyer, but a lot of lawyers call me for advice since I've had a lot of experience."

Kostuch, who spends thirty to forty hours a week working as a vet and the same amount of time on activism, excused herself for a few minutes to go downstairs. Returning several minutes later, she told me she'd just put a dog to sleep while the family watched; we talked about why it's important for kids to learn about death. It doesn't seem much of a jump when we start talking about tactics. Kostuch has developed a process for creating strategic plans, and she uses it to help advocacy groups as well as for the workshops she gives in schools. Anything goes during brainstorming, but when they get to the planning stage, Kostuch insists all violence—including property damage—must be weeded out. But that doesn't mean she shies away from conflict. "I think non-violent civil disobedience has a role to play. It has been an important tool for change throughout history," said Kostuch, who has read a lot by and about Gandhi. "Look at the civil-rights movement, which I grew up during, in the United States. Look at the women's movement. Look at what happened in India. Look at what happened in South Africa. Most people now would not dispute that those were valid reasons for using civil disobedience."

Kostuch began to talk more quickly and passionately than when I first arrived. She looks so much like the prototypical earth mother that if someone hit the mute button, I thought to myself, she'd be dismissed as a flake. But she is tough-minded and smart. "Would I ever consider civil disobedience myself?" she continued. "Yes, I would, but only if I were prepared to accept the consequences. Would I advocate others doing it? No, because that is an offence. Would I tell them not to do it? No, that's their choice, as long as they understand the consequences. But I will advocate against violence of any kind."

Surprisingly, court challenges have proven almost as controversial as direct action. Canadian conservatives, sounding as though they want the legal system to be their own gated community, now complain bitterly when activists seek satisfaction in the courts. F. L. (Ted) Morton, a University of Calgary political-science professor and co-author of *The Charter Revolution and the Court Party*, believes that since 1982, when Canada adopted the Charter of Rights and Freedoms, there has been a dramatic change in the way the country is governed. "Cheered on by its academic supporters," he argued, "the Supreme Court has consistently sacrificed claims of individual liberty on the altar of group equality."

In the same *National Post* op-ed piece, Morton accused the judiciary of getting too cozy with what he calls the Court Party, defined as "the now familiar coalition of interest groups that regularly appear in our courtrooms using Charter litigation to pursue policy demands that elected governments have rejected: feminists, civil libertarians, gay-rights activists, aboriginals, francophones outside Quebec, anglophones inside Quebec, environmentalists, immigration-advocacy groups, prisoners' rights groups, visible minority groups, and so on." The University of Toronto's Gregory Hein was so intrigued by Morton's argument, he investigated. His study, *Interest Group Litigation and Canadian Democracy*, looked at court challenges from 1988 to 1998 and confirmed that activists—including social-conservative groups that, curiously, didn't make Morton's enemies list—were frequently turning to the courts. But it also showed they weren't alone. Professional organizations, unions and companies were doing the same; in fact, corporate interests launched a whopping 38 percent of the court challenges.

For her part, Kostuch makes no apologies. The Oldman River Dam case reaffirmed that the federal government shares jurisdiction for environmental protection in Canada, and that the feds had an obligation to do an assessment because of that jurisdiction. "It was a turning point in a number of ways," she said. "It was one of the first environmental cases to go to that level, and with all the attention it got, a lot of others have followed and are now using the legal system as a tool." On the other hand, by the time the case was finished, the Oldman River had a dam. "We lost but we won. We knew going into the fight that we had very little chance of stopping it, but we felt we had a moral obligation to try, because if we didn't, we would be condoning the destruction caused by the dam. The bigger win has been for the environment of Canada."

While I sat on a stool on the other side of her kitchen counter, she boiled water to make chicken soup from a package for John, her 31-year-old adopted native son. (After having four children of her own, she adopted another two—and took three more under her wing when they lost their mothers. "I collect kids," she admitted.) "I believe the reason we have laws is so that people will obey them—including the government, including corporations," she said. "Our legal system is one of the best in the world, so why should we be reluctant to use it? And why should we be criticized when we do use it? I'm often criticized because I go to the courts. Well, forgive me for using the legal system that exists for precisely that reason."

Despite her success in the courts, Kostuch sees the legal route as just one option for activists. Most successful campaigns, she figures, combine lobbying politicians, generating media coverage and holding demonstrations, because each action reinforces the other. "You don't use a screwdriver when you need a hammer," she says, "but if you need a screwdriver *and* a hammer, you use them both. And often an array of tools, used together, works best."

BACK AT THE BARRON BUILDING in Calgary, Mike Sawyer was frustrated. For all his respect for Martha Kostuch and her ability to generate power through the courts, he knew that the Oldman River Dam still stood and the forest companies still hauled logs on the Sunpine road. Disappointed that so few Alberta environmental groups came out for the Sunday march and rally against the World Petroleum Congress, let alone the Monday street protest, he worried that the energy generated among the young people who organized the WPC protest might dissipate. Worse, he'd grown disillusioned at the general lack of maturity and professionalism among Alberta activists. "The level of knowledge about issues is generally pretty shallow, and the problem that creates is that the other side, which has virtually unlimited expertise, usually finds a lot of holes in the arguments," he said. "Our job is to convince enough people our perspective on an issue is correct, so we can change public policy."

Sawyer looked comfortable in the leather chair—and he was on a roll. With a masters degree in environmental science and three years of Toastmasters, a club for people who want to develop their public-speaking and leadership skills, to his credit, he is a thoughtful and articulate conversationalist. He takes everything, including himself, seriously, and though there's lots of ego at work here, he does have doubts about his own effectiveness. "I'm a bit frustrated at how I operate. I have a sense that we have to become more aggressive, but I can't convince many other people to go along with me. It's really a hard sell in this province," he said. "If we could clone twenty Martha Kostuchs and twenty Mike Sawyers, because all this stuff takes a lot of time and a lot of energy, then maybe things would move along faster."

Of course, Sawyer had more immediate problems than worrying about cloning for the public good. He admitted that the Citizens' Oil and Gas Council—known as the Rocky Mountain Ecosystem Coalition until 1999, when the group changed its name to reflect its emphasis on petroleum issues—was limping along with 180 members and a budget of $25,000. With no salary from the group, he must support his family on the consulting contracts he gets, and that means he can't devote all his time to COGC projects. The board remains in a formative stage; eager to give the organization a broader geographical perspective, Sawyer recruited people from Halifax, Alaska and Texas to join the board, but without money, the members have never had a meeting. Meanwhile, foundations—the best source of money for groups like COGC—won't donate to groups without charitable status. And since the federal government's position on charitable status is designed to silence environmentalists, Sawyer has been denied status three times, twice when his group was called the Rocky Mountain Ecosystem Coalition. "The unwritten policy of the government of Canada," said Sawyer, "is 'No money, no influence.'"

Groups such as the David Suzuki Foundation, the World Wildlife Fund and the Alberta Wilderness Association got status before the rules changed. But they need to be careful; in 1989, Revenue Canada revoked Greenpeace's status, which it had enjoyed since 1976. The group's appeals for reinstatement have been denied three times, most recently in 1999, when the taxman declared the group served "no public benefit."

That policy won't stop people like Sawyer. His favourite weapon is "regulatory monkeywrenching"—he challenges oil and gas companies in front of the National Energy Board and the Alberta Energy and Utilities Board. "I take as many of the bastards to regulatory hearings as I can, even though I know I'll lose," he said. It costs them money and he gets valuable press coverage, because it's a form of conflict. "If I can spend a month of my time costing a company several million dollars, that's pretty good leverage. And the companies hate to air their dirty laundry in public."

Still, he can't go to enough hearings to really make a difference. "In this business, it's very rare that you have big successes. You get a slow shift in perception about issues. To measure true success, you have to ask: Have you convinced a significant portion of the citizens that something is wrong, and have you been able to use that to change public policy? And we're not there yet." What he really wants to do is take the next step and launch a "markets campaign" to target natural-gas customers as a way to get at the producers. Such campaigns have proven successful in British

Columbia, where activists have won dramatic victories in the battle to save old-growth forests and change logging practices.

DURING THE AUGUST 2000 Campaigns & Elections conference in Vancouver, I attended a session called "The War in the Woods: The View from All Sides of a Key Western Issue." When it was his turn to speak, Tom Tevlin, from an industry-sponsored group called the Forest Alliance, announced, "The war in the woods is behind us." Chris Chilton, chief of staff with the B.C. premier's office, agreed by saying, "We have moved beyond war to periodic skirmishes."

However, Gavin Edwards, forest campaigner with Greenpeace and the third member of the panel, was far from declaring peace, especially since two of the six big forestry companies had left discussions aimed at improving logging practices. He admitted, "We're starting to get beyond conflict to solutions with four of the companies," but he warned that Greenpeace would be looking for ways to "access voters" in the ensuing six months: "It's time for government to get off the fence."

Those didn't sound like the words of someone ready to back off, so a few days later I visited the Greenpeace offices on a funky section of Vancouver's Commercial Drive. I was particularly interested in the organization's markets campaigns. "These campaigns have definitely been the breakthrough we've been looking for," said Edwards, though he assured me the group hasn't given up on civil disobedience. In fact, a couple of weeks earlier, Greenpeace activists prevented a ship carrying Canadian timber from docking in Germany. "Even within the Great Bear Rainforest campaign we're running now, markets campaigns are only one facet."

If that potent tactic hadn't quite brought the forest giants to their knees, it certainly put the environmentalists closer to protecting a huge chunk of B.C.'s west coast known as the Great Bear Rainforest.

A native of Birmingham, England, Edwards came to Canada in 1991 and soon joined the battle to save Clayoquot Sound. After seeing 850 protesters arrested there in one summer, Edwards co-founded the Forest Action Network to train people in civil disobedience. "A few of us in the peace camp figured maybe there was a different way of coming at this in terms of tactics," said the avid rock climber and mountaineer. "People were standing on a logging road at six in the morning and being arrested in about three minutes. The crews were going through and logging pristine areas. Our idea was to take civil disobedience a step further and actually try to stop them." In its first action, the group sent two climbers up trees in the path of a MacMillan Bloedel crew blasting a road. The pair stayed in the treetops for seven days, until the RCMP sent in a crack climbing team.

The fight over Clayoquot Sound was perhaps the highest-profile example of the valley-by-valley approach B.C. environmentalists relied on until a few years ago. That strategy was far from efficient, and the activists often couldn't save the valleys they blockaded. The activists also knew that as long as there was global demand for wood from old-growth forests, loggers would be eyeing new valleys.

After watching their colleagues in the U.K. convince Scott Paper to cancel a contract with MacBlo, Greenpeace realized there was another way. From polling in Canada and other countries, the organization knew consumers were concerned about the destruction of old-growth forests. Unfortunately, these people were several levels removed from the forestry companies. "We know the public cares about ancient forests, but a lot of the people in a position to do something about it don't care," said Edwards. "So our campaign is based on the idea that you follow the chain down until you find people who do care." That meant targeting the retailers, who are closest to the buying public, and getting them to send a message back to logging giants.

The markets campaign to save the Great Bear Rainforest, which is the world's largest remaining unprotected temperate rainforest, started to gather momentum in 1997. At the invitation of the New Hawk Nation, Greenpeace—and its ship, *Moby Dick*—joined a huge blockade against forestry giant Interfor. The protesters included not just Canadians but people from Belgium, Germany, the U.S. and other countries. Although the public and media in B.C. were outraged, people in countries that buy the province's lumber products reacted positively. "I'm not sure we could run a markets campaign without a presence on the ground—or without other groups on the ground—to alert people to the issues," said Edwards. "So within a markets campaign, civil disobedience is still a very valid and important tactic."

Meanwhile, campaigners from Greenpeace offices around the world contacted customer companies and urged them to discontinue buying from forest companies that refused to change their practices. In the U.S., the organization mailed out letters to 5,000 companies, including Xerox, Kinko's and large retailers. Because it would be pointless to stop purchasing wood from the Great Bear Rainforest only to buy it from another threatened area, Greenpeace asked companies to adopt a forest-product procurement policy that protects ancient forests and ensures responsible logging practices. After the mailout, the organization worked with twenty-seven corporations and later ran a full-page ad in the *New York Times* thanking them. It wasn't an endorsement, simply appreciation for moving on this specific issue. "We came along and said we'd like them to adopt a policy and we'd give them credit for adopting it," said Edwards. "Some saw it in a proactive way and saw they could actually gain some kudos."

In the beginning, the contracts cancelled were small, but soon retailers killed deals worth many millions. "Each contract

cancellation seemed pivotal," said Edwards, "but the real turning point came in 1999 when IKEA and Home Depot came on
board. Once we had them, we knew we were on the right track."

When Greenpeace International first approached the
biggest furniture retailer in the world in 1997, IKEA immediately expressed interest and began a slow dialogue with the
organization. Two years later, IKEA announced a plan to buy
only wood that doesn't come from ancient forests and meets the
standards of the Forest Stewardship Council, an international
eco-certification system.

Home Depot, the biggest retailer of ancient-forest products
in the world, proved a tougher sell. In the face of its intransigence, environmentalists—the San Francisco–based Rainforest
Action Network deserves most of the credit for this campaign—
began protesting at Home Depot stores in the U.S. and Canada.
These grew until, one day in the spring of 1999, there were
protests at more than a hundred outlets. At some stores, activists
set up information pickets; at others, they put warning stickers on
ancient forest products; and at some, tour guides took customers
through the aisles pointing out products such as mahogany from
the Amazon and western red cedar from B.C. In one suburban
Toronto store, an activist in a grizzly-bear suit and armed with a
megaphone climbed a ladder (rented from Home Depot) to the
store's rafters. He hung above the checkout counters and when
a patron walked by with a piece of wood, he'd say, "Hey, that's a
piece of cedar. Did you know that companies like Interfor are
destroying the Great Bear Rainforest?" By August of that year,
Home Depot cried uncle.

Once the industry leaders jumped aboard, more and more
companies followed suit. Within a year of Home Depot's capitu-
lation, six of the top ten do-it-yourself stores in the U.S. had
bought into FSC certification or an equivalent standard. More

importantly, Weyerhaeuser, Doman Industries, Canadian Forest Products (Canfor) and Fletcher Challenge agreed to negotiate with environmentalists through the Coastal Forest Conservation Initiative (CFCI).

While the logging giants may consider such markets campaigns as little more than extortion by another name, the tactic is really an attempt to use both the carrot and the stick to influence corporate buying decisions. When all six companies agreed to the CFCI talks, the campaign slowed down because of the progress being made, but after International Forest Products (Interfor) and West Fraser Timber dropped out, Greenpeace refocused its efforts against them.

"We're not saying, 'Boycott these companies.' We're saying, 'Discontinue business relationships, but leave the door open.' There has to be an incentive to change," said Edwards. "We don't want to destroy these companies necessarily, we want to reform them. If they disappear and someone else comes along and does a better job, that's fine. We really don't care who is logging the area as long as it's done in an environmentally sound manner and there is First Nations participation and local communities are getting some benefit."

Greenpeace and the other groups finally declared victory in April 2001, when the B.C. government announced a deal between environmentalists, native groups, forest companies and the province. Along with ensuring ecological logging practices, the agreement designated twenty valleys as off-limits to commercial loggers and set aside another sixty-eight valleys for further study. "These magical rainforests have witnessed the last millennium," said Merran Smith, of the Sierra Club of B.C., another of the groups involved in the campaign. "Now they are safe to witness the next."

MIKE SAWYER IS CONFIDENT a markets campaign can work for him too. In fact, he ran a successful pilot project in 1996 after watching in dismay as Alberta increased its exports to the U.S. by touting natural gas as a green fuel and ignoring environmental concerns such as the threat to wilderness areas and wildlife, the poisoning of farmers and the contamination of ground water. Sawyer countered by explaining the risks during speaking engagements—complete with slide show and handouts—in ten cities in the Pacific Northwest. He also met with politicians, bureaucrats and utility managers. As a result, a utility in Salem, Oregon, cancelled a gas contract and invested in a wind-power proposal.

While just the hint of a street protest thrills the media, more and more activists are learning that less colourful forms of conflict can be far more effective. With the success of the markets campaign against the B.C. forest industry, other activists—working on a variety of issues—are sure to try to do the same. One of the advantages of the tactic is it hurts business, rather than government, and corporations move quickly when their profits are at stake. Politicians, on the other hand, move slowly and only when they're in danger of losing their own supporters' votes.

Increasingly, activists see business as a more pliable target for their efforts. And while confrontation alone has rarely led to success for activists, people like Sawyer have become convinced that taking advantage of the power model is essential. "I am hardpressed to think of any issue in the environment, or any issue of social justice or human rights, that is resolved in the absence of conflict," he said. "Many campaigns start off with conflict, and because the activists have some power there, the conflict evolves into a reasoned negotiation and a resolution—not because of the reason, but because the parties know that if that doesn't work, they're back to conflict."

7

HEALTH

THE
DEMONIZATION
OF CRANKS,
ZEALOTS AND
LEFT-WING
NUTS

FOR CHRISTINE BURDETT, it was a memorably bad day. In November 1999, she'd gone to Calgary for a meeting she hoped would lead to the creation of a local chapter of Friends of Medicare (FOM). Only four people showed up. Worse, by cruel coincidence, Alberta Premier Ralph Klein appeared on television that same day to explain his plan to introduce the Health Care Protection Act, legislation allowing overnight surgical procedures at private clinics. Although Bill 11 would not allow clinics to charge fees directly to patients, Burdett and other opponents quickly feared an onslaught of private hospitals and the beginning of American-style health care. Horror and panic gripped the chair of the Alberta pro-medicare advocacy group, and the dismal turnout at the Calgary meeting didn't do much to fill her with confidence for the fight she knew was coming.

The next day in Lethbridge, where FOM already had an active chapter, two hundred people attended a meeting, and Burdett began to feel a bit more optimistic, enough that she and her colleagues started making plans for a series of information forums during a two-week tour of nine cities in February. At the first one, in Grande Prairie, 150 people showed up—about what Burdett expected. Similar crowds turned out in Hinton and St. Paul. And then in Red Deer, the fourth stop, 400 came, twice the anticipated crowd. More importantly, Burdett knew, these weren't just the usual suspects. These people were a little older than average, but they were so-called ordinary Albertans, including people who voted for the Conservative government.

When standing-room-only crowds crammed into meetings in Medicine Hat—a staunchly Tory part of the province—and Lethbridge, Burdett began to wonder if the rented hall in Calgary would be big enough. Good thing too, because the spectre of Bill 11 spurred 400 people (double the original estimate) from their previous complacency. And then, after scrambling to find a bigger venue in Edmonton, FOM attracted so many people to the Polish Hall (capacity 800) that the fire department arrived to enforce regulations. But because the indignation Burdett had seen in Calgary two days earlier had bloomed into full-fledged anger, no one had the guts to do anything about the overcrowding.

Flush with success, FOM planned large rallies in Edmonton and Calgary for mid-April. Believing that celebrity speakers would help generate publicity, the organizers lined up actor Shirley Douglas, the spokesperson for the Canadian Health Coalition and the daughter of Tommy Douglas, the father of national health care. They crossed their fingers that comedian Mary Walsh would also be able to speak at the rallies, and even asked about Douglas's son, Kiefer Sutherland, because they hoped the popular Hollywood actor would attract younger people to the cause. But he was too busy shooting a movie. Then a press conference to attract volunteers willing to deliver leaflets door-to-door produced more than 150 keeners the first night in Edmonton. In the end, the group delivered 32,000 leaflets in the provincial capital and 18,000 in Calgary.

Bill Blanchard, FOM's vice-chair, described the process as "jumping off a cliff and knitting the net on the way down." But the job became much easier when the premier clumsily tried to demonize his critics. First, at the prompting of a reporter, he described the team of MLAs he'd be dispatching to explain Bill 11 as "truth squads." Then, despite polls showing the majority of Albertans were against the proposed changes, he suggested his critics were "left-wing nuts."

For a politician justifiably proud of his rapport with Albertans, Klein's put-down didn't show a great deal of savvy. Opposition to the bill came from supporters of all parties and included non-nutty groups such as the Alberta Medical Association, the Canadian Nursing Association and the Alberta Conference of Catholic Bishops. FOM, which had to book halls, line up speakers and promote its rallies—not easy tasks without much money—quickly realized that the premier's comments were a gift. And soon Bill 11 opponents proudly wore small wing nuts attached to yellow ribbons.

Burdett's wildest dream came true when 2,500 people attended the rally at Calgary's Stampede Grounds. Even Sutherland, whose film had just wrapped, made it. Although FOM hadn't been able to promote his appearance, Burdett was pleased to see some young people at the rally. It meant the battle was broadening its appeal beyond the grey-topped crowds that dominated the information forums. The next day, despite some initial nail-biting over how ridiculous Edmonton's 6,000-seat Agricom might look half-empty, Burdett knew they'd be okay when she heard that the traffic was backed up to the river and there were no spots left in the parking lot. In the end, 8,000 people—including Douglas, Sutherland and Walsh, who was a last-minute arrival—showed up.

Standing at the podium in the Agricom, Burdett took the opportunity to defend Bill 11 opponents from government mudslinging. "Premier Ralph Klein has attempted to dismiss the legitimate concerns of people right across this province, people just like us. He's called us fearmongers, he's called us left-wing nuts and he's even accused this poor little old lady from Leduc"—here she touched her sternum—"of spreading malicious misinformation."

DESPITE THE SLAGGING from Klein, Burdett hardly had the resumé of a left-wing nut. A one-time Conservative and an early member of the Reform Party, she started supporting the provincial Liberals in 1994 because of her concern over the government's health-care policies. And then she found herself in the wrong place at the wrong time. After getting a job as a constituency manager for a Liberal MLA, she went to a 1995 meeting of citizens concerned about plans by a private company to lease parts of Alberta hospitals and provide private medical services. In Leduc's hospital, for example, the company wanted to offer hip replacements to American tourists, who could then vacation and convalesce in the Rockies. Much to her surprise, she left the meeting as a spokesperson for Friends of Leduc Hospital. "It wasn't by choice," she told me, laughing. "It crept up on me and happened when I wasn't watching. At the time, I was too quiet to say no. I was a shrinking violet."

But Burdett was also politically aware and opinionated. And with the help of Toastmasters—and the anger she feels over the government's plans—she soon outgrew her shyness and fear of public speaking. Soon she was the outspoken chair of Friends of Medicare, a 1,200-member group active in Alberta since 1979. Despite large and angry protests at the Alberta Legislature during the debate, the private-clinics bill passed, albeit with a few amendments. But Friends of Medicare—and Burdett—gained a national profile with the fight. "I had never given any thought to becoming actively involved," she said. "I don't think anyone does. If you gave it any thought, you wouldn't do it. You'd run in the opposite direction. It's not exactly a good way to save for retirement. Political activists tend to spend their money, they don't make money. And you set yourself up to be vilified by the authorities."

While most activists can't turn the insults to their advantage the way Burdett did, they all know—or quickly learn—that demonization from opponents and the media is part of the job description. Occasionally, the name-calling is justified: some activists *are* left-wing nuts, just as some are right-wing nuts. But many are not. And health activists suffer some of the worst attacks, even though their issues don't always fit neatly into the left-versus-right political debate.

WHEN I FIRST CALLED Christine Burdett about getting together, she told me she borrowed office space at the United Nurses of Alberta. I asked if it would be easier if I dropped by her home. Burdett, who hasn't quite lost her English accent after twenty-five years in Canada, would have none of it. "I don't let anyone come to my home," she said. "I haven't cleaned it in six months. I think twice before I let my dog in."

So, in mid-June 2000, Burdett and I sat at a conference table in a meeting room in the union's offices near the Alberta legislature. She wore a yellow ribbon attached to her black top with a safety pin; hanging from the ribbon was a small wing nut. As well as a symbol of the anti-Bill 11 forces, it showed how the 50-year-old has taken the inevitable vilification in stride. "I come from the North of England, and they would say you need to be brass-faced, which means you have to be cheeky enough to do whatever you decide to do and not care what people think about you," she said. "I know who I am and I know what I believe in. Does it bother me when people call me names? It depends on who's doing the calling, but when it's Ralph Klein and the government, no."

One of the stickier charges levelled against her during the fight against Bill 11 was that she was a union mouthpiece. Some of the $250,000 FOM spent on the campaign came from individual donations; at the Calgary and Edmonton rallies, for example, the group collected $27,000 by passing the hat. But three-quarters of the budget came from organizations, primarily unions. Given the rise of activism and the increasing irrelevance of unions in Canada, labour seems more likely to attach itself to activists than the other way around. But because I was talking to Burdett in offices of the United Nurses of Alberta, I started wondering myself.

Burdett, however, wasn't biting. "The government line is that we're very tied to unions and that we're out there trying to protect union jobs. But it doesn't hold water, because nothing we are doing directly will protect union jobs," she said, pointing out that Alberta already had unionized private, long-term care facilities. "What the Klein government is suggesting is not new or innovative, it's old and it's been tried. So quite frankly, it probably wouldn't have mattered if our money was coming directly from Satan, people had to believe the evidence. I don't speak for anybody, only what I believe in. If any part of the group says, 'Do this,' and I don't think I want to do it, well, tough. Someone else can do it, but I won't. Fortunately, we mostly agree on where to go. We're all supporters of medicare."

Although Bill 11 did become law, FOM managed to put the Alberta government—as well as other governments across the country—on notice: don't fiddle with public-health insurance and expect Canadians not to pay attention or care. Even after the passage of the controversial legislation, FOM urged Albertans to collect stories about queue-jumping at private MRI clinics, information the group would pass on to the federal health minister. And Burdett kept busy accepting invitations to speak in other provinces. Despite her initial reluctance to get into activism, she came to realize the sense of fulfillment that goes with achieving things. And that would be hard to give up. "It's like getting hooked on heroin or crack, I guess. Once you start, where do you stop? The fight is never-ending."

A WEEK AFTER I met Christine Burdett in Edmonton, I joined a standing-room-only crowd in a church auditorium on Toronto's Danforth. The air was hot and stuffy and there were four middle-aged women dressed in dark clothing on the stage: the emcee, local NDP MPP Marilyn Churley; and panelists Burdett, Shirley Douglas and Alexa McDonough. When Churley mentioned they were all wearing black, Douglas quipped, "It's serious business."

Billed as a Forum on Health Care Reform, the evening was really little more than an NDP rally. Everyone treated Burdett as the star attraction, even though she was the least well-known person on the stage. "She's been Ralph Klein's worst nightmare," said Churley, "and she's going to continue to be Ralph Klein's worst nightmare." Before telling the story of the birth of Canada's national health insurance in Saskatchewan, Douglas—who has a great voice, deep and strong, and sounds more like a preacher than an actor—declared, "You have a great friend in Christine Burdett. This is a woman who kept that coalition together." And when McDonough stepped up to the podium, the NDP leader said of the Albertan, "She's a dream of a community activist."

Though not the fiery orator Douglas is, Burdett went over well with the audience; they cheered her success and laughed at her winning sense of humour. After the question-and-answer session, the panelists said a few final words. And Burdett, who was wearing her wing nut, made the most of the opportunity. "As long as any government can write you off as a special-interest group, you can forget it," she said. "You need the broadest possible base of support. And quite frankly, I won't be happy until every person in this country is a left-wing nut."

AS IF THE ABUSE from political opponents wasn't enough, activists must also suffer at the hands of journalists. And, here, I suppose, I should take a look in the mirror. I first met Gar Mahood, the executive director of the Non-Smokers' Rights Association, in 1986. I had arranged to pick up some research at the NSRA office, a spartan space in a rather unsightly Toronto building at Bloor and Spadina. The glass windows of Mahood's office revealed a room that resembled nothing so much as a huge filing cabinet. There were file folders everywhere: on shelves made—student-style—out of bricks and boards, the table, the desk, the metal credenza, the chairs and even the floor. As we entered his office, I tried to make conversation: "This place looks like my office."

"No, your office is not like this," he snapped.

Nice social skills, I thought.

Two years later, I wrote a profile of the anti-tobacco activist for *Toronto Life* magazine. At the time, he was not exactly a popular figure in Hogtown. Mahood had been instrumental in passing bans on smoking in offices and public buildings, and his tough, uncompromising style didn't go over well with a lot of people.

And I said so. Using quotes from foes—and even allies—to back up my claims, I called him obnoxious, I described him as a bit of a social misfit, and I suggested that while he was respected, he wasn't much liked. It wasn't a complete hatchet job, though; in fact, the piece was an attempt to show that underneath this prickly exterior was a decent, honest—sensitive, even—man, passionately committed to making the world a better, safer place. I genuinely admired the guy, and I think that came through to most readers. One colleague, a smoker, even sent me a postcard saying my story had made him realize Mahood wasn't so bad after all.

Once the article appeared, Mahood called me up and invited me to lunch. I said sure, expecting he'd ask me to do some writing for NSRA. (I'd say no, of course, but that was no reason not to have lunch with him.) At a restaurant near his office, he unloaded on me; he was polite and dignified, but he made it clear I had hurt him deeply. And then he gave me a fourteen-page letter rebutting my story.

That might have been that, but it turned out to be a bit more complicated. He called me a couple of times to see if I wanted to play shinny at a nearby rink (where he knew I played). Once he got my machine; the other time I was too busy, so he didn't get his chance to exact revenge in the corners. A couple of years later, at the rink, I came off the ice and walked into the change hut only to find him putting on his skates. When he introduced me to his friend as the guy who'd profiled him, there was, I'm convinced, a certain measure of pride in his voice. The same thing happened at a party to celebrate the twenty-fifth anniversary of *Toronto Life* at the Art Gallery of Ontario; he introduced me to lawyer Clayton Ruby as "the guy who skewered me in *Toronto Life*." Just after Christmas 1999, we finally played shinny together, but because it was cold and I wore a black watch cap pulled low, he didn't recognize me. As I left the rink, I shook his hand and revealed who I was. I could tell he was disappointed I was done playing. So it was with a bit of history that I interviewed Gar Mahood again.

Although he grew up on the edge of Ontario's tobacco farming district and as a teenager even spent a summer picking suckers off tobacco plants, Mahood has devoted more than a quarter of a century to taking on the tobacco industry. It's all quite obvious to him: there's a preventable epidemic that, every year, kills 45,000 Canadians and more than three million people around the world, so he's going to do something about it.

By the 1980s, many Torontonians—especially nicotine fiends— thought of Mahood as the jerk behind the movement to ban smoking in public places; the city's groundbreaking bylaw requiring every employer to establish and enforce a non-smoking policy; and the legislation controlling smoking in the federal government, Crown corporations and federally regulated industries. The anti-smoking bylaws were a great way to build a reputation and get the debate going, but the tobacco industry was always his main target. And that meant working at the national and international level. As early as the late 1970s, when he wrote his first brochure on the subject, he demanded an end to tobacco advertising. In the 1980s, he convinced several Canadian newspapers, including the Kingston *Whig-Standard* and the *Globe and Mail*, to refuse tobacco ads. Finally, in 1988, the federal government passed the Tobacco Products Control Act, banning advertising and promotion by tobacco manufacturers. Those were high-profile days for Mahood. He often appeared on TV and he'd made a name for himself, even if he wasn't universally loved. After that, his public profile decreased even as his clout increased; today, he remains the most effective anti-tobacco crusader in Canada, but his influence now extends around the world.

One of Mahood's major triumphs, one that has gone largely unnoticed by the public, has been to change the tactics of the anti-smoking movement. "Advocacy is the key to the tobacco issue," Mahood told me back in 1988. "Education can't compete with tobacco industry advertising. Instead of mopping up the floor, you have to turn off the pump." He never blamed smokers for their addiction because he realized it could easily have happened to him. As a 14-year-old, 125-pound guard on the high-school football team, he hoped smoking would make him seem tougher. He bought a pack of Sportsman cigarettes, smoked three—without inhaling—and threw the rest away. So rather than fault the addicts, Mahood attacks the pushers. But to do that effectively, he knew he had to discredit the "blame the victim" approach favoured by health agencies such as the Canadian Cancer Society, the Heart and Stroke Foundation and the Lung Association. These groups and the government insisted on running campaigns that essentially told tobacco addicts to "just say no." He made some enemies along the way, but with his aggressive tactics—and his attacks on the industry—Mahood showed at least some of the groups they had take the gloves off. The Canadian Cancer Society, for example, hired Ken Kyle to be its first full-time Ottawa lobbyist in 1986, and the CCS has been a staunch ally of NSRA ever since.

While Mahood dismisses any suggestion that he's mellowed over the years, he admits the response to his work is different now. Cigarette manufacturers have long seen him as a zealot intent on threatening their freedom of commercial expression, and that's not about to change. But ten or fifteen years ago, the tobacco industry had an easier time getting its way with government than he did. Now the industry is on the outside, and Mahood has earned the respect of politicians and bureaucrats. "They take us seriously, " he said. "To get the ear of government, first you have to show that your advice is worth listening to. Secondly, you have to be able to demonstrate that you can develop public support, that you speak for a substantial body of public opinion. Thirdly, you have to show them that you can punch them in the nose if they don't pay attention. And I think we've demonstrated all three things."

OUR ODD RELATIONSHIP has always been polite and, in a way, friendly. When I got together with him again in the fall of 2000, I realized his appearance hadn't changed much over the years. He'd softened the monkish haircut, the hair was a little whiter and he'd started wearing wire-rimmed bifocals, but he'd kept the beard and stayed in shape and, as ever, he was well dressed—tie, blue-and-white-striped shirt, khakis and polished brown loafers. NSRA's office space, just down Spadina from the old one, was bigger, less spartan and tidier, though there were still stacks of paper everywhere.

NSRA began with a phone call in February 1974. Rosalee Berlin, then a nursing instructor who was allergic to tobacco smoke, had heard of the Group Against Smoking Pollution (GASP) organizations being formed in the U.S. under the auspices of the Lung Association. She wanted to start one in Toronto. Believing that smoking was an environmental issue as well as a health one, she phoned CELA (the Canadian Environmental Law Association) in search of a lawyer to help her group. Mahood, then CELA's 33-year-old layman executive director, answered the phone. As it turned out, he'd recently started keeping a file on smoking as an indoor environmental problem and had begun to see it as the tobacco industry's soft underbelly.

Berlin had stumbled onto a born fighter with a knack for ballsy showmanship. For Mahood, it was a chance to make an issue his own. It was a perfect fit. Back in high school, for example, he had helped a classmate running for the student council presidency. To the candidate, Wes Wilson, it seemed hopeless. He was only in grade 11, and his two opponents, one a popular athlete, were both in grade 13. But Mahood felt spurned because, despite his reputation as a promoter, he had not been asked to join the frontrunner's campaign. He decided to work for the underdog. Mahood talked the principal into announcing that, on skit day, a maharaja would visit the school to study the Canadian education system, then convinced the local Cadillac dealership to provide a car. And wearing dark makeup and a makeshift turban, Mahood rode alone in the back of the limo as it followed its police escort through the streets of Brantford to the school. Facing the auditorium full of students, teachers and the local media, Mahood said a few words about the importance of elections in a democracy. He then urged everyone to vote for Wes Wilson and made a speedy exit. The escapade earned Mahood front-page coverage in the Brantford *Expositor* and won Wilson the election.

In 1972, after graduating from Toronto's York University, he joined CELA as executive director. In 1975, while still with the group, Mahood, who then as now lived in downtown Toronto, became involved in People or Planes, the group that stopped the proposed Pickering Airport, and organized "A Tribute to Ernie," to publicize the plight of Ernie Carruthers, whose farmhouse was scheduled for demolition. That same year, the Ontario government dragged its feet on a proposed Environmental Assessment Act, hoping to get by with a weakened bill. A deputy minister warned that if CELA didn't stop its tenacious lobbying, there would be no legislation. The next day Mahood exposed the intimidation at a press conference, and a week later the government introduced the promised law. That campaign earned CELA the White Owl Conservation Award, and Mahood delighted in the irony of the $10,000 cheque from Imperial Tobacco, the award's sponsor, helping to pay his salary, part of which he funnelled into the NSRA.

Early in 1976, Mahood left CELA to become NSRA's full-time executive director. His immediate goal was a municipal bylaw banning smoking in public places. When Toronto's city council debated the law in 1977, Mahood filled the council chamber with four hundred supporters. The proposal passed unanimously, a triumph that gave the group much-needed credibility and led to a string of other victories. Filling council chambers is, of course, a time-honoured practice in activism. But one of Mahood's great strengths is his ability to combine guerrilla tactics and standard corporate techniques. Long before other groups started seeing the benefits of professionalism, NSRA used many trappings of the corporate world, including direct-mail campaigns, orchestrated press conferences and prominent honorary directors. "Not only do we use unorthodox, surprise tactics, but we use the same tactics the tobacco industry would use," said Mahood, who doesn't like the term activist because he thinks it comes with a derisive, left-wing tinge. "We just do a better job."

In a 1987 direct-mail campaign, for example, NSRA sent letters to all 30,000 constituents of Conservative MP Ron Stewart. He'd been lobbying hard against two of the Mahood's pet bills, but the letter explained that Stewart was in a conflict of interest because he owned a tobacco wholesaling business. A few days later, he resigned as a parliamentary assistant. Then, worried the bills would be weakened by the clout of Bill Neville, a tobacco lobbyist with impeccable Tory connections, NSRA took out a full-page ad in the *Globe and Mail*, with this line in bold type: "Given the enormous death rates caused by the tobacco products Bill Neville is defending, there is a danger that every point he wins and every compromise he extracts could have the potential to translate into tens of thousands of deaths over time."

Although he happily steals from the corporate playbook, Mahood's style inevitably invites comparisons with the late

American community organizer Saul Alinsky. But Mahood believes Alinsky's tactics are more suited to organizing disadvantaged people than lobbying politicians. "I play the game the way people are used to having the game played," he said, admitting he will use Alinsky's approach when it makes sense. "If I'm in a news conference and it's dragging, I'll just come out and say something about getting the sons-of-bitches, and they'll sense that they're dealing with someone like Saul Alinsky, someone who is prepared to get in a brawl."

FOR DECADES, HOLLYWOOD STARS helped sell cigarettes by looking so glamorous when they lit up on the silver screen. Closer to home, plenty of everyday people have the same effect on young people. Every time parents, older siblings or respected peers pull a cigarette pack out of a pocket or a purse, they are giving smokes a strongly implied endorsement. And Mahood knew that even if tobacco companies couldn't advertise, the power of cigarette packaging would remain.

The Tobacco Products Control Act, passed by Parliament in 1988, phased out advertising and promotion and called for warnings on packs. Pushing for the world-precendent-setting statute was a long, tough fight for Mahood, and it remains one of the highlights of his career. "I'm happy to say we put over $1 million into the Tobacco Products Control Act," he said. But he soon realized the manufacturers were determined to fight the legislation in court and, if they didn't win, to adopt the weakest possible warnings. So Mahood got to work. With the help of documents obtained through the Access to Information Act, he discredited the industry's proposals by showing how the companies had lobbied against effective warnings. He also came up with six samples—"Smoking can kill you" and "Cigarettes are addictive," for example—and when the bureaucrats dragged their feet on offering their own suggestions, Perrin Beatty, then the Conservative health minister, adopted Mahood's handiwork. The battle didn't stop there, though. It took three years of litigation—and pressure from groups such as NSRA, the Canadian Cancer Society and the Canadian Council on Smoking and Health to stop the government's backpedaling—before the warnings started showing up on cigarette packs in 1994. Canada became the first country in the world to insist on warnings about addiction and death from second-hand smoke. Soon other countries followed Canada's lead, including Australia, Poland, Singapore, South Africa and Thailand.

As groundbreaking as the warnings were, Mahood wanted better ones. He wanted graphic pictures on the outside of packs— and more detailed information about the hazards of smoking on the inside. He continued to press the government, and in January of 1999, Liberal Health Minister Allan Rock announced new warnings. Everything about them was wrong, Mahood thought. The biggest problem was the language. He argued, for example, the use of highly scientific words, such as "nitrosamines," wouldn't mean much to anyone who wasn't a chemistry major. (The proposals compounded the problem by listing the amount of nitrosamines as 0.0001 mg—suggesting concentrations were too low to worry about.)

Despite his disappointment, Mahood took care not to attack Rock. "If I had totally panned it," he said, "it might have killed the whole initiative. I wanted to encourage them." He also gave Rock's staff and the bureaucrats a heads-up about his plans to push for better warnings. The purpose of the campaign was not only to convince the government, but also to move public opinion so when Rock did make an announcement, he wouldn't be seen as extreme. "We had to get out in front of the health minister," said

Mahood, who gave Health Canada colour photos of his proposals two months before launching the public campaign in May.

The national "Tobacco OR Kids" campaign showed Mahood at his entrepreneurial best. Working with the Canadian Cancer Society and Physicians for Smoke-Free Canada, he sent over a thousand large black boxes to MPs, senators, members of the parliamentary press gallery and the editorial boards of major newspapers. The top of each box read: "What would be a fair warning for a lethal product that addicts children and causes more preventable death than murder, traffic accidents, alcohol and AIDS combined? At a minimum, warnings that tell the truth . . ." Inside, there were six package mock-ups and a list of the 150 endorsing organizations, including health, church and labour groups. The budget for the campaign was $60,000, most of which he raised through personal contacts. "I held dinners at my home—you know, the guy who has no friends," he said, in what was clearly a jab at me for what I'd written a dozen years earlier. "I had dinners at my home with the presidents of corporations and got $10,000 per dinner."

Unlike American cigarette packages, Canadian ones include an outer shell and an interior "slide." Mahood was happy with the dramatic warnings that featured pictures of, for example, diseased gums, lungs and hearts, which the government planned for the outer shells of packages. They were, after all, quite similar to the ones he'd proposed. But the interior slide provided an ideal venue for a health-information campaign, and Mahood was convinced that messages inside cigarette packs had the potential to be even more effective because they would be more detailed.

And yet, for a variety of reasons—cautious Health Canada lawyers who feared the courts would rule they were going too far, lack of resources within the health department to test the options, perhaps even industry lobbying—the opportunity was slipping away. Worse, Mahood knew that whatever Canada set-tled on would soon be copied around the world, just as the origi-nal text-only warnings had been.

"By the time you regroup and run another campaign and have another fight, you could be ten years down the road," he said. "And when you think of the importance of both aspects of the warning system as a precedent for other countries, because this is going to go around the world, it's very easy to come to the con-clusion that literally tens of thousands of people will die. So you can set a good model or you can set one that has only the exterior warning system. We were on the verge of losing this."

Mahood sat down on a Friday night in 1999 and started to write a series of interior warnings; on Saturday he consulted a constitutional lawyer to make sure he'd have no legal problems; by Sunday morning, he'd finished eight proposals. That afternoon he and a designer came up with the right look. At 10 p.m., he fin-ished printing the proposals at a local copy shop and then drove them to the airport so they would be delivered to the minister's office by ten the next morning. In a meeting later that week, he aggressively challenged Health Canada officials, pointing out that packages of Advil and Aspirin—products that don't kill people—had more detailed warnings than the department planned to put on cigarette packages. Soon, Mahood's logic won the day. "That meeting," he said, "was as important for the interior warnings as the black box was for the exterior warning."

BLACKMAIL. THAT WAS THE WORD beside Mahood's name in the desk calender of a Philip Morris executive. Mahood learned he might have been a target when Minnesota sued the tobacco industry, and, as part of the settlement, the companies had to hand over millions of documents. Anyone who has seen the movie *The Insider* knows about the smears and harassment former tobacco executive and whistle-blower Jeffrey Wigand suffered when he testified in court about the dangerous additives in cigarettes—and how the industry fought to suppress information about the addictive nature of nicotine. And Wigand is a friend of Mahood's. "I know what happened to Wigand and I know these warnings are a huge threat to the international industry," said Mahood, who adds that he doesn't spend a lot of time worrying about retaliation from the industry. It is, after all, a point of pride for him that in 1990 a leaked document from Infotab, the international tobacco industry's research and intelligence-gathering agency, described Mahood as the top individual threat to the industry in the world.

No one will be shocked to learn that tobacco companies loathe Mahood, but the activist's rough treatment at the hands of journalists may seem less predictable. And yet Mahood has long had a difficult relationship with the media. Yes, he's had some good press, and his biographical notes include a list of publications that have profiled him. My story isn't on it, of course, but even I had high praise for his work. Others haven't.

"The media, of course, likes conflict, and the conflict has always been the smoker versus the non-smoker," said Lorraine Fry, NSRA's general manager since 1996. "The industry is never happier than when it's smokers versus non-smokers. So it's our job to reposition the conflict: the industry has to become the new demon." As public attitudes changed, the media's take also shifted. "He was considered a zealot for saying things that are now accepted," Fry said. "Now he won't be portrayed as a zealot or a radical so much, simply because the government and the public have caught up to him."

Smoking is an issue that crosses political lines. When Fry started working at NSRA, a friend from her days in Ontario's NDP government said, "My God, you aren't going to work with him, are you? He's a zealot." Still, Mahood faces the sharpest criticism from the conservative media. Perhaps his most persistent critic has been Terence Corcoran, now a columnist with the *National Post*. In 1994, when he was with the *Globe and Mail*, Corcoran accused David Sweanor, NSRA's Ottawa-based senior legal counsel, of lying and lacking evidence when he said that reductions in tobacco taxes would lead to increased consumption. As part of the out-of-court settlement, the NSRA got a cheque and apologies from both the paper and Corcoran. But just a few weeks after that settlement, Corcoran accused Mahood of using government money to attack politicians in a February 15, 1997, column entitled "Garfield Mahood's lobbying guide." Armed with a leaked NSRA discussion paper, Corcoran wrote: "In a campaign to embarrass the Liberals and discredit opponents, Mr. Mahood proposes plans to manipulate the media, smear individual tobacco officials, attack Liberal politicians and undermine the credibility of others, including the *Globe and Mail*."

Mahood responded by launching a libel suit against Corcoran, the *Globe* and Jane Gadd, a reporter who wrote a front-page story the same day. "I tend to be aggressive and a little rough and tumble," he said, "and I'll defend my integrity." While Mahood admits NSRA and its sister organization, the Smoking and Health Action Foundation, do receive funding from the federal government, he insists the group has never used that money for campaigns against politicians or any other political activity. The suit remained unsettled in the spring of 2001, but Corcoran had moved to the *Post*, which took over from the *Globe* as the leading NSRA critic. In Mahood's opinion, "Terence Corcoran is a mouthpiece for the tobacco industry. If you want to see tobacco industry press releases reprinted in the form of columns, then read Terence Corcoran."

A libertarian and an unabashed contrarian, Corcoran regularly takes on activists in his columns, dismissing as "junk science" all scientific evidence supporting causes he disagrees with. "He attacks junk science when, in fact, he's the living, breathing example of junk science," said Mahood. "We now have thirty to forty million documents in the public domain as a result of U.S. litigation that show we were bang on the money in virtually every aspect of our work."

While the demonization obviously gets under Mahood's skin, it doesn't surprise him. "It's classic shoot-the-messenger," he said. Unlike most Canadians, he doesn't try to conform, and he's not much interested in compromise. "Society doesn't always welcome people who dance to their own music, and that's always been my style. What the critics tend to do is suggest that people like that are a little bit outside normal social circles." Here again, I detected another not-so-subtle swipe at me. But I knew he had a point when he said, "At this stage of my career, it's pretty difficult for people to do a credible attack on me."

No one can reasonably dismiss him as a crank because, for more than twenty-five years, Mahood has been one of the most effective activists on any issue in Canada. This feat is all the more remarkable given that he faces not only the legislative and bureaucratic resistance all activists face, but also entrenched attitudes and an industry famous for its dirty tricks. Yet, he still has trouble getting due credit from those outside the health community.

In the summer of 2000, Mahood flew to Chicago to accept the inaugural Luther L. Terry Award in the outstanding organization category on behalf of NSRA. Former U.S. Surgeon General C. Everett Koop made the presentation. Given that Mahood was winning a prestigious international honour, he can be forgiven for expecting a little laudatory media coverage. But the *Globe and Mail* ran only a small news brief, and other papers simply ignored the event. And my guess is the non-coverage hurt him far more than all the blackmail threats, libelous columns and nasty magazine profiles.

EVEN WHEN ACTIVISTS don't face personal vilification from opponents or the media, they can find it difficult to get their message out because of demonization of their issue. That, according to Jim Wakeford, is the case with medical marijuana. The evil weed could help thousands of Canadians with AIDS, cancer and other health problems, he maintains, but the federal government remains unmoved.

The tidy living room of Wakeford's apartment in Toronto's gay village has Georgia O'Keefe prints—and photos of him smoking up—on the wall. His video collection includes a copy of *Reefer Madness*, and there was a plateful of sweet-looking buds drying in his kitchen. But I quickly realized Wakeford is no "head," we weren't going to giggle over old Cheech and Chong routines, and I would not be sampling any of the primo crop he'd boasted about in the *Globe and Mail* that very morning. Wakeford does not smoke dope for fun. A slight, soft-spoken, gentle man, he learned he was HIV positive in 1989. And every year since 1995, his doctor has given him two years to live. Back in the 1960s, Wakeford experimented with pot, mescaline and LSD, but he stopped in 1967 when he founded Oolagen House, a refuge for Toronto street kids with drug problems. (It now handles a range of mental-health problems in youth.) Thirty years later, he turned to dope for salvation. He needed something to suppress the nausea created by all the pills he must take and to increase his appetite. The problem, of course, is that marijuana is illegal in Canada. So Wakeford, who worked with the Casey House hospice and AIDS Action Now after leaving Oolagen, became Canada's leading medical marijuana activist.

Unwilling to put up with the cost, inconsistent quality and legal risks that go with buying grass on the street, Wakeford, who smokes about an ounce a month, launched a constitutional challenge in 1998. In May 1999, an Ontario judge ruled in his favour, and Health Minister Allan Rock granted Wakeford a Section 56 exemption, allowing him to use and cultivate marijuana for medical reasons. (By April 2000, about two hundred other Canadians had won the same exemption.)

While a couple of callers to a talk show he was on called him "a fag" and "a druggie," Wakeford faces little personal demonization. Instead, politicians made him fight for every concession, bureaucrats stalled, and too many doctors weren't up to speed on the medical benefits of marijuana. Meanwhile, disease advocacy organizations—including the Canadian Cancer Society, the Muscular Dystrophy Association of Canada and many AIDS groups—refused to support him financially or even morally. And some people called him to thank him but wouldn't send a cheque, out of fear. "People won't talk about it," he said. "It's not unlike being gay thirty years ago. It's very closeted."

Desperate for money to fund his legal battle and remembering how Casey House had successfully sold T-shirts and sweatshirts, he ordered a hundred T-shirts with a chest logo consisting of a medical insignia over a marijuana leaf and the words "Medical Marijuana Wakeford." But he sold fewer than fifty and didn't raise a nickel. Only a $50,000 grant from the Court Challenges Program and $10,000 he raised from his own contacts allowed him to pursue his case with the help of Alan Young, the Osgoode Hall law professor who has helped many activists and has a habit of taking on cases involving sex, drugs and rock 'n' roll.

Although Wakeford won a Section 56 exemption, he wasn't satisfied. While it allowed him to use marijuana for medical purposes, it didn't help him—or anyone else in his position—get it. He never wanted to become a grower, and because of his health, he can only grow his plants with the help of friends. Instead, Wakeford wanted the government to provide him with free, high-quality pot—and he launched a court challenge to back up his position. In March 2000, police arrested him because he had more plants than his exemption allowed (he said he was only trying to help other sufferers). A month later, Health Minister Allan Rock announced plans to dramatically loosen the regulations for both patients and their caregivers.

The two-storey apartment Wakeford lives in has balconies on both levels, which came in handy during the growing season. As the afternoon wore on, he showed me pictures of his crop, which he'd harvested a few weeks earlier. In one photo, Farmer Jim, as the Saskatchewan native now likes to think of himself, was all but obscured by the tall, leafy plants.

After two and a half hours, during which I watched my host suck on countless Craven 'A' Special Milds, I could see he was getting tired. A 57-year-old with glasses and closely cropped hair, Wakeford was generally feeling better of late and proud to be up to 139 pounds. Realizing death wasn't far away, he declared his determination to fight for the right to die by physician-assisted suicide. Like homosexuality once was, like AIDS remains for some people, like medical marijuana continues to be, euthanasia is a subject most Canadians don't want to talk about. But Wakeford will spend the rest of his life fighting society's desire to stigmatize and criminalize issues that make some people uncomfortable. "I see myself," he said, "as a closet-door opener."

POVERTY

FIGHTING
FRUSTRATION
WITH SMALL
VICTORIES

AS JIM GREEN WALKED around Vancouver's Downtown Eastside on a sunny mid-August day, he issued hellos, raised his arm in salutation and accepted hugs. He seemed to know everyone. His short hair is thinning and greying; he has a paunch and a round, not-quite cherubic face; and he wore a dark, double-breasted suit, black shirt, black-and-grey tie and dark sunglasses with black rims. It was a good look for him, but it made comparisons to a Mafia don inevitable. And, in many ways, Green is Godfather to this neighbourhood, the one that always gets tagged as "Canada's poorest postal code."

With the long-time anti-poverty activist were two bureaucrats on a Downtown Eastside tour that included non-profit and co-op housing projects, a bottle depot created by a formerly homeless man and other points of interest. There may be no better person than Green to show people around the area. The former executive director of the Downtown Eastside Residents Association (DERA) led the fight against the evictions of tenants to make way for Expo 86, built social housing and opened the Four Corners Community Savings, a bank for the kind of people the big banks don't want anything to do with. His tour featured tales—often success stories about the local residents—and jokes. Outside the Four Corners building at Hastings and Main, for example, he explained in a conspiratorial tone that it had previously been a

Bank of Montreal branch, but when the bankers left, they took the clock. Since many people in the neighbourhood don't own watches, the clock was more than just a local landmark. One day a woman approached Green and asked what happened to the clock.

"The Bank of Montreal took it," he explained.

"Fucking Frenchmen," she replied.

The potentially off-colour anecdote got a good laugh from the bureaucrats. Occasionally, as he talked to them, Green touched one or the other of the women on the arm, the way politicians do. He has a certain, undeniable charm. Of course, charm is just one of the assets the 58-year-old has needed over the years, as a champion of Downtown Eastside.

As he strolled around the neighbourhood, his cellphone rang frequently. Most of the time, he let Carla, his assistant, answer it; and she often used his phone to make calls, because there was a problem with his schedule for the next day. Near the end of the tour, Green walked by a man with a baseball cap and a moustache who said, "Staying out of trouble?"

"About as much as you."

It's just jocular banter, of course, because Green doesn't even try to stay out of trouble. A former stevedore and draft dodger, he didn't become a household name in Vancouver by leading an uninvolved life. When he ran for mayor against Gordon Campbell in 1990, he got 46 percent of the vote. Six years later, in a provincial election, he got the same level of support when he took on Campbell in Vancouver's tony Point Grey riding. Although he became a provincial bureaucrat—executive director of the Social Alternative Unit of the Ministry of Community Development, Cooperatives and Volunteers—no one is suggesting he has mellowed. "I never thought I'd be a banker, I never thought I'd be a bureaucrat, I never thought I'd be a politician. But nobody has ever said to me, 'Oh, you're a fucking bureaucrat and you've sold out.' And I know they certainly don't think that in Victoria."

After the tour, we all piled into his black, late-model Volvo. As we passed Victory Square, he pointed out a park bench where, six weeks earlier, his 33-year-old nephew died of a heroin overdose. That sent his passengers into a thoughtful silence until, a few blocks later, it was time to drop off the bureaucrats. Before he let them go, he insisted on telling them a story about Verdi. An opera buff, Green organized free performances in the Four Corners Community Savings building. The yarn, though, turned out to be a joke, which ends with Verdi, in a mausoleum, using an eraser to rub out an opera and saying, "Can't you see I'm decomposing?"

As soon as the bureaucrats are out of the car, Green began talking louder, faster and more profanely. He had, apparently, been on his best behaviour. A few blocks later, he dropped off Carla and headed to Panama Jack's Bar & Grill for his weekly pool game. As he drove, I wondered if he was frustrated, because, for all his effectiveness, for all the small victories, poverty and home-lessness are getting worse in this country, not better.

"Do I look frustrated?" he asked me.

"No," I answered honestly.

"You know what keeps me going? Walking around down there today and saying Hi to everybody and looking at, as you say, the small victories. Yeah, small victories, but with amazing human beings who are developing there. We could be running around in paradise in this world, but there are a lot of things that have to be done to get us there. It ain't going to be easy."

For Canada's anti-poverty activists, "ain't easy" is wild under-statement. It is easy to get politicians to pay lip service to the problem, but getting money or effective action from them is something else entirely. Nowhere is the frustration greater than in Toronto, where an estimated 10,000 people now live on the streets. Canada's biggest, richest and most powerful city has a burgeoning underclass: food banks, soup kitchens and over-crowded hostels have been around so long they seem normal.

The best-known—and most vilified—anti-poverty activist in this city is John Clarke, of the Ontario Coalition Against Poverty. Over the years, OCAP supporters have demanded discounts at supermarkets in wealthy neighbourhoods, chanted at diners in posh restaurants and yelled, "Homeless in, tourists out," as they followed a bagpiper through the city's tourist districts. The motto on the group's Web site is: "Whatever it takes." And, lately, they'd been thinking it takes more than disruptive protests. So the group, which gets most of its money from unions, demonstrated at the opening of the 1999 edition of the Toronto International Film Festival, faced pepper spray on Parliament Hill and occu-pied Allan Gardens, a downtown Toronto park. And then, on a Thursday afternoon in June 2000, several hundred OCAP sup-porters marched from Allan Gardens to Queen's Park and demanded the right to address the legislature. They wanted the provincial government to restore the 21.6 percent cut in welfare benefits it had made in its first term, to end landlord-tenant rules that left tenants vulnerable and to repeal the "safe streets" legis-lation aimed at aggressive panhandlers and squeegee kids. OCAP sees that as "legalized persecution of homeless people."

The government, predictably enough, refused to hear from OCAP in the legislature, and the afternoon ended badly. The pro-testers—who threw rocks, hunks of concrete and paint bombs—blamed the police for starting the violence; the police—who used pepper spray, batons and horses—blamed the protesters. Whoever started it, both sides came prepared: some protesters sported goggles and bandanas to protect themselves from pep-per spray, while the police wore full riot gear. Clarke and several supporters wound up in jail, and in the aftermath, city councillor

Olivia Chow had to resign her post on the Police Services Board because she'd criticized the actions of the cops during the confrontation. The donnybrook stunned a city inured to protests but not to violence.

A *National Post* editorial summed up what most conservatives and the suburban middle class thought of the protest: "This was an organized, military-style attack on law and order itself, the legislature and the police." Meanwhile, most people on the left side of the ideological divide offered Clarke and OCAP only muted support, if they offered any at all. NDP MPPs and city councillors, for example, distanced themselves from Clarke's tactics, even as they reiterated their commitment to the poor.

Many activists who don't work on poverty had no time for Clarke or his tactics. "OCAP, ugh, God, I don't think they're effective," said Lorraine Fry, general manager of the Non-Smokers' Rights Association and a former chief of staff in Ontario's NDP government. "John Clarke deserves his label as a zealot; he's a terrible activist." But anti-poverty activists were less willing to criticize Clarke, perhaps because they understand the frustration of working on such a difficult issue. "I've never met John Clarke, but I have a ton of respect for him," said Vancouver's Green. "What happens if people like John Clarke and me aren't doing this? You'd have a hell of a lot more homeless people. You'd have a lot more people in poverty, because they haven't got opportunities to get out."

IN THE LATE 1980S, Jim Green sat in his office at DERA and looked across the street at prostitutes turning tricks in rooms with no curtains. Vancouver's Rainbow Hotel had fallen into ruin and become a place for hourlies, and Green vowed to do something about it. He went to war with the owner, threatening the hotel's bar license, which the city could take away under its standards-and-maintenance bylaw. The owner agreed to fix up the place, but the hourlies continued. So Green got creative and eventually worked out an arrangement to take over the hotel, while the owner continued operating the pub. In 1991, after putting $150,000 into the building, he renamed it the Portland Hotel and re-opened it as social housing.

Some of the project's funding was to pay for a mental-health worker to care for ten residents. But Liz Evans, a registered nurse with psychiatric experience who joined DERA in 1991 to work on the project, got so many referrals that more than thirty-five people with chronic mental illness moved to the hotel in the first few months. Sometimes called "hard to house," these people often have no other place to live. So they became the Portland's mission.

When Green left DERA, Evans and her partner Mark Townsend took up the cause. After an attempt by the hotel owner to evict everyone so he could sell the place, and knowing the lease would expire in mid-2000 anyway, Evans and Townsend set about creating a new Portland Hotel in 1993. As the Portland Hotel Society—and with the help of Green, who'd joined the bureaucracy—they raised more than $7 million from four provincial ministries, the federal government, the city and three foundations. Once they had the money lined up, they wanted an architect who had no experience with social housing, because the people who would live in the building are typically excluded from social housing. And Arthur Erickson was perfect for the job.

"We wanted someone who would do what needed to be done, rather than what it said in the rule book about what you're allowed to do," said Townsend. "We liked that Arthur was controversial because what we try to do is controversial. It was useful to have a name, because it brought profile and some respect to the residents. And we liked his architecture; we liked the juxtaposition that he designs rich people's houses. Some of the houses he designs cost as much as this building."

A few days after Green showed me around Vancouver's Downtown Eastside, I visited Mark Townsend at the new Portland Hotel. Located a block away from the old one, it had been open only two weeks, and tradesmen were still working on the final touches; some of the public spaces were still bare because there was no money for furniture yet. But the building had a staff of seventy to serve the residents, who face mental illness, behavioural problems, drug and alcohol addiction and HIV. And each of the eighty-four rooms has its own shower and toilet, a big step up from the four showers for seventy rooms at the old property. The rent is $325 per month. A few apartments have kitchens, but most don't, so there are communal kitchens on each floor. The building also has a waterfall in the lobby, a meeting room, a gym, a movie theatre and a barber shop, which opens every few weeks and offers free haircuts. When Townsend showed me around the ten-storey building, I got to see Teresa Bassani's room. In the old hotel, where she lived for two and a half years, she had a tiny room with no bathroom and no closets. Now she lives in a 475-square-foot, one-bedroom apartment—hers is one of the fourteen largest suites, which means plenty of room for her and her cat. Bassani has a stove and small fridge, a heated concrete floor and a view of the garden. "I always heard traffic at the old place, but this is nice and quiet," she said. "This is perfect."

The Portland Hotel is more than just a good place for people to live. During Green's tour of the neighbourhood, he'd taken us to the garden atop the Four Sisters Housing Co-op and pointed to the $750,000 condos across the street. It was a stark illustration of the problem facing the community: developers want to push out the poor in order to create plenty of high-priced places to live. "If you look at it as a land issue, the people who live in the

Downtown Eastside have had their land squeezed out by development," said Townsend, who pointed out that the Portland Hotel's location—in the middle of a block in the heart of the Downtown Eastside—is strategic. "It says the people are staying and this is their home. Even though it's a cheap building, it's designed by Arthur Erickson and it looks different. So it makes a political statement and it holds a piece of land."

Townsend and I sat outside in the courtyard garden and he held his cooing four-month-old son in his arms. Far from a wild-eyed radical, the 39-year-old was calm and soft-spoken, with red hair going grey at the temples. Green had lamented his failure to bring along a generation of organizers to follow him, but he'd been clear that Evans and Townsend were the exceptions. "Liz and Mark are going to change the world," he told me. That's not really what they created the Portland Hotel Society to do, though. "We're a housing provider," said Townsend. "But we've taken up some slack in the community because things upset us. We've done stuff because it's upsetting to see people you like die. We didn't set out to be a political organization, but obviously everything is political. It's something we're doing more and more of."

Drug addiction, for example, is one of the major problems in the community. The PHS has staged demonstrations with thousands of crosses, one for every person who has died of a drug overdose, in Oppenheimer Park, a Downtown Eastside park known for attracting drug users. The group also works toward the decriminalization of drugs. "What's needed is a realistic and pragmatic approach," said Townsend. To that end, the group held a conference in a big tent in Oppenheimer Park. Area residents showed up and sat with politicians, academics and others, while speakers from around the world talked about how other countries are dealing with the problem. Frankfurt, for example, offers safe injection sites.

Despite the group's work—and successes like the new Port-land Hotel—Townsend saw frustration building in the area and thought something like OCAP's Queen's Park protest could hap-pen here. In fact, he'd noticed an increase in police presence at demonstrations lately. Where once fifty or sixty protesters would attract five cops, now twenty or thirty police are showing up. "It's out of all proportion to what's going on, but they get pressure from developers, so they have to send undercover cops with cameras to film children painting daisies on old pieces of plywood," he said. "But if we call the police, we don't have the same clout."

After Townsend arrived in Canada from Bristol, England, he lived in the Downtown Eastside with Evans. When she needed an assistant, but couldn't find anyone willing to do it, he said he'd do it for a year. That was in 1992. "I'm not very good with com-mitment, but I'm thinking I'll stay for the big fight, which I'm sure is coming. Things are going to get worse for the people in this neigbourhood. It's an easy target, and I think the community is really going to get the shit kicked out of it in the next little while," he said. "Communities like this always lose, so I'm going to stick around to try to help it win a little bit."

WHILE THE PORTLAND Hotel Society notches victories in Vancouver by building housing, at the other end of the country, Halifax legal aid lawyer Vince Calderhead racks them up in the courts. One of his favourite wins came after Irma Sparks walked into his office in 1991 and told him she was about to be tossed out of the apartment she and her children had lived in for more than ten years. After the police charged her son with selling drugs, the Dartmouth/Halifax County Regional Housing Authority gave her thirty days to get out. Normally, that would have been an illegal eviction, because of the province's security-of-tenure provisions, which protect tenants who've been in the same place for five years. But Sparks lived in public housing, so her landlord was the government—and it was exempt from its own Residential Tenancies Act. Calderhead argued that the exemption discriminated against women, blacks and people in poverty.

After losing in lower courts, he won in the Nova Scotia Court of Appeal. "That was a nice win," he says of the 1993 decision. Not only did Sparks get to stay, the 10,000 other families living in public housing also benefited. And the decision gets cited by other courts in the province and elsewhere in Canada. "In this work, the progress is slow and hard to measure, but when your slogging culminates in a nice test-case victory, well, then that's your payday."

If I didn't already know what Vince Calderhead did for a living, it became painfully obvious when I visited him at his north-end Halifax office. Before he'd answer any of my questions, the 47-year-old interviewed me for twenty minutes. His lawyerly caution surprised me, because Calderhead has an impressive record of fighting against the powerful on behalf of the poor. But, I suppose, it's tough to take the legal training out of the lawyer, even if he is an activist. Apparently satisfied, he agreed to answer my questions over lunch on the noisy patio of a nearby pub.

The barrister and solicitor with Nova Scotia Legal Aid explained that, rather than attacking poverty politically, he's chosen to do it by pursuing legal rights for the disadvantaged. "The constitution provides the rights, and it's the poor who come to me and want their rights respected, so that's where I get my mandate," he said. "To raise questions of political accountability is to raise the wrong questions. I'm not claiming I have any political mandate, it's a legal mandate."

Aside from his precedent-setting cases in Canada, his work has twice taken him to the United Nations in Geneva. In 1995, the federal government was about to scrap the Canada Assistance Plan, a policy that required the feds to fund 50 percent of social programs (such as welfare) in exchange for the right to set national standards. Many anti-poverty activists saw it as the cornerstone of the country's social security system. Calderhead asked the U.N. to advise Canada that repealing of CAP would violate the 1966 Covenant on Economic, Social and Cultural Rights, which guarantees the right to adequate food, clothing, housing, health care and education. The Committee on Economic, Social and Cultural Rights expressed grave concern. It said that repealing the national standards was regressive and represented a departure from Canada's obligations under the covenant. Then in 1999, Calderhead made similar arguments before the U.N.'s Human Rights Committee. That committee also said Canada was not respecting the civil and political rights of poor people. In the end, two senior U.N. human-rights bodies condemned Canada, but Calderhead admits nothing really changed.

"So do you consider those hollow victories?" I asked.

"No, not at all," he said. "They're important because they allow Canadians and others, internationally, to see Canada's real standing in terms of observing basic human rights. These U.N. reports allow us to see Canada's human-rights observation for what it really is."

To most North Americans, human rights mean the right to freedom of expression, the right to vote and similar democratic rights. But Calderhead sees human rights the way they're viewed internationally, as basic social and economic rights, including the right to an adequate income, the right to health care and the right to education. And he pointed out that Canadian courts are paying more attention to the international view of human rights when interpreting the Charter. "There's a fusion between what's happening internationally with human rights and what the courts in Canada are doing."

The political right decries such developments as "judicial activism," and Calderhead knows that what he does drives conservatives crazy. But he believes the Constitution is there to protect the politically voiceless. "Many of these critics are the first ones to go to court to enforce what they feel are their legal rights. It's not so much the appeal to the legal process they're criticizing; they're opposed to legal protection for disadvantaged groups," he said. "It reveals a horrible double standard." And he insisted opponents who suggest he's bringing forward frivolous legal claims to generate media coverage for his pet issues just don't know him. "I won't go anywhere near a legal claim unless I think I'm going to win," he said, "because I'm a sore loser."

While homelessness is not as flagrant in Halifax as in Toronto, the Maritime city has plenty of poverty. And Calderhead, who always has about a hundred cases on the go, often feels as though he's banging his head against the wall. "The fact that I'm still in it, in all honesty, is because I feel it's worthwhile and progress is happening," he said. "My heart gets torn out when I see the misery a lot of people are going through, the real anguish and the waste of human potential. That spurs me on. Once you've seen the horror of it, it's not easy to turn away."

"I CAN BE QUITE pessimistic, but it doesn't get me anywhere," Sarah Kerr told me. "I can get all down in the dumps, but then what? So I have to imagine change." Actually, it's a little hard to imagine the 34-year-old Queen of Kensington, as her friends call her, being anything but gregarious and enthusiastic and chatty. And determined: not only does she imagine changing society's values, the Calgary anti-poverty activist takes a practical approach to it. She's the program director of the Bow Chinook Barter Community, a local currency system designed to help the working poor.

The June 2000 day I'd arranged to drop by Kerr's office turned out to be the day after the demo that turned violent at Queen's Park in Toronto. The nastiness there seemed foreign to Calgary's peaceful Sunday march and rally against the World Petroleum Congress, which was where I'd met Kerr a few days earlier. But she didn't seem terribly surprised by the news coming out of the east. "It demonstrates the desperation of people," she said. "They're at the point where they're willing to engage in combat with riot cops. Doesn't that tell you something?"

Coincidentally, poverty in Toronto helped redirect her from environmental activism to her current work. After completing her masters in environmental studies at York University, Kerr got a job with a pro-bicycle transportation group. But working in a poor section of Toronto made her realize that people in poverty can't get too worked up about the environment. "You can't really ask people to change their lifestyles and live more environmentally sensitive lives when they're just trying to feed their kids and meet their basic needs," she said. "They don't have space in their heads to think about the environment; they're just trying to survive."

When she returned to her hometown, she thought about starting a local currency system and discovered one was already in the works at Calgary's Arusha Centre. While local currencies flourished in Alberta and elsewhere in the 1930s, they didn't last long. But barter systems started reappearing in the 1980s, and today there are over 2,500 of them around world and eighty or so in Canada. (The best-known Canadian one is LETS, which started in Comox, B.C.) Since the launch of the Bow Chinook

Barter Community in 1996, it has grown to three hundred members and over forty companies, including video stores, grocery stores, clothing stores, flower shops, hairdressers and various home-based businesses.

Based on a system first developed in Ithaca, New York, the local currency is the HOUR. An HOUR bill is worth $10, or one hour of labour. A member might, for example, fix a bike for two HOURs and then use that to buy other goods or services. "It's best for the working poor, people who have a job and pay the rent, but are making minimum wage," she said. "They're the same people who use the food bank. They cruise along and lose their job and don't have any cushion." By taking part in the barter community, people who can't afford skis can go skiing or arrange for professional-quality photographs of their grandchildren. The monthly pot-luck dinners attract eighty or ninety members, many of whom bring handicrafts or garage-sale items to sell.

Though local currency systems exist in big cities, most of the ones that really thrive are in small towns. But Kerr believes the Calgary system can work, and help people in poverty. More importantly, the Bow Chinook Barter Community is a means to an end—as much as an end in itself. "Our goal is not to have people use local currency, our goal is to help people strengthen community connections and use their skills to meet their needs."

The Sunday before we got together, Kerr had planned a community block party. But with all the paranoia surrounding the World Petroleum Congress protests, Calgary police cancelled all permits. By pulling a few strings, Kerr got the go-ahead, so thirty people could play road hockey and eat hot dogs. "I'm obviously not the only one who thinks a block party is political," she noted slyly.

Despite her interest in community-building, Kerr doesn't restrict her activism to local issues. She took part in Clayoquot

Sound protests and said, "I was incredibly moved by people putting themselves in the way. They felt so strongly, they put themselves on the line to say no." She also went to Seattle, where she was tear-gassed and spent four and a half days in jail for failure to obey an order to disperse (even though she was trying to do just that).

She considers Seattle the opening ceremonies for a movement dedicated to social change, but she knows it will take more than a bolt of lightning like Seattle to get there. In the meantime, it's important for people to reach out locally. "If we're looking at changing values on a widespread level, we have to do it on an individual level. But you have to start with something in common, and perhaps the only thing I have in common with the cop who lives across the alley—or the CEO who lives next door—is that we share the same little corner of the world," said Kerr, who says she draws courage from the American civil-rights movement. "That's the connection between the personal and the political. That's where the barter community comes into it all. When you lend your lawnmower or borrow a cup of sugar or make a trade, you start building those relationships and trust. So the idea that 'Oh, my God, they're all freaks down in the streets, I don't know who they are or what they do, but they weird me out' becomes 'Well, they're my neighbours and they have a job, they even have hope.' That's the seed that takes a long time to grow."

JIM GREEN AND I sat on stools at the bar of Panama Jack's Bar & Grill. Sports memorabilia decorated the walls, and rock music pounded out of the sound system. We ordered draft beer, and after he groused about the music, the opera lover began to tell me how he ended up coming to Canada in 1968. The son of an abusive, alcoholic master-sargeant in the air force, Green was born in Alabama and raised in South Carolina. He began organizing blacks to vote when he got out of high school in the early 1960s; later he moved to Colorado for grad school and started organizing for the United Farm Workers, then led by Cesar Chavez. "I never really got involved in the anti-war movement. I had other issues, and I saw a lot of the anti-war movement as university-based, middle-class and full of rhetoric," he said. "The people who were going to Vietnam were people like me and my brother and the black kids."

As we talked about this, his cellphone rang. He answered it and stepped away from the bar. Soon Crosby, Stills, Nash & Young's "Ohio" blared from the speakers. Written by Neil Young, the haunting song about the shooting of four students by the National Guard at Kent State University had always been one of my favourites. And when Green returned, I naively said, "Pretty appropriate . . ." But before I could finish, he made it clear he had a different take on the song than I did.

"It exactly defines what's wrong with the anti-war movement to me. Four dead in Ohio. Absolutely. Unbelievable. But in that same month, seven blacks students were killed at a southern university, and that got a little blurb on the back page of the papers." I didn't detect any dismissiveness or arrogance in his voice when he said this. Instead, he was simply using that song to make a point, and it struck me that his attitude toward "Ohio" is probably typical of the way he thinks. The luxury car, the fancy clothes, the love of opera—all his contradictions—don't diminish the fact that Green has devoted his life to fighting for what he believes is right.

When Green came to Canada and Vancouver's Downtown Eastside, he had a Jeep but no money. He soon got a job teaching anthropology at what is now Vancouver Community College, and he started getting involved in city politics and the student movement. After finishing his master's degree, he started working on a

Ph.D. thesis about the Canadian Seamen's Union, a militant union that the government outlawed in 1950 for being a communist organization. He finished the thesis but never got his degree. "I got kicked out of UBC for being a socialist and not a sociologist," he said, "and for writing a paper called 'The Anthropologist as Imperialist.'" In 1986, Green published a book called *Against the Tide: The Story of the Canadian Seamen's Union,* and he's now an adjunct professor in the Department of Anthropology and Sociology at UBC.

While writing his thesis, he worked as a longshoreman and marine boilermaker and then became a union organizer. In 1981, DERA offered him a job and he took it. Founded in 1973, DERA was an effective grassroots advocacy organization dedicated to improving life in what was then known as Skid Road. An important first step was to give the neighbourhood a new identity by changing its name from Skid Road to the Downtown Eastside. Unafraid of confrontation, DERA forced landlords to fix up their rooms, marched against both drug dealers and politicians and generated attention by staging cockroach races in slum hotels. Green, who'd picked up a lot of valuable organizing skills while working with unions, was an ideal choice to succeed founders Bruce Eriksen and Libby Davies. "Homelessness was not something we really threw around as a term in those days, but you could see it coming," Green said. "Our major issues were gentrification, redevelopment, poverty and democracy. I didn't see myself as being involved with homelessness issues, it was more trying to stop homelessness from happening."

It didn't take long before Green made waves. In 1983, to protest several Social Credit policies, including government restraint, he led a contingent that occupied then premier Bill Bennett's Vancouver office. Meanwhile, the city started preparing for Expo 86. "I got to watch, before my eyes, public policy create homelessness. That's exactly what happened. In those days, tenants had no rights and could be evicted without notice, without cause, at any time day or night." When people were thrown out of their lifetime homes, Bennett called it "slum clearance."

But Green was fighting for more than just people's homes. "It was a major, major, major battle, and it still haunts to me to this day," says Green. "It was a battle for hegemony over not only this neighbourhood but the way that things happen in our city." Even today, Vancouver has no democratic neighbourhood structure and since councillors aren't elected by wards, an area like the Downtown Eastside has no way to get a champion in power. Green, however, had always sworn he'd never become a politician. After he went to work for DERA, that stance became even more important, because his predecessors, Davies and Eriksen, had gone on to city council, and Green didn't want people to think of DERA as a political machine.

But in 1990, he took on mayor Gordon Campbell as part of the Committee of Progressive Electors slate. Though he lost, the rest of the slate won, and Green was fine with that, figuring, "Gordon can be the pretty boy who cuts ribbons; I'll go down and do the work in the community." That doesn't mean he would have been disappointed if he'd won. "I'd have used that American thing, the bully pulpit, as a platform to build this town and do some of the creative things that we can't get done now. I wouldn't have been disappointed if I'd won, but I'm not disappointed that I lost. It was a victory for me either way."

Even without a bully pulpit, Green can take pride in some creative achievements. He brought government, community organizers and residents together to create Four Corners Community Savings, a financial institution owned by a crown corporation. The bank, which opened in 1996 and still loses money, not only welcomes the poor but treats them with respect. The day I joined Green on his tour of the Downtown Eastside, I waited for him at Four Corners. It's a beautiful building from the days when bankers believed in bricks and mortar and customer service. Green, who is chair and CEO of Four Corners, saved the terrazzo floor, and while he couldn't remove the false ceiling, he did take out part of it to let people see the original craftwork. A huge anti-racism mural fills one wall, and the employees represent several races and speak many languages. While there's an automated banking machine in the corner, most customers take advantage of the tellers. They don't have to line up to get service, though; instead, they take a number and grab a seat.

More importantly, he developed safe, clean and livable housing projects such as the DERA Housing Co-op and the Four Sisters Housing Co-op, which won the Architectural Institute of B.C. Award for its innovative design and success in housing a diverse mix of tenants. Most proud of his work on the Portland Hotel, he believes building housing is the most political act there is—and some of his opponents agree. "Jim Green is not building housing, he's building an army," fretted one city councillor.

"She was dead right," Green said. "People were getting secure housing, so they would be rooted in the neighbourhood, and their skills and knowledge were developing. When you develop housing, you develop people, and you become a dangerous fellow."

9

JUSTICE

THE SECRETS

OF SUCCESS

PRISCILLA DE VILLIERS lived a lovely life. She'd followed her husband Rocco, a doctor, to Canada from South Africa at the end of 1979. They didn't have much money in the early days, but they and their two small children were happy. By 1991, she had plenty of marvellous friends, painted every day and played lots of tennis. "I had a very spoiled existence," de Villiers told me, "and then, suddenly, it came to an end."

On a Friday evening in August, de Villiers's 19-year-old daughter, Nina, set out for a jog at a Burlington, Ontario, tennis club. She could not have known that less than an hour earlier, an officer with U.S. Immigration and Naturalization Service at Niagara Falls had turned away a man with a gun, a bail-release form and a suicide note. Despite his eleven-year history of attacks on women, Jonathan Yeo continually slipped through the cracks of the justice and mental-health systems. On August 9, 1991, he was out on $3,000 bail for charges of sexual assault and using a firearm, but his bail conditions came with no weapons restrictions. Despite a heads-up phone call from the Americans—and even though trying to skip the country was a violation of Yeo's bail—Canadian Customs and two police forces did nothing. Free to do as he pleased, Yeo abducted Nina in Burlington and killed her with the same rifle he'd used in his previous assault. (He later murdered Karen Marquis in New Brunswick, and he finally turned the gun on himself after police cornered him in Hamilton, Ontario.) Nine days after she disappeared, Nina's body turned up by a creek near Napanee, Ontario. She'd been shot in the head.

Maybe it was all the media attention—and by her own admission, de Villiers was so frantic to find her daughter she was willing to talk to anyone at anytime—or maybe it was because Nina's disappearance came on the heels of several other tragic incidents involving young women. Whatever it was, the case caused an outpouring of support from Canadians. A group of truckers across the country had taken out a full-page ad showing Nina's picture in the Sunday edition of the *Toronto Sun* and truckers and cab drivers posted the pictures on or in their vehicles. After 5,000 people showed up to help with the search, the local police chief went on the radio to say there were more than enough volunteers.

Several weeks later, de Villiers went on the radio to thank people for their support. A young police officer (who'd helped out on the search off-duty) called in to the station and talked about how scared people were. He echoed what de Villiers had heard from friends, neighbours and the strangers who stopped her on the street or phoned her or sent her faxes. "What are we going to do?" they said. "We're so frightened." But when the officer asked de Villiers what she was going to do, she blurted out that she wanted to start a petition. It was not something she'd thought about; in fact, she still doesn't know where it came from. But it struck a chord with the people listening to the radio, and by the time she got home, there were TV cameras waiting at her house. Then her tennis partner called to say that if de Villiers wrote a petition, her friends would distribute it.

After coming up with wording that called for Parliament to change the criminal code, bail legislation and the parole act "to reflect societal attitudes," de Villiers and four friends worked on the petition campaign. Within six weeks, they had 100,000 signatures. In June 1992, they set up CAVEAT (Canadians Against Violence Everywhere Advocating its Termination). Although they still had no interest in establishing an advocacy organization, they needed something formal so they could handle the donation money that was coming in. In February of 1994, when the group gave the de Villiers petition to Justice Minister Allan Rock, the names of 2.5 million Canadians were on it.

By then, CAVEAT had morphed into a full-fledged victims' rights group. It provided support to victims, worked on education and prevention, intervened in high-profile Supreme Court of Canada cases and advocated for numerous changes to the justice system. Typical of CAVEAT's approach was the 1994 SafteyNet Conference, which brought together over a hundred experts, representing victims, victims' rights activists, politicians, judges, police and customs officers, educators, psychiatrists and legal experts. The three days of sessions produced 146 recommendations on everything from crime prevention to young offenders to parole reform. After presenting its report to federal, provincial and territorial governments, the group began pushing politicians to make the necessary changes.

The first four or five years were heady; there was so much progress. After that, changing the way Canadians think about victims became the bigger challenge. "I started this in a fog of despair, but I had a sense of purpose," de Villiers said. "I had spent ten years having a wonderful life. I'd done charitable things and donated my art to charity, but I had abdicated from taking an interest in government. I'd joined the millions of Canadians who say, 'Let's leave it to them.' I felt my child had paid with her life partly because of that, and I felt that if another young woman dies and I do nothing to prevent it, that death is on my head."

BOILED DOWN TO ITS ESSENCE, activism is the struggle for justice. It's fitting, then, that activists who work on justice issues—including freedom of speech, gay rights and newer ideas such as victims' rights—are some of the most successful in the country. And so I drove to CAVEAT's office in Burlington, near Hamilton, to visit one of Canada's most effective advocates. The late November rain had stopped but the roads remained wet, and when I stopped at a crosswalk, a van rear-ended me. That left me a bit jumpy, but I was really more anxious about meeting Priscilla de Villiers.

To be honest, I'd been putting it off. I'd spent the summer travelling across the country, talking to activists with varying ideologies, but I never felt uncomfortable with their views. Whether it was conservative Walter Robinson of the Canadian Taxpayers Federation or the young socialists fighting economic globalization, some of what I heard I agreed with and some I didn't. Either way, I figured, it didn't really matter what I thought.

With de Villiers, though, I knew the subject of capital punishment would come up. And that's an issue that really does matter to me. The only time I ever wrote a letter to a politician was just before a free vote in the House of Commons on reinstating the death penalty. At the time, the *Toronto Star* surveyed local MPs about where they stood on the issue and reported—erroneously, it turned out—that my MP, Tory Barbara McDougall, had yet to make up her mind. So I urged her to vote against bringing back capital punishment. Fortunately, McDougall and enough of her colleagues voted to defeat the proposal.

As is so often the case, de Villiers turned out to be quite different from what I expected. Once I learned that her anti-apartheid work in her native South Africa had jeopardized her father's job as chief of defence staff, I began to relax. And despite what I'd been told, she's against the death penalty. "I personally can't deal with the concept," she said. "I'm a pacifist and I'm against violence." CAVEAT never took a position on the issue, and that, de Villiers knew, cost the group money and support. (The group's involvement in the campaign for gun control had the same result.) I quickly realized that a lot of what I'd heard and read about CAVEAT was wrong. While the group certainly pushed for tougher sentences and stricter parole—arguing, "Life means life"—it never was a bloodthirsty gang of hang-'em-high fanatics. We typically think that human rights apply only when it's the state against an offender, but de Villiers wanted a new definition, one that would also include the state's responsibility to protect victims.

De Villiers had plenty of experience being misunderstood. "There are all these myths about victims," she said. "The minute somebody doesn't agree with what you're saying, they say you're vengeful, you're vindictive and you have to let it go and forget." However she knows better than anyone that letting go and forgetting is not possible. Even nine years after her daughter's death, I could see the toll it had taken—mixed with the passion, there was pain and sadness and a certain weariness that I imagine will never go away. And during our long conversation, she kept returning to Jonathan Yeo and the mindset that allowed so many people, who could have stopped him, to do nothing. "With violent crime, there's no way to repair the harm. You can never undo that hurt," she explained. "People come up to me in airports, in trains, in stores, all over the country, and start telling me what happened to them, and I do not know if it was yesterday or thirty years ago."

Despite the rawness of her pain, de Villiers insisted that CAVEAT sought balance and protection, not vengeance. She believes offenders do have rights, and that many able advocates work on their behalf. But victims should also have rights. She wants them to be allowed some presence in the process, have access to support systems, be treated with courtesy and be kept fully informed during trials and parole hearings. Instead of focusing solely on the crime, the justice system should pay due attention to the outcome.

"Yes, we have to protect offenders in the courts, because they're just accused at that point," she said. "But that's exactly when victims are feeling emotionally abused beyond speech." De Villiers argued that, at best, the system shuts victims out, while, at worst, they're treated shamefully, like the rape victim who was expected to testify in court after travelling two hundred miles in the back of a truck with her rapist sitting across from her. "All the focus is on the offender, but if you have to make a choice—and this is where I am, I suppose, hardline—you have to make it on the side of the innocent and the vulnerable."

As CAVEAT achieved one goal, it moved on to the next, so the group's main focus changed each year or two. "It's no good solely targeting one law or one statute or one bit of the process," said de Villiers. "I wasn't interested in finding scapegoats at all. My feeling was that the system needed a thorough overhaul and a shakeup, because it had gone so far away from a balance at every level." The organization's broad approach to victims' rights had its roots in the original petition, which touched on so many issues, and in de Villiers's insistence at looking at the big picture. At times, de Villiers and the other board members did think about narrowing their focus, but they never wanted to miss an opportunity to have their say when there was proposed legislation, a relevant court case or some other event.

It didn't hurt that there were plenty of victories along the way. In the 1990s, the federal government introduced legislative changes that may not have gone as far as CAVEAT would have liked, but were nonetheless crucial improvements. De Villiers was happiest to see Justice Canada create the Policy Centre for Victim Issues, and Corrections Canada establish a protocol for dealing with victims. Meanwhile, the provinces, led by Ontario and Manitoba, also made headway. Ontario, for example, introduced a victims' hotline and opened the Office for Victims of Crime, which de Villiers helped design.

Still, such success couldn't free CAVEAT from its constant financial struggles. De Villiers's office was a jumble of donated old furniture, and the table we sat at had nails poking through it. The group had an annual budget of $250,000, but it had little luck raising funds from corporations, because no company wanted to be linked to victims. CAVEAT needed money to host conferences and workshops and to help finance victims' attendance. As president, de Villiers was a volunteer; so were the rest of the board members. But two full-time employees and two part-timers were on salary. And it was particularly frustrating watching so many good staffers leave because the group couldn't pay them enough.

De Villiers herself almost left in the fall of 2000. That's when she made her ill-fated stab at electoral politics, running as a candidate for the provincial Conservatives in a local by-election. (Because CAVEAT was non-partisan and prided itself on being able to work with governments of all stripes across the country, she took a leave of absence.) After she lost, though, she returned to devoting up to eighteen hours a day to the cause. But that also meant worrying about funding once again. "Our stated goal, right at the beginning, was that we become redundant, that this work should not be done by a bunch well-meaning amateurs," said de Villiers, who worried that burnout would kill the group long before redundancy did. "We may close up just because we're tired. We're all so weary and we get so tired of begging for money. The work is the reward, but you still have to pay your expenses."

Given those words, I wasn't terribly surprised when, six months later, I read that CAVEAT had decided to wind itself up at the end of May 2001. In a press release, de Villiers made it clear there was more work to do, but the group didn't have the resources to tackle the increasingly complex projects it wanted to take on. "As we close our office, let us be clear that there is still a need in our communities for the work of organizations like CAVEAT," she wrote. "Stay involved, stay active; shape your community and your Canada. One person does make a difference."

In ten years of activism, de Villiers certainly made a difference and set an example for others, but she also realized that changing society takes a lot of money, a lot of energy and a lot of time. As CAVEAT shut down, the emergence of a new attitude toward victims and a greater voice for victims remained two not-quite-accomplished goals. Before 1992, for example, victims weren't even informed about parole hearings; now they're allowed to attend—though they aren't allowed to speak. That policy is endlessly frustrating for de Villiers, who sees it as part of the mindset that allowed Jonathan Yeo to slip through the cracks, a mindset that has to change. "My goal is a peaceful, just and safe society," she said. "I believe we have an obligation to protect and to do our best to rehabilitate offenders—and to support them when they go back into the community. Absolutely. That's not in question, it never has been. But I also think we have to look at the larger picture and say why does anyone expect Canadians to be complacent about their sense of safety. Despite injections of money and expertise and conferences, we've made dismal headway compared to other areas—like smoking or drinking and driving—where we've made extraordinary strides."

JOHN FISHER and Laurie Arron sat in the House of Commons gallery in 1996 and watched a ten-year struggle come to an end as our politicians made an extraordinary, if long overdue, stride. Finally, Parliament amended the Canadian Human Rights Act to include sexual orientation, a decade after Conservative Justice Minister John Crosbie first promised to do so. Before the vote, Fisher, who is the executive director of Equality for Gays and Lesbians Everywhere, and Arron bought a card for Liberal Justice Minister Allan Rock. As MPs indicated their yeas and nays, Rock opened the card and read a message thanking him for his support and hard work, and then mischievously saying EGALE looked forward to his support on the issue of gay marriage. After laughing at the card, Rock looked up at the gallery, smiled and wagged his finger at them.

While they were on the Hill, Arron was amazed to see Fisher in action with the politicians. "Every MP in that place knew John Fisher," said the Toronto lawyer and former EGALE president. "They either came up to shake his hand and congratulate him or they scowled at him. And it was clear from the MPs that the legislation looked the way it looked because of John."

Outside of Parliament and Canada's gay community, Fisher may not enjoy the high profile that Priscilla de Villiers does, but that doesn't mean he's any less influential. Along with legislative and judicial victories, the 35-year-old lawyer has built EGALE into one of the most reputable advocacy organizations in the country. "Our biggest victory is not any one piece of legislation," said Arron, "it's the respect EGALE has from the media, the courts and the politicians."

In 1986, gay activist Les McAfee and some of his friends created EGALE because they wanted to ensure Crosbie kept his promise to protect gays, lesbians and bisexuals in the Canadian

Human Rights Act. By the early 1990s, though, the group was adrift and in danger of falling apart: the Human Rights Act remained unchanged, McAfee had died of AIDS in 1991, and criticism swirled around the organization. For all its claims about being national and inclusive, EGALE was really a male-dominated Ottawa group without proper internal accountability.

That wasn't enough to scare off Fisher, a New Zealander who moved to Ottawa in 1992 after finishing a masters degree in law at Queen's University in Kingston. He helped mediate between the group's old guard and its critics, while they came up with a new structure and mandate. Then, after serving as chairman of its human-rights committee, Fisher became president in 1994. At the time, he was still doing legal research and support work for an Ottawa lawyer, but soon EGALE's responsibilities ate up so much of his time that he stepped down as president and returned as a paid, part-time executive director, working out of borrowed office space. Within a year, the position was full-time.

When Fisher met Allan Rock on Valentine's Day, 1994, it was the first time EGALE had met with a justice minister. Even better, Rock clearly indicated he would amend the Human Rights Act that year. Meanwhile, the group had its first legislative triumph with the passage of the 1994 Hate Crimes Bill, which included among its provisions increased penalties for gay bashing. But by the end of the year, Fisher learned Rock wasn't going to be introducing amendments to the Human Rights Act after all. Nor was he willing to say when he would; it was still a government commitment, he insisted, but there were other priorities. EGALE had heard that story again and again over the years; a justice minister wants to do the right thing, but faces more opposition than he expects.

Rather than simply maintain the pressure on Parliament Hill, Fisher decided to do something that would help the campaign, build the group's relationships with Canada's far-flung gay and lesbian communities and impress everyone in the organization. In 1995, he flew to Vancouver and began a cross-country train trip, stopping along the way to stay at billets. In Toronto, a train strike forced him to switch to buses, but by the time he flew back from Newfoundland, he'd visited about twenty cities, including places like Medicine Hat and Moncton, where the gay and lesbian communities are small and isolated. Not only did he make valuable contacts across the nation, he helped build a 20,000-name petition calling for the government to amend the Human Rights Act. (He went to even more cities when he reprised the tour in 1997, but now such trips are less important because the Internet makes keeping in touch so much easier.)

On the May 2000 day I got together with Fisher in his Ottawa office, he talked as quickly as people warned me he would. And I could see the easy manner that has endeared him to so many people, including the politicians he lobbies. "He's the right guy for the job because he's low-key, respectful and non-threatening in the way he presents himself and the issue," said David Corbett, counsel for the Foundation for Equal Families, a litigation group that works toward equality for same-sex couples. "He's very articulate in both official languages and always well prepared. He's done a good job, without the sheen of the American lobbyists, the sheen that says, 'I'm being paid a fortune to say what I say.'"

But it also wouldn't be fair to suggest he's just an establishment activist—or anything like an American lobbyist—because he's not afraid of using more creative tactics. "There are all sorts of tools open to a group like EGALE," Fisher said. "The court system and the political system are two of them, but there's a role for protest and for direct action. A group like EGALE has to choose its tools carefully, in accordance with what the issue is and what's the best means for accomplishing a particular goal."

In 1996, for example, Prime Minister Jean Chrétien broke a promise by announcing there would be a free vote rather than a party vote on amending the Human Rights Act. So Fisher and his supporters donned giant red flip-flops and waddled up to Parliament Hill, where they burned Chrétien's letter by the ceremonial flame. Even his allies in government were displeased, but Fisher believes the protest was needed. "If we ever have a Canadian Alliance government, we might be protesting a lot. You have to tailor it to the circumstances," he said. "But as long as you're willing to do it, most of the time you don't have to."

By the time EGALE had won the changes to the Human Rights Act, it had transformed itself into a group with three main goals: political lobbying, legal challenges and public education. Playing the role of intervenor in court challenges has provided the group with some of its most important gains. As part of *Egan v. Canada*, for example, EGALE challenged the "opposite-sex" definition of "spouse" in the Old Age Security Act. In 1995, the Supreme Court of Canada agreed that the "opposite-sex" definition of "spouse" was discriminatory, but gave the government time to bring its laws in line with the Charter of Rights. A spousal support case, known as *M v. H & Ontario*, proved a more clear-cut victory. In 1999, the Supreme Court ruled that Ontario's Family Law Act's opposite-sex definition of "spouse" was unconstitutional. This time, the court ordered the government to change the law. And the judgment quoted EGALE four times, even though the court rarely quotes intervenors.

Despite its solid track record, the future may be tougher for the group, because it must take positions on matters such as censorship, age of consent and marriage—all issues that, unlike Human Rights Act protection, have the potential to split the community. EGALE is building on the success of the Women's Legal Education and Action Fund (LEAF), a group that argues for equality for women and girls before courts, human-rights commissions and government agencies, and provides public education on the issue of sex equality. But LEAF is in turmoil because issues such as censorship are tearing it apart.

Already, the sniping at EGALE has begun. The gay magazine *Xtra*, for example, attacked it as too mainstream. Fisher admitted that some of the criticism is valid, because the group has tended to put more emphasis on relationship issues, but that's a natural outgrowth of all the court cases that have presented opportunities to intervene. "The opponents of particular issues tend to polarize things more than is necessary," said Fisher, who figures if he's getting criticized from both sides, he's doing his job about right. "We're a diverse community, and a group like EGALE should seek to support legal structures that maximize people's ability to decide for themselves what kind of life they want to lead."

More of a concern is that it's easier to mobilize the community around a threat, such as the lack of human-rights protection for gays and lesbians. "The challenge for EGALE is to keep itself relevant and grounded," he said. "It's harder to define a proactive platform that people can sign on to than to respond to negative stuff. As we overcome many of the clear legal obstacles and legislation, there will be differences of opinion about where we should put our efforts and resources. We may find fundraising gets harder once people feel their rights have been secured."

Fisher, who quickly discovered the job required a jack-of-all-trades person, started at the organization with lots of training in law, but none in politics or media relations or financial management. Although a fast learner, he's never enjoyed or excelled at fundraising. Board members such as Arron, though, are more worried about burnout. "EGALE is incredibly stretched, and for John to work twelve- to fourteen-hour days is typical," he said. "The board has big eyes and takes on too much, and poor John is the one the work falls on. And he's very hesitant to say, 'I have too much on my plate.'"

Despite the long days and a salary of only $33,000, Fisher is happy with the job. And if he does leave, he's not likely to head up to the Hill. "I enjoy politics from the outside; I don't think being on the inside would be a lot of fun," he said. "There are too many compromises required. One of the things I value about this job is there is as much conformity between what I actually believe and want to do and what I get to say and do as I could hope for in any job."

CRAIG JONES LIKES to say he was a protester for exactly fifteen minutes of his life—and that was the fifteen minutes right before he got arrested. In November 1997, Jones was a law student at the University of British Columbia, watching with dismay as police trampled the constitutional rights of other students in the lead-up to the Asia Pacific Economic Co-operation Summit. What disturbed him most was what happened to Jaggi Singh, a member of a group called APEC Alert. On the day before the world leaders arrived—and in an eerie harbinger of what would happen to Singh at the 2001 Summit of the Americas in Quebec City—plainclothes cops grabbed the activist, whisked him into an unmarked car and sped off. They charged him with assaulting a campus security officer, alleging that he had yelled in the guard's ear with a megaphone.

"It was simply an arrest of convenience, but a very scary one, because it was very Latin American in its execution," said Jones. "I couldn't believe the lengths the police and the federal government were going to, to make sure these kids weren't heard. It seemed completely out of proportion with any threat that they could present."

So, the next day, Jones staged a little protest of his own. On the morning of November 25, he went to the motorcade route and put up signs that read "Democracy" and "Free Speech." When he refused to take them down, the RCMP wrestled him to the ground, arrested him and held him in jail for fourteen hours without laying any charges. Though the Mounties claimed the signs were a security risk, they completely ignored Jones's backpack, which was lying on the ground nearby.

In the aftermath of the APEC scandal, Jones became the best-known of the protesters—and not just because he was the recipient of the infamous e-mail from CBC television reporter Terry Milewski that jokingly referred to those in the Prime Minister's Office as "the forces of darkness." Jones was, after all, a clean-cut law student who usually appeared on television in a suit, so he wasn't threatening to middle-class Canadians who were trying to figure out the whole mess.

"I've always felt like a bit of a fraud as an activist," he admitted. "I feel bad I usurped the attention from people who had something to say about APEC, because all I had to say was something about the people who had something to say about APEC."

Jones is far from a fraud, though. The 36-year-old is a litigation lawyer for the blue-chip Vancouver law firm of Bull, Housser & Tupper, where he spends most of his time representing the provincial government in its suit against tobacco companies to recover health-care costs. The rest of his practice is devoted to civil litigation with a constitutional bent. But he's also the president of the British Columbia Civil Liberties Association. Formed in 1963, the BCCLA was the first of its kind in Canada, and it remains among the most active. So while APEC is a fading memory for most Canadians, Jones is more influential than ever.

When I showed up at his Kitsilano townhouse on an early August evening, Jones poured me a glass of red wine, and we walked out to a leafy backyard and sat on Adirondack chairs. He wore a white T-shirt and blue shorts; his feet were bare, and he had splotches of blue ink on his right hand. A native of England, Jones came to Canada when he was five. He started law school at 29, after a "misspent youth" that included a foray into student politics at a community college, a stint in the army and a tour of duty with a folk-rock band called Poetic Justice.

He has an affable manner and an easy laugh, as I quickly found out. While in Vancouver, I was staying with an old friend who is a zoology professor at UBC. Upon learning I'd be seeing Jones, my host had asked, "Are you going to ask him if he used APEC to launch his career?" When I relayed this question to Jones, he started laughing even before I could add that he must hear that a lot. "I don't get asked it a lot, but I'm glad you did, because it's always in the back of my mind that people are thinking that," he answered. "I'm exactly where I would be—my wife was my girl-friend before APEC; I work at the firm I worked at before APEC; I do volunteer work at the Civil Liberties Association, which I did before APEC. I think it has given me a lot of profile, for better or worse. It's pigeonholed me with some people, and maybe has given me opportunities in other ways. Early on, the question I asked myself was if this was going to affect my career positively or negatively—and at first, of course, it looked like it was going to be a big, huge negative—would I do anything differently? Once I decided I wasn't going to do anything differently, no matter what the answer to that question was, then I stopped worrying about it."

He takes the same attitude to his work at the BCCLA, even when it requires taking flak for unpopular positions, such as questioning the constitutionality of Canada's child-pornography laws. That position also meant that his wife, a kindergarten teacher, had to go to work and hear people ask, "Why is your husband in favour of child pornography?" But the value of civil liberties associations has long been misunderstood by too many people who should know better. And such organizations have ranked high among the favourite whipping boys for conservatives; south of the border, in fact, it's a vicious insult to call someone a "card-carrying member" of the American Civil Liberties Union, a group dedicated to standing up for the American Constitution.

The BCCLA faces the same demonization, even though there's no political consensus in the organization. Former Conservative Prime Minister Kim Campbell and NDP MP Svend Robinson both sit on the honorary board, for example, and the directors include a former bigwig from the Fraser Institute. "The beautiful thing is the degree to which we agree, and that's what really attracted me to civil liberties work," said Jones. "I've always been interested in politics, but I've never been a member of a political party, because you have to take a lot of baggage that you might not agree with in order to get electoral support. The Civil Liberties Association just doesn't work that way. It honestly works from a position of principle—not from coalition-building or who our friends are and who are enemies are. The positions we take are vigorously debated simply on issues of principle."

He admits things can get complicated when rights collide. After the Surrey School Board banned gay-themed children's books, for example, the BCCLA sided with the Gay and Lesbian Educators (GALE). But when a parents' group put together a bill of rights saying their children had a right not to be exposed to gay and lesbian literature—a move GALE denounced as hate speech—BCCLA took the side of the parents. "Everyone has this urge to censor," he said, "and it really does cross from left to right. If your activism is centred on civil liberties as opposed to straightforward politics, you never keep your friends for long. You will be supporting the Fraser Institute's right to say something one week," said Jones, laughing, "and then criticizing the hell out of it the next."

Although he describes himself as "a classic pro-choice, atheist, godless man," he took the case of an anti-abortion student group at UBC that had its display torn apart by pro-choice students. That file was one he worked on as part of his own civil litigation practice, but in October 2000, as BCCLA president, he spoke out against student leaders at the University College of Cariboo in Kamloops who revoked the club status of a group called Students for Life. The latter case earned Jones a laudatory, if somewhat amazed, editorial in the *National Post* that ended, "Canada's civil liberties community, whose support for civil liberties often appears to be coterminous with its left-wing political opinions, should look upon Mr. Jones as a role model."

IN THE FALL OF 1991, just months after her daughter's death, Priscilla de Villiers travelled to Ottawa to speak before the Senate Committee on Legal and Constitutional Affairs. Her appearance was part of an effort to ensure that the upper house would pass gun-control legislation introduced by Kim Campbell, then the Conservative justice minister. De Villiers was there at the request of Suzanne Laplante Edward, the mother of one of the fourteen young women gunned down by Marc Lepine during the massacre at Montreal's l'École Polytechnique on December 6, 1989. Though de Villiers was still reeling from her own tragedy, she readily agreed, because Jonathan Yeo had killed Nina with a gun that didn't need to be registered. Soon de Villiers and CAVEAT were part of one of Canada's most success-ful, and controversial, activist campaigns.

Led by its president, Wendy Cukier, and its first executive director, Montrealer Heidi Rathjen, the Coalition for Gun Con-trol won effective legislation in the face of fierce opposition from pro-gun groups. Unlike a lot of activists, Cukier and Rathjen did not have to change the minds of most Canadians. "We didn't shape public opinion," said Cukier. "All we did was try to mobilize public opinion. When I started, 70 percent of Canadians wanted stronger gun control; today 70 percent of Canadians support stronger gun control." Even though her views were mainstream, they weren't reflected by politicians, because those in the vociferous minority were highly motivated; they wrote letters, packed angry meetings, protested on Parliament Hill and threatened to defy legislation. And they made it clear they would cast their votes only for candidates who shared their views on guns.

Few Canadians who wanted gun control, on the other hand, were prepared to do anything about it. "My problem wasn't my opponents," said Cukier, "it was my supporters." So Cukier built a coalition of 350 endorsing organizations, including various unions, church groups and professional associations. Cukier calls the strategy the "unusual suspects" because she was able to attract such diverse interests. The Canadian Association of Chiefs of Police and the Canadian Labour Congress both signed on, as did CAVEAT and the John Howard Society, an offenders' rights organization. "That undermined efforts by the gun lobby to dismiss us as the usual suspects who are uninformed, emotional and hysterical."

Despite favourable polls, sympathetic justice ministers and the credibility a coalition offered, Cukier and Rathjen did not have an easy time. It took two pieces of bitterly fought legislation to get what they wanted. In May 1990, Campbell unveiled Bill C-80 to improve the screening process for Firearm Acquisition Certificates, define safe storage and ban some military weapons and large-capacity magazines. Although it did not ban semi-automatic military weapons, require the registration of firearms or control the sale of ammunition, the bill got a rough ride. Due to opposition within the Conservative caucus, it failed to pass second reading and had to go to Special Committee for further review. The committee, which included seven gun owners among its eight members, recommended several changes to weaken the legislation. The bill died on the order paper anyway, when Parliament prorogued. In May 1991, Campbell introduced Bill C-17, a revised version of the previous proposal. Opponents, both inside and outside Parliament, continued their efforts, but the legislation passed in November of that year and moved on to the Senate, where the battle continued and de Villiers and others spoke in support of the law.

When the Senate passed the legislation, though, Cukier and Rathjen weren't satisfied because it didn't go far enough. All along they'd bitten their tongues, knowing they had to be supportive or there'd be no legislation at all. Besides, they realized the justice minister was doing her best in difficult circumstances. "We never attacked Kim Campbell, but we attacked some members of her caucus who tried to undermine her," said Cukier. "I wish that law had gone further, but it was a good first step." The danger with that approach, though, was that people would say, "What are you complaining about? You've got your gun control." But they took their chances, got what they could and then started working on the rest.

In 1994, Allan Rock, the new Liberal justice minister, promised to look at ways to strengthen gun control. This only intensified the lobbying by those for and against gun control. Pro-gun groups organized rallies and spread ludicrous rumours that Rock would ban all guns. In September of that year, 10,000 gun owners protested on Parliament Hill; the Coalition for Gun Control responded with a press conference stacked with the families of victims of gun violence.

The following February, Rock tabled Bill C-68 to make the licensing and registration of all firearms mandatory, ban semiautomatic military weapons and some handguns and stiffen penalties for firearms offences. The House of Commons passed the legislation in June of 1995, but in September, as senators tried to derail Rock's work, the Province of Alberta, supported by Ontario, Manitoba, Saskatchewan, Northwest Territories and Yukon, announced a constitutional challenge. Canada's Firearms Act became law in December 1995, despite the determined efforts of pro-gun senators and like-minded activists—and in June 2000, the Supreme Court unanimously upheld the law's constitutionality.

Still, opponents of gun control—who include hunting groups, target shooters, collectors, retailers and manufacturers, as well as advocacy organizations such as the National Firearms Association and various responsible firearms owners groups—never wavered. In the 2000 federal election, as before, the Canadian Alliance and the Progressive Conservatives continued to stand firm against the law. The NDP was split on the issue, and the Liberals and Bloc Québécois were strongly in favour. The NFA and other gun groups tried to defeat pro-control candidates, and tops on their hit list was Anne McLellan, the Liberal justice minister from Edmonton. And they nearly pulled it off. In fact, when Wendy Cukier went to bed on election night, she thought McLellan had lost.

The next morning, I met Cukier in her office at Ryerson University, where she's a professor of information technology management and justice studies. It had been a busy morning for the 44-year-old, with phone calls from the media and supporters, but she was feeling great relief—not because she's a dedicated Liberal, but because a strengthened majority for the government meant the law was safe. "I'm a single-issue girl," she said. "I have no political ties. I'm interested in who supports the legislation."

She found her issue on December 6, 1989. As she watched the television coverage of the massacre, she thought, "There's something wrong with this picture, and I am so ordinary that if I think this, everyone thinks this." Cukier, who'd been active in industry associations for years, tried to find a gun-control group to join. But there weren't any in Canada. After speaking to Bob Crampton, a Toronto police officer who'd written a 1984 report calling for gun registration, as well as to criminologist Darryl Davies and others, Cukier launched a group called Canadians for Gun Control. She also began working with Rathjen, a witness to the Montreal massacre and the co-ordinator of a petition, which initially just called for a ban on military assault weapons, put together by students at l'École Polytechnique. So while Cukier had started to build a network of experts, Rathjen was the focus of intense media attention around the petition. Eventually, in April 1991, the students of l'École Polytechnique and Canadians for Gun Control formally merged, forming the Coalition for Gun Control.

I'd met a lot of activists with post-graduate degrees—and Cukier has an M.A. in history and is working on a Ph.D. in management science—but she was the only one I came across who has an M.B.A. In the early 1980s, she worked in the vehicles-and-drivers section of Ontario's Ministry of Transportation (an experience that came in handy in the fight for gun registration), and then she became a telecommunications consultant working with clients such as Bell Canada and IBM. The gun-control campaign allowed Cukier to put her business training to good use.

"Moral indignation is not a strategy," she likes to say, so she created a coalition as a way to build critical mass quickly—and because one of the fundamental principles in organizational theory is that the complexity of an organization needs to match the diversity of the environment. The coalition meant she could match the messengers to the target audiences. Rather than having Toronto academic Wendy Cukier speak in Winnipeg, for example, she could get the local chief of police and someone from the John Howard Society to give a press conference. "Coalitions are particularly valuable in Canada because of the diversity of the audience, whether it's the public, the politicians or the media," she said. "In the corporate sector, there's a real move toward virtual organizations that are flexible. That's the principle I apply. It used to be that your big focus was strategic planning and building a big solid bureaucratic, stable organization. But if you're in an environment that's very changeable, a big solid organization can be the *Titanic*."

Although her coalition finally won the legislation it sought, Cukier believes there will always be a need for something like the Coalition for Gun Control to play a watchdog role. "It's one thing to get legislation through, it's another to get legislation implemented," she said, "and it's another to preserve it from constant attack." Cukier's contact with politicians had already decreased as the group became more concerned with education and keeping supporters informed as the law's measures gradually come into effect until 2003. One task was to ensure that police, as well as health-care and crisis workers, understand that if they go on a domestic-violence call, one of the first things they must do is check for—and remove—any guns.

As the focus shifts away from advocacy, Cukier hopes to extricate herself from the coalition, which will be good for her personal life, her academic career and the Ph.D. she's trying to finish. She'd also enjoy not being the lightning rod for people who don't like the legislation. In 1995, as part of a "Bricks for Wendy" campaign, gun owners sent her bricks, manure and men's underwear, postage-collect. Over the years, they've also sent her lots of anti-Semitic hate literature and violent pornography. And she's received many death threats. But even as she reduces her domestic role, she plans to increase her international work. She's helped on Brazilian, South African and French projects—and a United Nations Crime Commission targeting the illicit traffic of guns. If she were to move onto another cause, it would be children's issues, primarily child poverty.

"The kids agenda hasn't really been as central as it should be. Strategically, there are things that could be done to bring in more of the 'unusual suspects,'" she said. "The state of children in this country is an issue that tends to be spoken about by a particular segment of the population. Every once in a while, they'll bring in a Bay Street guy in a suit, but not very often. It would be an interesting challenge to bring an issue like that into the mainstream." But she's in no rush to move on, because there's much work to be done on guns internationally. "We now have so much experience in Canada that's almost directly transferable. So that's the clear priority."

For all her success, Cukier doesn't discount the role played by timing and trends. After all, the push for tougher regulations had been building for a long time. The Trudeau government proposed registration of rifles and shotguns for its 1978 gun law, but removed that provision and others as a sop to gun owners. Still, NDP leader Tommy Douglas supported the bill as a good first step. "Half a loaf is better than none," he told the House of Commons. "I believe that someday we will have the techniques to register all guns." A decade later, the Mulroney Conservatives planned to introduce improved gun control, even before the Montreal massacre. "We were activists with an agenda that fit," admitted Cukier. In a 1999 paper called "A Social Marketing Approach to Advocacy: The Canadian Gun Control Story," she wrote: "Depending on one's perspective, the Coalition for Gun Control was either enormously successful, because it got legislation passed, or terribly ineffective, because it took seven years, despite the fact that most Canadians supported it."

That statement reveals as much frustration as humour. If more people had let their feelings be known to the politicians, the country would have had effective gun control long ago. The silent majority isn't doing itself any favours by waiting for someone like

Cukier to come along. "The only thing that makes me different from a lot of other people—aside from a large ego and thinking I can do things and it not occurring to me that I can't—is a sense of personal responsibility. I grew up with a sense that if you don't stand up for what you believe in, in a very active way, you're a collaborator," she said. "I realize when I talk to other people that they think exactly what I think, they read the newspaper and they cry, they're horrified by things that go on, but somehow there's a disconnect between them and all that stuff."

She admits that some people don't know what they can do to make a difference—or simply don't believe anything they do matters—while others can't even see the direct impact on their lives. But the bigger problem is complacency. "I believe to my toenails that people who believe in things have to fight for them. That's the biggest challenge in our society. It's not just for gun control. I don't care what the issue is, the biggest problem is that Canadians take things for granted. They don't feel they have a responsibility to preserve what we have, because they don't appreciate it."

10

DUFF CONACHER

AND THE

DRIVE FOR

DEMOCRATIC

REFORM

DUFF CONACHER'S LIFE would be so much easier—and perhaps higher profile—if he'd just become a corporate lawyer. After all, his pedigree is perfect for it. Tall, athletic and possessing patrician good looks, he has a private-school education and the connections that go with it. And it doesn't hurt that his last name echoes with memories of all the famous athletes in his family.

Conacher did get the law degree, but he never considered Bay Street. After studying activism under the master, Ralph Nader himself, he launched Democracy Watch. It's an Ottawa-based citizen watchdog group that works on some of the most powerful issues in the country: improved government ethics, registration of lobbyists and more truly democratic governments and socially responsible corporations. A big fan of coalitions, Conacher chaired the Canadian Community Reinvestment Coalition, an alliance of more than a hundred groups, which pushed for more accountable banks—and successfully scuttled the proposed bank mergers in 1998.

Despite that success and Democracy Watch's impressive advisory committee, which includes actor Dan Ackroyd, Hall of Fame goalie Ken Dryden and lawyer Marilou McPhedran, most Canadians don't have a clue who Conacher is. I suppose that doesn't really set him apart from the other activists I met, most of whom enjoy, at best, a regional profile. But given that the

Democracy Watch coordinator works out of Ottawa and that his issues are so central to the way the country operates, I would have thought he'd be able to garner as much name recognition as, say, Walter Robinson, the federal director of the Canadian Taxpayers Federation.

His quiet style partly explains it. While Conacher gets on television often enough, he rarely leaves a lasting impression. Although he may use words like "outrageous"—as in "The fact that government does not consult with the public in a meaningful way to develop policy and ends up imposing stupid decisions on everyone's lives, that I find outrageous"—his behaviour is anything but. That understated approach not only fits with his personality; it's one he learned from Nader, who became famous and influential despite eschewing guerrilla tactics in favour of methodically plugging away.

Conacher started pushing his reform ideas in 1993 as coordinator of Democracy Watch, and although his goal of expanding democracy ought to be an obvious crowd-pleaser, the public— and, worse, other activists who stand to benefit from many of his ideas—has been slow to join forces with him. Still, activism is a long game, and the 38-year-old hopes to generate a steady light rather than a blast of heat. So even if his fellow Canadians are too apathetic to notice, he keeps working at giving them a greater voice in the way their country works. "We need a citizen movement," he said. "Right now we have citizen groups, but we don't have a citizen movement."

DUFF CONACHER WAS CALM. Casually dressed in a green button-down shirt and blue chinos, he waited patiently in his office, just east of Parliament Hill. There was no hint in his demeanour that as soon as colleague Doug Gabelmann arrived with copies of the *Task Force Report on the Future of the Canadian Financial Services Sector* (a study that would influence the future of the banking system), this drizzly mid-September day in 1998 would become one of the busiest in Conacher's career.

At 9:20, Gabelmann returned from the Department of Finance and announced, "It was like a Spice Girls concert up there." Conacher moved slowly to the newspaper-covered table in the middle of the office, gently picked up the report and sat down to read it. Within ten minutes, the media started calling. A little after eleven o'clock, Conacher slipped into a sober blue suit, crisp white shirt and paisley tie; suddenly, he looked more like a Bay Street bond trader than someone determined to change the way Canadian banks operate.

After an interview with Rafe Mair, the popular and influential Vancouver talk-show host, he realized he didn't have much time to get to the Press Building for an appearance on Newsworld. He walked quickly—not difficult, given his long legs—across the street to grab a cab. Hopping in, he told the driver, "We're in a hurry." It was the closest to panic he came all day.

That composure may hurt him with the public, but not with the media. Later, as he left the Press Building, several reporters greeted him warmly. While some advocates and lobbyists schmooze journalists with lunches—something he neither enjoys nor can afford—Conacher made his contacts the hard way; before the days of e-mail, he delivered his press releases in person. It paid off: Democracy Watch has had national media coverage every month since its first campaign in 1994.

Conacher launched the organization with $60,000 in royalties from *Canada Firsts: Ralph Nader's Salute to Canada and Canadian Achievement*, a 1993 bestseller he co-wrote with Nader. The money gave him a chance to pursue the creation of Democracy Watch, an idea he'd been harbouring for several years. True to form, he began a six-month feasibility study to determine how and where to set it up. He also came up with a mandate called "20 Steps Toward a Modern, Working Democracy." It's a broad catalogue designed to "empower Canadians" as voters, citizens, taxpayers, consumers of information and services, and shareholders of private and public wealth. Some of the items on the wish list—including electoral reform and ways to hold politicians accountable—are ideas that would fit comfortably in a conservative manifesto. But where Democracy Watch parts company with the right is in its insistence that corporations also consider the desires and needs of citizens, consumers and stakeholders when making decisions.

Conacher believes governments communicate well with business, and they don't do a bad job of getting advice from experts and academics, but they aren't as successful at conferring with advocacy groups. And when it comes to consulting individual Canadians, they're a complete failure. "The more meaningful the decision, the more meaningful and widespread the consultation should be," said Conacher. "And it should be a direct avenue for individual citizens. The government should hold a series of meetings—not just travelling road-show, town-hall meetings—where interest-group representatives are not allowed to come, where it's just individual citizens."

One of his ideas would see governments adopt study circles, which are common in Sweden, as one way to engage in meaningful consultation with citizens. Canada tried it once in 1994 on the issue of immigration. First, the government produced a tabloid-style newspaper that said these are the facts and figures of immigration and here are the options, including the option favoured by the party in power. Anyone—excluding members of advocacy groups—could sign up to join a study circle. Those who did came together with a small group of people, usually at their local school, and for a few hours had a facilitated discussion about the issue. The facilitators were professionals, not government employees, and instead of being a focus group, it was a learning process. The experiment was a success, and the government acted on two of the recommendations. But to really work, study circles would require Canadians to become much more engaged citizens than most are now.

Another of Conacher's ideas—Step 15 in his mandate—could be a much easier triumph, if only the government would try it. He wants banks, insurance companies and utilities to include flyers (with their bills) inviting customers to join consumer associations that would act as watchdogs for each industry. It works in the United States; with 100,000 dues-paying members, the Citizens Utility Board in Illinois, for example, fights for lower rates and better service from the state's electric, gas and telephone companies. And Conacher hopes to see similar CUBs in Canada. "You would have a third sector that is actually balancing. It wouldn't have the same resources as corporations, but the resources would be exponentially larger than they are now," he said, adding that unlike small groups such as Democracy Watch or the Consumers' Association of Canada, flyer-generated organizations would have real power, which governments and corporations couldn't ignore. "It would balance the policy-making process greatly, because you would have these large citizen groups, which really don't exist except in the environmental area, and you'd have more of a tripartite system. But instead of business, government and labour, you'd have business and government and citizen groups."

He estimates it would cost $8 million to do a direct-mail campaign to every Canadian bank customer—assuming he could get the addresses. But if the banks enclosed the campaign flyers with their customers' account statements, the only cost would be

$300,000 for printing. Bank executives, needless to say, are cool to the suggestion, but in April 1996, then Industry Minister John Manley said if there were broad support from consumers, he'd be willing to push the banks to enclose flyers if they refused to do so voluntarily. So far, though, the government hasn't followed through, and the banks haven't jumped at the opportunity to do something on their own.

The idea of using flyers to help consumers help themselves is typical of Conacher's practical, rational approach. While many activists prefer to play the street fighter, Conacher stands out because of his refusal to use inflammatory rhetoric or publicity stunts calculated to attract media attention. "Sometimes you have to break the mould of expectations to be effective," said Richard Remillard, who left the Canadian Bankers Association to work as a public-policy consultant, "and his tack can be better than always saying the sky is falling." Instead of staging angry demonstrations on Parliament Hill or in front of bank towers in downtown Toronto, Conacher put together the Canadian Community Reinvestment Coalition in 1996. When the banks announced their intention to merge, the coalition jumped from sixty member groups to over a hundred. Although most CCRC members are on the left—including the Council of Canadians, the Canadian Auto Workers and the Canadian Federation of Students—he insists it is non-partisan. But while the Canadian Federation of Independent Business supported the CCRC's goals, it wouldn't sign on because of the unions in the coalition.

The CCRC's fingerprints—and that means Conacher's—were all over the government's task-force report. It was cited in several footnotes, and all of its proposals—including calls for an independent ombudsman and rules governing community reinvestment—were dealt with, though not necessarily to Conacher's satisfaction. "He's been able to influence the political debate about the banks by defining the issues," said Remillard. Or, as Conacher matter-of-factly put it, "We are the citizen voice that's heard most strongly through the report."

His critics weren't impressed, though. Doug Peters, for example, who was secretary of state for finance in Jean Chrétien's first government, and then became a financial and economic consultant, said Conacher was "a single voice with a not very effective organization—and he doesn't have the analysis." Peters suggested Conacher ought to tackle privacy issues and the way credit-card interest is calculated instead of worrying about community reinvestment and service fees. "I don't think many of the issues he's followed are the ones concerning consumers."

Predictably enough, the bankers were even less complimentary. Although the CCRC represents over a hundred groups, Scott Mullin, vice-president of public affairs for the Canadian Bankers Association, dismissed it as a one-man band, with no annual report or transparent decision-making process. "He's become a professional critic and gained a profile for himself," he said. "And there hasn't been anyone else for the media to turn to." Mullin is equally dismissive of Conacher's community-reinvestment proposals, claiming they are American ideas not suited to Canada's system of national banks. "Rather than working toward a solution," he said, "Conacher seems to be working to establish a position for himself."

Sniping from bankers and other opponents goes with the territory, of course, but Conacher doesn't always get the warmest reception from other activists. Upon meeting Conacher at a party, the director of one advocacy organization said, "So you're the competition." Some resent his influence with the media and see Democracy Watch as a threat to their turf—despite Conacher's efforts to ease some of these fears by creating coalitions. But even within the alliances, rivalries are hard to avoid; the Council of Canadians, which was a member of the CCRC, likes to take the credit for the bank campaign. At the Campaigns & Elections conference in Vancouver in August 2000, Jo Dufay, who is now with Greenpeace, gave a workshop detailing how the council killed the mergers.

It doesn't help that Conacher's ideas and his approach to activism are often at odds with conventional thinking in the activist community. For one thing, he wants all activists to register as lobbyists, something many of them don't think they should have to do. For another, plenty of groups—including the Public Interest Advocacy Centre, which operates out of the same building as Democracy Watch and has joined some of Conacher's coalitions, and the Consumers' Association of Canada—aren't keen on the flyer idea because they're protective of their turf. It's the same with environmentalists who don't want anyone else working their corner. But most of them are ineffective.

"If they're doing such a great job, then why did Walkerton happen?" he asked. "A healthy citizen movement prevents crises, it doesn't just react to them." More than that, he believes Canadians would be better off with larger, more-democratic organizations. "There are groups that get quoted all the time in the paper that have five hundred members and an appointed board, and they're against the flyer idea to create a group with 500,000 or a million members," said Conacher, who knows Democracy Watch is not large enough to be able to truly represent what citizens want. "There are citizen groups that say just government and corporations have to be democratized, but we all have to be, because we are self-appointed watchdogs."

AS A SCION OF ONE of Canada's greatest sports families, Conacher was born to be on the other side of the struggle for reform. His grandfather Lionel "Big Train" Conacher was selected by reporters as the country's male athlete of the first half-century, and his great-uncle Charlie "Bomber" Conacher was a captain of the Toronto Maple Leafs. Big Train later sat as a Liberal in the Ontario legislature and then became a member of Parliament, but politics doesn't run in the family, sports does. Several members of the next generation were pro athletes, including Duff's father, Lionel Jr., who played football for the Montreal Alouettes and then had a successful career in insurance and as the owner of a Canadian Tire store.

True to his genes, Conacher is a jock. An avid ultimate Frisbee player, he excelled in football, basketball and track at Upper Canada College and then played university football. Though he read a lot of books by peyote philosopher Carlos Castaneda, a counterculture favourite in the 1960s and 1970s, there was little to suggest he'd take a markedly different course from the one taken by his classmates or his older brother, another Lionel, who is an investment banker in Toronto. "Lionel's doing the banking thing full tilt, and Duff is doing his thing full tilt. They're very close, but they're very competitive," said Tom Digby, a friend since their days at UCC. "Duff is in every way a true Conacher— smart, tough and competitive. But like all Conachers, there is a sensitive side."

Before I met him, I wondered if Conacher would be a silver-spoon rebel, a pampered brat who was rebelling against his privilege out of some inchoate anger or hurt. But I quickly realized that wasn't the case, though even his friends weren't really sure what does motivate him. He wasn't much clearer about it himself, except to say he enjoys it. "I like to tackle issues," he said, "and come up with solutions that work for the whole society." If there was a turning point, it may have come in 1985. After a summer of tree-planting, he and Digby travelled to Central America and ended up in Nicaragua. Building houses with various groups, including Habitat for Humanity, exposed Conacher to activism, but he also saw how difficult it was to make a difference in the war-torn country, especially when a housing project he'd worked on was attacked by the Contras. "In my mind," Digby told me, "he never really came back."

Physically, of course, he did return to Canada, but six months later he left again. This time he went to Washington and a job with Nader's Raiders, the team of interns who assist the great consumer advocate. It was an idea his uncle Brian Conacher, the former Toronto Maple Leaf, heard from Ken Dryden, the one-time Montreal Canadiens goalie who had enjoyed his own experience as a Raider in 1971. In Nader, Conacher found a compelling role model and mentor, and he became intrigued by democratic reform ideas while working on projects such as improving the quality of U.S. drinking water. He realized if citizens had a stronger voice in the way governments make decisions and corporations operate, advocacy work on specific issues—clean water, for example—would be a lot easier. "Duff saw a set of issues that underlay all the other ones, and he saw the potential to fix so many problems," said Aaron Freeman, a founding director of Democracy Watch. "They're the reforms that make all other reforms easier."

DEMOCRACY WATCH has its office on the edge of Ottawa's Byward Market. I went there twice—once in September 1998 and once in May 2000—and both times the room was broken into cubicles with dividers and overflowing bookshelves. It was decorated with posters and two Group of Seven fakes by the entrance. The many documents that covered Conacher's desk were staggered in neat rows, and there was a copy of the Canadian Constitution on his wall. As the only full-time staffer in the group, he pulls in just $30,000 annually. Life as an activist is a tough slog for little pay and less thanks, but Conacher can imagine the day when the mandate of Democracy Watch, broad and utopian though it is, will be a reality—and he can stop campaigning. "If we achieve the 20 Steps," he says, "we go out of business."

All activists say that, but few get their wish. Yes, of course, plenty go out of business because of burnout, bankruptcy or lack of public interest. But complete victory is rare. The exception that proved the rule was the Canadian Coalition on Acid Rain. Created in 1981 by the Federation of Ontario Naturalists, Pollution Probe and others, the group pushed state and provincial governments to pass acid-rain legislation. While Michael Perley and Adele Hurley, who ran the organization from offices in Toronto and Washington, did get the laws they sought—and wound up operations in 1991—the problem of acid rain certainly never went away.

Unlike Hurley and Perley, Conacher has not staked out one easily winnable goal. But in December 1998, he enjoyed a sweet victory when Finance Minister Paul Martin nixed the proposed bank mergers. Although Conacher saw the decision as a good sign, he was not ready to celebrate just yet. "Stopping the mergers is not enough," he said at the time. "Canadians want better banks, and the only way to get that is to pass accountability and consumer-protection laws."

His "better banks, not bigger banks" refrain is an echo of how the CCRC defined the campaign. That forced the banks to react, and only too late did they attempt to push the dubious notion that bigger banks are better banks. Conacher cites *The War Room*, a documentary film about Bill Clinton's 1992 presidential campaign, as a great example of how to define a campaign. In the movie, spin doctor James Carville comes up with the famous "It's the economy, stupid" line that helps propel Clinton to the White House.

Of course, winning an advocacy campaign—especially against a powerful business lobby like the banks—requires far more than a snappy line. Conacher remains convinced he's found the right formula. First, he got a lot of groups working together in a broad coalition. "We're dealing with a federal government that has to have more people applauding than screaming whenever it does something," he said. "So you have to build a broad base of people who will applaud and then show the government that the applause will happen if it does what you want. If groups think they can move things forward alone, they're not only fooling themselves, they're fooling their donors, because there isn't a group large enough to do it." He added that representation from across the country, including Quebec, is crucial, but too often organizations neglect *la belle province* even though it accounts for nearly one-quarter of the nation's population and is a major consideration whenever the federal government makes a decision.

Second, the CCRC put forth a positive set of rule changes that it wanted. Conacher argues that one of the biggest weaknesses among Canadian activists is their insistence on believing effective activism is simply stopping things. "All they do is maintain the status quo and they actually lose in the long run, because the rules never change and there are all sorts of things they're not stopping. They're just stopping a few symbolic things." So instead of simply demanding there be no mergers, the CCRC suggested alternatives and ideas, such as a flyer-generated citizen group to act as a bank watchdog, which would change the rules of the game. He argues that one of the reasons the environmental movement has been so successful in Canada is that it changed the rules by entrenching the need for environmental assessments.

Third, the CCRC did its research and put out six carefully considered position papers. This set it apart from activists who are only too happy to make pronouncements before they know what they're talking about.

Fourth, the group lobbied politicians directly, rather than simply through the media. Many organizations have a bias against lobbying that baffles Conacher. In fact, he wonders how any government can know what people want unless they explain their positions to their politicians.

In the end, the CCRC not only stopped the mergers, it won about 75 percent of what it wanted. And yet no other group has shown any interest in learning from the experience. "You'd think there would be curiosity across the citizen movement about how we actually won re-regulation, including the creation of a regulatory agency, in so-called deregulatory times," said Conacher, adding that no one has ever asked him how the CCRC had so much success. "But there's no curiosity at all." He doesn't say that because he wants to be the centre of attention; it's just that he's increasingly fed up with the immaturity of other advocates. Rather than thinking strategically and learning from the success of others, too many activists prefer to blame their lack of success on cuts to government funding and the refusal of politicians to listen to them anymore. That's left progressive groups licking their wounds and looking inward, while conservative organizations like the Canadian Taxpayers Federation are reaching out and winning battles.

Conacher is equally disappointed with the attitude of other activists when it comes to electoral reform, which is Step 1 in his 20 Steps. It's a classic example of a rule change that would give citizens a greater voice. As I travelled across the country talking to activists, I was surprised at how many activists are keen on changing the way we send people to Parliament. On three consecutive days in Alberta, three different people brought up the subject before I did: Christine Burdett, chair of Friends of Medicare, environmentalist Mike Sawyer and anti-poverty activist Sarah Kerr. Burdett told me that while she was driving around the province to the group's information forums on Bill 11, she began to wonder if she was working on the right issue, and it dawned on her that maybe she should be working on electoral reform.

But few organizations have the resources to devote to an issue that presents so many hurdles. Only one of the five federal parties, the NDP, has electoral reform in its platform. Worse, the three parties with the most seats in the House of Commons all benefit from the first-past-the-post system, and the ruling Liberals publicly criticized Elections Canada for even holding an info session on proportional representation. In addition, any major change would probably require an amendment to the Constitution, no small feat in this country. And then there's the problem of deciding what should replace the current system. "Everyone agrees the system should be changed, but there are all sorts of models and no agreement on which one is best," said Conacher. "It will take a lot to get citizens to rally behind one model."

Despite the enormous external barriers that pro-reform activists face, their own inability to think strategically and get past petty differences may be bigger problems. When Conacher and the CTF's Walter Robinson tried to launch a voting-reform coalition in 1999, they were disappointed to discover that most groups wouldn't park their ideological baggage long enough to work together. Groups on the left refused to work with the CTF; organizations on the right wanted nothing to do with a coalition that included unions. The likely solution will be two coalitions, one on right and one on left, a situation that would weaken an already flimsy movement. "There's no way around it. The so-called leadership of citizen groups is not mature enough to set aside differences and work together in coalition for systemic changes on issues where there is agreement," a frustrated Conacher told me early in 2001. He won't give up on electoral reform, but he plans to put most of his energy and resources toward democratic reforms that actually have a chance of happening. "It's easy to be active; it's not easy to be effective. There are a lot of activists out there, but not many effectivists."

EVEN AFTER THE PROPOSED mergers put banking issues in the spotlight, Conacher and Democracy Watch remained a long, long way from achieving household-name status. He admits a lack of resources has stunted Democracy Watch's reputation. As it is for all activists, funding is a constant struggle. The group has an annual budget of $60,000 and doesn't seek money from government or business. That leaves individuals (the group has just a thousand members) and foundations, so along with fundraising and public-speaking engagements, Conacher wrote *More Canada Firsts: Another Collection of Canadian Firsts and Foremosts in the World* to raise money. A third volume is in the works.

His low-key approach doesn't do much to fill the coffers. Rather than staging colourful stunts, Conacher prefers to prepare well-reasoned, well-researched reports, press releases and briefs to ministers and committees. That's just his style. In its first campaign, in April 1994, Democracy Watch produced *Spring Cleaning*, a report comparing lobbying legislation in sixty jurisdictions in North America. In June 1995 and 1996, it issued report cards on how well the federal Liberals did in keeping their promise to improve government ethics (the Liberals failed both times). Along with the CCRC's six position papers on the banking issue, such reports are typical of Conacher's efforts, but they are time-consuming and expensive to produce. But more than that, these efforts rarely attract the amount of media attention he needs to get most Canadians excited about the possibility of democratic reform. If he were more of a showman, he might have a higher profile. If he were more ruthless, he might be a greater threat to the banks. In the fall of 1998, I called James Laxer, a political scientist at York University and a savvy political observer, to see what he thought about Conacher. After saying he didn't know enough about him to comment, Laxer went on to suggest a little more volume might be in order, adding, "He's not getting through to me."

In person, Conacher is an extremely likable man, personable and unfailingly polite as well as smart and thoughtful. But the truth is he has all the charisma of a small-town bank manager. The day I followed him around in Ottawa, I kept waiting for something to happen—I wanted to see him lose his temper and swear a blue streak or break out in whoops of glee or do something to suggest his passion is more than just intellectual. But unrestrained displays of emotion are rare, though Tom Heintzman, a long-time friend and a lawyer who once worked for the Sierra Legal Defence Fund, once saw him dancing on a table in a pub. That happened after the Quebec Public Interest Research Group he'd helped organize at McGill University won a referendum that gave it funding from students' fees. "He's the antithesis of what society thinks of as a rebel," said Heintzman. "He appeals to common sense because he's better read, calmer and more rational than his opponents."

The problem is that Canadians need to see or hear more of him to make the comparison. A potential appearance on CTV's *Canada AM* the morning after the release of the task-force report fell through, and CBC's *The National* considered booking him for its discussion on the report, but instead opted for the human-interest story of Betty Hyde, an Ottawa woman who became a local folk hero when she forced the Royal Bank to reverse its decision to close her branch. Rafe Mair may have 100,000 listeners, but *The National* attracts over a million viewers. Unfortunately for Conacher, the media, especially television, often prefer colour to content, an unspoken fact that may go a long way to explain why the leading anti-bank activist in a country with a long-standing antipathy to banks has such a low profile. This is not a good thing for someone whose opponents are richer, more powerful and better connected. While the banks spend millions getting their message out—one estimate put the Royal Bank's public-relations budget for the merger campaign at $7 million—the CCRC earmarked $70,000 for its 1998 campaign. But Conacher doesn't believe that giving in to the cult of personality will make up any of the deficit. "Where the U.S. system is different is that Ralph Nader, as one person, can have a great influence," he said. "In Canada, we don't have icons the way they do in the U.S., so it's necessary to build broad-based coalitions."

Accordingly, Democracy Watch has put together several alliances aside from the CCRC. The Money in Politics Coalition, which is Aaron Freeman's project, has fifty member groups and campaigns for changes to Canada's electoral finance laws with the hope of reducing the influence of wealthy interests in Canadian politics. The Government Ethics Coalition includes thirty-one member groups, ranging from the British Columbia Civil Liberties Association to the Sierra Club of Canada to the Canadian Labour Congress. In February 2001, it called on Prime Minister Jean Chrétien to strengthen the ethics code for cabinet ministers and to pass similar rules for all MPs and senators. Meanwhile, the Corporate Responsibility Coalition, which has thirty-two member groups, campaigns for changes to Canada's corporate laws to ensure companies act responsibly—and are held accountable if they don't. That would give legislative weight to consumer boycotts and markets campaigns such as Greenpeace's successful efforts to convince retailers to stop selling wood from old-growth forests. As Conacher points out, activists against genetic engineering have had great success targeting

Monsanto, but few people know about Cargill, another company that sells genetically modified agricultural products. "I'm not saying they're unsuccessful or unnecessary, but it can be ad hoc," said Conacher. "It can change one company rather than one industry, let alone a whole sector." So his coalition wants to replace the ineffective patchwork of rules and weak penalties that now exist. "That would bring some teeth—a legal requirement—to what is becoming a political, social, cultural mandate that consumers are pushing."

He isn't surprised that the public has been slow to get excited about his work—it does, after all, focus on murky areas like government policy, instead of more Technicolor issues such as battered seal pups—and he's willing to be patient. Although his conviction that a larger-than-life persona isn't necessary to succeed as an activist may seem naive, his supporters are convinced it's the right approach. "There are different ways to wage battle," said Doug Gabelmann, a former political aide turned advocacy consultant who served as the CCRC's part-time co-coordinator. He pointed out that the phones in Democracy Watch's office wouldn't be so busy if Conacher weren't effective. "You can try to beat the banks using the same methods as Greenpeace, or you can try to reform the system," said Rick Wallace, a human-rights consultant in Toronto. "I don't think he's trying to nationalize the banks or dismantle them. He's willing to have a dialogue and believes in persuasion." Political analyst and author Linda McQuaig also thinks he's effective. "There's a need for people to organize protests, but there's also a need for serious analysis," she said. "His role is educating the public, and I think that's a good goal."

Of course, an activist can be loud as well as smart, but Conacher is doubtful about the benefits of traditional protesting—and wary that it would just make it easier for his opponents to marginalize both his position and his organization. "You can have a few people protesting outside a bank branch and get on the national news. So you get media coverage, but what is a policy-maker supposed to do with that?" he asked. "Is that really how our democracy should work?"

REVEILLE FOR CITIZENS

BACK HOME TO VISIT her parents in New Glasgow, Nova Scotia, Mary Gorman decided to head down to Lighthouse Beach. She'd played there as a little girl and had fond memories of it. But upon returning in 1988, she was disgusted at the sight of black waves of effluent from the Scott Paper plant rolling up on the shore. Furious, she went to the nearest phone and called the company.

That was just typical of the woman whom many now consider the Erin Brockovich of Nova Scotia. After ten years in New York City, where she'd tried to make a go of it as a screenwriter (and where she got her start in activism by working with the homeless), Gorman soon found herself living once again in her old stomping grounds—and at the centre of countless battles, big and small. She took on the phone company over its policies, fought a planned rock quarry, battled Nova Scotia Power Corporation over chronic outages and challenged Shell's decision to take the gas pumps from a local rural store. And she led a group of protesters who occupied the office of John Hamm for three weeks. Now Conservative premier of the province, Hamm was the leader of the third party at the time, but he wouldn't fight the government's proposal to close rural schools and replace them with big regional schools. Although Gorman has no kids of her own, she joined the campaign because parents asked her to help them out. "I have to learn to say no," she said. "I don't know what propels me to do this stuff. Quite frankly, I wish I wasn't doing it a lot of the time, because it really is a burnout—it's an exceptional burnout. Just because I do this stuff doesn't mean I enjoy it. I'm fed up with it."

By the summer of 2000 when I visited her, Gorman had found herself in the midst of her biggest struggle yet. She was fighting plans to allow oil exploration along coastal fishing grounds in the southern Gulf of St. Lawrence. She organized the founding meeting of the Save Our Seas and Shores Coalition in October 1999. It brought together all sorts of "unusual suspects," including fishing, native, environmental and tourist groups from Nova Scotia, New Brunswick and Prince Edward Island. Environmentalists and fishermen are rarely allies, but the even bigger surprise was the presence of both native and non-native fishermen, despite the acrimony over fishing rights. Irene Novaczek, a PEI scientist and environmentalist who is a member of the coalition, said, "When it comes to rubber hitting the road, Mary Gorman is a perfect example of just getting out there and doing it." But the multinational petrochemical industry turned out to be a foe like no other she'd faced, and politicians who once listened to grassroots concerns were turning a deaf ear to the issue. So she spent a lot more time writing press releases than screenplays. "It's been virtually full-time and I'm absolutely zapped."

Gorman kept telling me she was burned out. And I believed her, but I quickly became convinced she couldn't help herself. Even as Canadian activism becomes more sophisticated, using all manner of professional techniques, it's still ultimately about ordinary people standing up for what they believe in. Since so few Canadians are engaged, though, we're really talking about extraordinary people—people like Mary Gorman. But even the extraordinary get frustrated. "The difference between Erin Brockovich and me is she did it after the damage had been done.

What she did was admirable; she mobilized people and made them realize they were dying because of this corporation. But there's nothing more difficult than fighting a preventive battle. Listen, in ten years, if our fishery and our shoreline are wiped out, everyone will be behind us. But it will be too late then, because once the fish are dead, they're dead."

MARY GORMAN LIVES just outside Merigomish in a cheerful, turquoise house with a red door at the end of long gravel driveway and beside a big lawn. As she greeted me at the door, she said, "Sorry for not mowing the lawn for you." Inside, she pointed proudly to the big old pink stove that dominates the kitchen, its bubbled paint a reminder of the fire it survived, and an old black-and-white photo of her among a group of young girls wearing short dresses and hairbands on a day they served society women at a tea party.

There was an uncommon amount of nervous energy at work here; as she talked—and she barely stopped to breathe—she tugged at her reddish hair and curled it behind her ears, she took off her necklace, knotted it in a chain, then unraveled the knot and put it back on. After a while, her partner, Percy Hayne, came home and joined us. He's a leader among local fishermen, and they met when Gorman yelled at him during one of her early battles. A shy man with big hands, sausage-like fingers and mussed hair around the crown of his bald head, he wore work clothes, including a well-oiled T-shirt and cap. Getting the occasional word in edgewise was not easy for him, and he doodled while Gorman talked. When he left, he said, "I can't compete with her anyway."

Gorman worked on Hayne's 42-foot boat for four years filled with "you're fired" and "I quit" fights. When they're fighting to save the fishery, though, they have a much better working relationship. Both are leaders in the Save Our Seas and Shores Coalition, and they believe it is the only way to prevent the government and oil companies from using a divide-and-conquer strategy to pit fishermen against each other and against the environmentalists. With tensions between native and non-native fishermen still bubbling over in the wake of the Supreme Court's Marshall decision, Hayne was the first to embrace First Nations leaders. "It's necessary to form alliances today, because in the global economy the big people are forming alliances against the little people," he said. "So the little people have to form alliances to compete against that."

The Coalition wants the government to halt all exploration until the completion of proper studies to determine the effect on the fish stocks. Gorman wonders why anyone would be willing to throw away renewable resources, such as the fisheries, to accommodate primarily transnational corporations that export Nova Scotia's non-renewable resources while paying the province a pittance. "How much are Nova Scotians actually benefiting from all this?" she asked. Despite the press releases, the local news coverage, a submission to the House of Commons Standing Committee on Fisheries, a four-thousand-name petition and a twenty-vessel sail-by protest at the Pictou Lobster Carnival in the summer of 2000, Gorman finds it hard to get her message across, because politicians and the national media no longer listen to people. "It's a Catch-22. We can yell and scream until the cows come home, but we can't get any media attention unless we go out and do something—like block a highway—that will turn the public off us. It's the same with drama—if you don't have conflict, you don't have a story," said the author of five screenplays. "But if we do, then they come out and say, 'Aren't these people awful.' I cannot stress to you how much democracy has eroded in this country. You really have to be in a rural area, powerless, penniless and trying to mobilize people to understand. Canada gives the illusion of democracy. They let us all yell and then they go and do what they're going to do anyway. And that has never been truer than it is right now."

People often suggest Gorman should run for office, but she can't imagine ever doing it as long as she would have to vote along party lines. Besides, she wants to write scripts, not be a politician. "I don't enjoy this anymore. I am so burned out. Honest to God, I would stop tomorrow if my elected MLA would do his goddamn job," she said. "The reason why there is a surge of activists—both on the left and the right—is because Parliament isn't functioning."

She was just as irritated with her fellow citizens, especially the members of the middle-class silent majority who are hard to mobilize even when they know there's a problem. "I get so frustrated at the people who agree with me but won't write a letter or make a phone call. Why won't they do anything?" she said. "These environmental battles are our generation's war and I get so profoundly discouraged at the apathy of the middle class. Taking their kids to hockey is more important. I know they love those kids, but don't they care what water they're going to be drinking, what food they're going to be eating? There's a take, take, take mentality that I see today. We don't give back the way previous generations did."

As I settled into my car and put the key in the ignition, the irrepressible Gorman leaned in the passenger side and continued talking about activism and why she does it. "I wouldn't have to do what I do if the elected people did what they're supposed to," she said. "If they did, I'd stop in a minute."

PHILOSOPHERS AND ACADEMICS tend to define citizenship in esoteric ways, most of which I have trouble fully wrapping my head around. It's easier for me to point at Mary Gorman and say, "There." After all, she is everything a citizen should be: informed, passionate and engaged. I can only imagine what kind of world we'd live in if all of us—including those who disagree with her—were as active as Gorman. And yet I continually hear complaints about activists: they're noisy, they're obnoxious, they're unelected. Well, maybe they are, but nobody ever said democracy should be neat and tidy. And those doing the complaining are usually people with something to lose or—and this is the really scary part—people who are too lazy or self-satisfied or complacent to get involved themselves.

We take for granted our freedom, our wealth, our ability to pursue happiness. It rarely crosses our minds that people once had to fight to win every one of our democratic rights. And then other people fought to preserve them. It may have taken place on a battlefield or in the streets or even in the corridors of power, but there was always a struggle. Since we live with an embarrassment of riches, there's little incentive for most people to want to change the world. That doesn't mean the world doesn't need changing, because even the most comfortable do plenty of carping. But only a few people are prepared to act on their complaints. Through our complacency and inaction, we've allowed our citizenship to atrophy. Unless we start exercising our rights again, democracy itself will inevitably suffer the same decline.

With only a relatively small number of citizens actively trying to make the world a better place, most of the power in society stays in the hands of a few people—who may or may not give short shrift to our interests. Early in April 2001, during the run-up to the Summit of the Americas in Quebec City, protesters concerned about the secrecy of the talks on a hemispheric trade agreement staged a demo against finance ministers of the thirty-four countries who were closeted in the Four Seasons Hotel in the chic Yorkville section of Toronto. The day before, Julian Fantino, Toronto's police chief, had been spoiling for a fight. And sure enough, police cordoned off several blocks around the hotel and prepared for battle. Some wore bullet-proof jackets; some rode horses; and some, armed with guns that fire plastic bullets, positioned themselves high atop scaffolding. Predictably, fewer protesters—350 or so—than cops showed up.

Before the throng arrived from nearby Queen's Park, I watched a man walk down the middle of a closed-off Bloor Street. Apparently, drugs, alcohol or mental illness had altered his reality, and he was ranting. "This is my street," he insisted as he tramped along the yellow line. "You know it is." At the time, I didn't think much about him, but he ended up being the only person the police arrested at the protest. When I thought about it later, the cruel irony of his words began to bother me. Even if he was a homeless man—and he might have been—that certainly wasn't his street that day. It made me think of the standard protest chant: "Whose streets? Our streets."

It is, alas, just wishful thinking. Our streets, our governments and our democracy are all increasingly bought and paid for by corporations. That no doubt sounds like knee-jerk anti-corporate rhetoric, but it's not meant to be. Companies are not, of course, inherently evil. If they spend a lot of time, money and energy trying to influence governments and international bodies, they're only doing what's in their best interests. And because we let them.

The problem is that when their interests and ours don't coincide—and despite what some conservatives insist, they don't always—we don't stand up for what we believe in. Even when those interests and ours are in sync—which happens sometimes, despite what some liberals argue—we allow corporations, rather than citizens, to make the decisions. "If you took away activism, you'd find government is run by elites, not necessarily entirely self-serving elites—doctors and nurses aren't entirely self-serving, they do actually care about the health-care system—but it would probably be government by elites," said John Willis, a Toronto consultant and the chair of Greenpeace USA. "The good thing about activism is it brings into government ideas and programs and policies and ways of behaving that may be just the right answers to the problems. So I generally see it as a good thing, since activists don't write legislation; if they did, then we might have to worry."

Activists aren't elected, don't pretend to be and don't try to do the job of those who are elected. Still, some activists do worry they might have too much influence. Before the last provincial election in Ontario, the NDP approached Annie Kidder of People for Education about running for office. Aside from some reservations about that party, Kidder had two young daughters in school, so the time wasn't right for her. Still, she would like to go into politics some day, because she is uncomfortable about the influence of both wealthy corporate lobby groups and loud activists.

"Organizations, even teeny-tiny ones, can wield an enormous amount of power," she said. "Look at us, we're just twelve women in Toronto, really, and I think we've done a lot. If governments just end up being run by whoever can scream the loudest on the outside, you have exactly what we have now—a government that feels it doesn't have to listen to the two opposition parties or anybody who isn't one of the loud screamers on their side. I know we're one of those groups on the outside, but I have a real fear when you start to set up your country as a balance of power between all these screaming groups. Because money will win then."

Not true, according to Lorraine Fry, the general manager of the Non-Smoker's Rights Association. For proof, she points to her boss, Gar Mahood, who has taken on the well-funded and ruthless tobacco industry with great success. Nor does she think volume is necessary. "You don't have to be the loudest," she said, "just the most consistent, most relentless and the most vigilant."

In hindsight, many people would agree that Canada is a better, safer place because people like Mahood and some environmentalists, for example, started working on issues long before the government or the people cared about them. But sometimes activists can push through unpopular measures or make their issues seem far more important than they really are. When cities ban pesticides, for example, it's usually at the insistence of environmentalists, but a lot of people would rather use the chemicals than have weeds in their lawns. Right or wrong, that's the way they feel. Similarly, the work of the Canadian Taxpayers Federation pushed tax cuts to the top of the political agenda, even though all the polls showed taxes were well down the list of concerns for Canadians. (In the meantime, we made little progress on health care, which was top of the pops.)

Democracy Watch's Duff Conacher says conservative activists, with the help of the media, exaggerated the need for tax cuts. "That's a successful campaign and that's great, but it's a distorting campaign at the same time," he said. "Any of us can have a distorting effect if we do our campaigns the right way." Still, he believes distortions aren't that common because, generally, groups are not successful if they aren't representing the majority. The problem is that, too often, citizens groups aren't successful even when they do represent the majority. "That's why I work on democratic reform," he said, adding that advocacy groups need to be citizen-driven too. "We need to downplay the influence of all lobbyists—particularly corporate lobbyists, because their influence is much greater and disproportionate, but also citizen lobbyists. I'm not saying we're all bad or that we're generally not representative. I just think much more can be done. All citizens should have more of a voice, not just ones I happen to agree with."

Needless to say, the most biting and most persistent criticism comes from people who aren't activists. When the International Olympic Committee awarded the 1996 Games to Atlanta, many observers—including Paul Henderson, one of the leaders of the Toronto bid—blamed the failure to win the Games on the work of an anti-poverty group called Bread Not Circuses. In 1991, I profiled Michael Shapcott, the group's spokesperson, for *Toronto Life* magazine. When I called Henderson to get his opinion of Shapcott, he gave me one of my favourite lines: "The indictment on this city is that we took this guy seriously," he said. "This city has to do some soul-searching to find out why we feel so comfortable with the Michael Shapcotts, Jack Laytons and Toronto Maple Leafs."

Since Shapcott had helped scuttle Henderson's dream, and Layton was—and continues to be—one of the most effective city councillors in Toronto, Henderson's venom had more than a whiff of sour grapes to it. (He did, however, have a point about the Ballard-era Leafs.) Newspaper editorialists, on the other hand, don't even have a stinging defeat as an excuse. Yet, they seem particularly chagrined by the rise of activism. "Shelley got it wrong. It's not poets who are the unacknowledged legislators of the world, it's Greenpeace," began one editorial in the *Globe and Mail*. "Unelected, unchecked by the discipline of power, Greenpeace somehow makes public debate revolve around its preoccupations and prejudices." After the street protest against the International Monetary Fund and World Bank meetings in Washington, the *Ottawa Citizen* asked, "Who elected Maude Barlow?" Meanwhile, a *National Post* editorial attacked Duff Conacher as undemocratic, even though Conacher is the head of a citizen watchdog group that fights for greater accountability from government and business. It's true, of course, that no one elected Conacher, but no one elected anyone on any newspaper editorial board or any of the corporate lobbyists who wield so much power at all levels of government.

Since editorialists once enjoyed considerable influence, their bleating about activism as a threat to democracy increasingly sounds like the last gasp from an old guard bitter about changes it is powerless to stop. "It's always been who screams the loudest; the only difference is that in the old days it was a very small group of essentially male, moneyed interests who screamed the loudest, and that was the end of the story. Now it's broader," said Craig Jones, the president of the British Columbia Civil Liberties Association. He doesn't have much time for the newspaper editorialists who denounce the protesters at trade meetings as unelected, because the World Trade Organization isn't elected either. "No one ever said that to have a voice in a democracy you had to be elected or somehow have a constituency. That's almost antithetical to democracy. What we want is a vibrant exchange of ideas."

In the face of the increasing centralization of power in Canada, advocacy is the only way that vibrant exchange can take place. "There's going to have to be a stronger role played by extra-parliamentary opposition or we're simply not going to have good public policy formed," said Mahood. "It's obvious we have major issues, and somebody has to raise the debate or we simply will not address them. I'm thinking of everything from poverty to air and water quality to the education of our kids. At least if you have a debate, you get a better-informed public." Lyndsay Poaps, an anti-globalization activist and co-director of the Vancouver group Check Your Head, goes a step further, arguing that a healthy democracy depends on people getting out and making their voices heard. "Activism keeps democracy working," she said. "If citizens weren't active, then why would we have democracy? For democracy to work, we have to make it work, right? We have to keep using it and challenging it. Nobody elected me, but I'm allowed to voice my concerns because I live in a democracy. I'm allowed to be an active citizen, and if I weren't, the system wouldn't be worth anything."

The critics of activism, not surprisingly, usually come from the right—especially Jones's "essentially male, moneyed interests"—but Walter Robinson of the conservative Canadian Taxpayers Federation doesn't agree with his ideological brethren on that point. Citing *The Decline of Deference*, a book by University of Toronto professor Neil Nevitte, Robinson suggests that the increase in activism is connected to the increased willingness of Canadians to challenge authority—whether it's the government, corporations, medical experts or the church. "Activism is a form of citizenship," he said, and then dismissed those who try to discredit advocates as unelected and unaccountable. "My answer to them is very simple: Nobody elected us. There's a group of people who support an issue—whether it's Greenpeace or the Canadian Taxpayers Federation—exercising their democratic right to freedom of expression. If you don't like it, to be very blunt, exercise yours and show us where our ideas are wrong. If you don't like our influence, strive to have your own."

BACK IN THE 1980S, Lorraine Fry taught refugees at a community college. Since most of her students did not come from democratic countries, toward the end of the course she'd always talk a bit about what it means to live in a free society. "What do you think is the biggest enemy of democracy?" she would ask them. And after they'd made a few guesses, she'd write the word "apathy" on the board and say, "That's the enemy of democracy." When she told me this anecdote, she added, "And the opposite of apathy is activism."

Apathy's smirking sidekick is cynicism, something I spent a great many years indulging in. I am now at an age when my friends are starting to hit the mid-life crisis, complete with affairs, failed marriages and odd choices. I find this all a bit baffling, because I have cheerfully spent so much of my life in a state of non-stop adolescence. I didn't get a driver's licence until I was 38, for example, and after living with the same woman for eleven years, I finally eloped with her a few weeks before I turned 40. And then, following years of—in my wife's withering words— "focusing on fun," I decided to write a book about activists. It seemed a good topic for me, one that I was interested in and had written about. But now that it's over, I'm starting to think there was something else going on at a subconscious level. Even I know my exit is closer than my entrance and it would be only natural for me to finally start wondering what it means to be an adult in a world full of immaturity.

During my university days, I spent a little time in the McGill student pub, which was named for Gertrude Stein, the writer who famously told Ernest Hemingway, "You are all a lost generation." Sometimes I would weep a pint with Matthew Church, another member of my lost generation. He was the kind of guy who might wear a "McGill Out of South Africa" button but, by his own admission, only pay lip service to campus activism. Overwhelmed by the size and complexity of the problems—and reluctant to appear too passionate about anything—he opted to stay above it all.

After university, we both ended up in the same city and in the same industry. Eventually, he became a committed stay-at-home dad—and, much to my surprise, an activist. In an effort to understand how this had happened, I dropped by his home west of downtown Toronto on a muggy day in early May 2000. We sat in his backyard as his youngest daughter napped, and he told me how he led a group of parents who saved the local school. It had been a lot of work, but he discovered he was actually a pretty good activist and someone others would listen to. As he said, "It was a form of alchemy taking all that anger and anxiety and converting it to reasonable, logical arguments."

When he finished his story, I asked him if he was surprised he became an activist. "I'm amazed," he said. "I had no faith whatsoever that anything I did would actually make a difference. And beyond that, there's also this thing about being cool. Staying home with Olivia and being involved with Alice's school transformed me. It became less important for me to be cool, less important to be obviously cynical. I learned I could be completely committed to something and not be embarrassed by it."

Despite his journey from youthful cynicism to adult activism, Church remains pessimistic about electoral politics. In fact, he turned down the inevitable entreaties to run for office. "What a loser job. I'd rather be on the outside screaming in," said Church, who prefers to help out other parent groups. "Of all the people I've worked with, not one has wanted to be on the inside."

I've never wanted to be inside or outside. I stay informed and I vote (even in municipal elections) but I've never been engaged, except as the kind of colour commentator only my friends will tolerate (and even then only barely). But after meeting so many committed people in 2000, I now see that my citizenship is sadly impoverished. It's never been enough just to vote, and these days, between our dysfunctional political system and the increasing power of international agreements to limit what even well-adjusted legislatures can do, a vote means less and less.

I keep thinking about something Jim Green, the Vancouver anti-poverty activist said: "We could be running around in paradise in this world, but there are a lot of things that have to be done to get us there." A lot of people may think they live in paradise—or they're too busy with the kids, the job and the mortgage to even give it much thought—but the truth is there is a lot of work to do. And the politicians have proven they aren't going to do it for us.

That doesn't mean that all of us should drop everything and rush into the streets. Wendy Cukier, for one, worries that too many activists put too much pressure on their fellow citizens. The president of the Canadian Coalition for Gun Control thinks there's an activism scale that, at one end, has all the people who do nothing but vote; at the other end are all the people whose whole identity is wrapped up in changing the world. And she worries that giving people an all-or-nothing ultimatum is sending the wrong message.

"If you give people the choice between spending forty hours a week working for free and getting yelled at by a bunch of unattractive people or doing nothing, that's a hard choice to make," she says, "But you can ask people to express their opinions by writing to their member of Parliament or writing a letter to the editor. Or they can spend an hour a week—or a month—as a volunteer. I don't even care what it is. Activism or participation or whatever you call it doesn't have to be all-consuming and take over your life."

It should, however, be a part of our lives. Unfortunately, lulled by our own relative wealth and success, we've become democratic dropouts. Worse, too many people seem to be going in the opposite direction. They want private schools, private health care and gated communities. Since more and more people can't even be bothered to vote anymore, it's not going to be easy to get them to spend even a few hours working on the important issues of the day. That, of course, means they are ceding their voice to others who are louder or richer or wilier—or simply more active. But that's their choice.

"The fact that we have to have a word to describe someone as an activist is a bad thing in a democracy," said Garth Mullins, a Vancouver anti-globalization activist. If we had a healthier democracy, if more people were engaged, what the Garth Mullinses, the Wendy Cukiers and the Mary Gormans do wouldn't be out of the ordinary. And we wouldn't call it activism, we'd call it citizenship.

APPENDIX: ACTIVIST WEB SITES

More information about the organizations mentioned in *Watchdogs and Gadflies* is available by visiting these Web sites:

Alberta Home Education Association:
    <www.abhome-ed.org>
Alberta Wilderness Association:
    <www.albertawilderness.ca>
Alliance for Employment Equity:
    <www.web.net/~allforee>
Amnesty International:
    <www.amnesty.ca>
APEC Alert:
    <www.cs.ubc.ca/spider/fuller/apec_alert>
Bow Chinook Barter Community:
    <www.calcna.ab.ca/bcbc>
Bread Not Circuses:
    <www.breadnotcircuses.org>
British Columbia Civil Liberties Association:
    <www.bccla.org>
Campaign Life Coalition:
    <www.lifesite.net/clc>
Canada Family Action Coalition:
    <www.familyaction.org>
Canadian Environmental Law Association:
    <www.web.net/cela>
Canadian Environmental Network:
    <www.cen-rce.org>
Canadian Health Coalition:
    <www.healthcoalition.ca>
Canadian Peace Alliance:
    <www.acp-cpa.ca>
Canadian Taxpayers Federation:
    <www.taxpayer.com>
Canadians Concerned About Violence in Entertainment:
    <www.media-awareness.ca/eng/med/home/advoc/c-cave.htm>

CAVEAT:
   <www.caveat.org>
Check Your Head:
   <www.checkyourhead.org>
Citizens' Oil and Gas Council:
   <www.rmec.org/cogc/>
Coalition for Gun Control:
   <www.guncontrol.ca>
Co-Motion:
   <www.co-motion.net>
Consumers Association of Canada:
   <www.consumer.ca>
Council of Canadians:
   <www.canadians.org>
Green Web:
   <fox.nstn.ca/~greenweb>
David Suzuki Foundation:
   <www.davidsuzuki.org>
Democracy Street:
   <www.democracy-street.tao.ca>
Democracy Watch:
   <www.dwatch.ca>
Earth Action:
   <www.flora.org/earth-action>
End of Oil Coalition:
   <www.tao.ca/~no_oil>
Energy Probe:
   <www.energyprobe.org>
Environmental Coalition of P.E.I.:
   <www.upei.ca/~cmartin/ecopei>
Equality for Gays and Lesbians Everywhere:
   <www.egale.ca>
Fair Vote Canada:
   <www.fairvotecanada.org>
Federation of Ontario Naturalists:
   <www.ontarionature.org>
Forest Action Network:
   <www.fanweb.org>
Foundation for Equal Families:
   <www.ffef.ca>

Friends of Medicare:
   <www.friendsofmedicare.ab.ca>
Greenpeace:
   <www.greenpeacecanada.org>
International Fund for Animal Welfare:
   <www.ifaw.org>
LEAF (The Women's Legal Education and Action Fund):
   <www.leaf.ca>
National Firearms Association:
   <www.nfa.ca>
Non-Smokers' Rights Association:
   <www.nsra-adnf.ca>
Ontario Coalition Against Poverty:
   <www.tao.ca/~ocap>
Organization for Quality Education:
   <www.oqe.org>
People for Education:
   <www.peopleforeducation.com>
Pollution Probe:
   <www.pollutionprobe.org>
Public Interest Advocacy Centre:
   <www.piac.ca>
Rainforest Action Coalition:
   <www.ran.org>
Ruckus Society:
   <www.ruckus.org>
Save Our Seas and Shores:
   <north.nsis.com/~egilsson>
Sea Shepherd Conservation Society:
   <www.seashepherd.org>
Sierra Club of Canada:
   <www.sierraclub.ca>
Sierra Legal Defence Fund:
   <www.sierralegal.org>
Sierra Youth Coalition:
   <www.sierrayouthcoalition.org>
The Wakeford Medical Marijuana Website:
   <www.interlog.com/~wakeford>
Links to these sites can be found on the author's site:
   <www.timfalconer.com>

ACKNOWLEDGEMENTS

The cover of this book bears the name of just one man, but many other people deserve much of the credit.

Since I first met her at the Banff Publishing Workshop in 1984, Lynn Cunningham has been something of a guardian angel to me. And I don't mean that just because she keeps finding me work. When she asked me to profile Gar Mahood for *Toronto Life* magazine in 1988, Lynn unwittingly sparked my fascination with activists, which ultimately led to this book.

Alison Maclean first got me thinking seriously about writing a book and then found me a great agent: her husband David Johnston. Wisely, as it turned out, he made me rewrite my proposal several times. Finally, I was fortunate to have two wonderful editors: Jackie Kaiser, who pointed me in the right direction, and Diane Turbide, who helped get me there. Copy editor Dennis Mills and production editor Shannon Proulx were also a great help.

This book would not have been possible without the friends who graciously put me up as I travelled the country, talking to activists. My hosts were Peter Cronyn and Liz Barrett in Ottawa; Blake O'Brien in Calgary; Richard Leggat in Halifax and on the St. John River; Rick Taylor and Nini Gibson Taylor in Vancouver; Ruby Andrew in Victoria; and Monica Merrifield and Filippo Miglior in Burlington.

Jocelyn Laurence, then an editor at the old *Financial Post Magazine*, worked with me on my profile of Duff Conacher, which forms the basis of chapter ten. David Hayes read an early version of the proposal, provided advice all along the way, and even read some of the first draft; his counsel was invaluable. Frank Addario, Malcolm MacRury and Paul Rush helped me get my thoughts together while I worked on the proposal. Many people—including David Brooke, John Brooke, Alex Campbell, Tom Heintzman, Doug MacLeod, Jeannine Mitchell, Bruce Ryder, Robert Stack, Paul Washington and Hugh Wilson—suggested activists to write about. Doug Bell and Moira Farr guided me through the book-writing experience. David Shannon helped in several ways, including brainstorming over the subtitle. Grahame Arnould, Brian Banks, Joseph Blasioli, Matthew Church, Janet Cornfield, Georgette Gagnon, Bruce Gillespie, Timm Hughes, Marni Jackson, Mike Harper, Catherine Lewis, Andy Malcolm, Jonathan Marshall, Don Obe, Ian Pearson, Kim Pittaway, Claire Sibonney, Simon Smith, Amy Spach, Jessica

Wong and the Pistols hockey team offered various other ideas, advice and support. And though he died around the time I first started working on the proposal, I want to thank my friend, editor and hockey buddy Jim Cormier.

Chris Goldie took on the brave task of reading the first draft and gave me excellent feedback during many long gab sessions. Dave Paterson, Steve Watt and Felix Vikhman also helped me with their thoughts on the first draft.

Special thanks to my mom and my four sisters for all their support. Thanks also to Donnie Shannon, Biff Norris, Scott Tomenson and all my other friends who picked up the tab far too often.

Finally, there is the incomparable Carmen Merrifield, who has—against all odds—put up with me for eighteen years. While I worked on this book, she provided always-sensible advice, gave me pep talks (including stern ones when necessary), read pre-release drafts, helped out with the research and even donated frequent-flier miles to the cause. But mostly she gave me her love and patience.

Tim Falconer
www.timfalconer.com
Toronto
April 2001

INDEX

Abbey, Ed, 129
abortion issue, 18, 52
access to information process, 57, 59, 166
activism/activists. *See also* various groups and issues
  incomes and, 68, 72, 143, 211, 233
  politicians and, 25–27, 34–35, 37–38, 41–43
  politics or, 12–14, 17–22, 51–57, 195, 204, 251, 257
  tradition of, 4–6
  training (*See* training)
"adopting the issue," 20, 60
advocacy groups, 14, 15, 19, 227. *See also* various groups
affinity groups, 104, 112
Against the Tide, 194
AIDS, 173, 175
AIDS Action Now, 174
Alberta Energy and Utilities Board, 144
Alberta Home Education Association (AHEA), 79–81
Alberta League for Environmentally Responsible Tourism (ALERT), 138–39
Alberta Wilderness Association, 123, 144
Alinsky, Saul, 4, 166
Alliance for Employment Equity, 37
American takeovers, 94
Amnesty International, 28
Anderson, David, 42

anti-globalization movement. *See* globalization issues
anti-poverty. *See* poverty issues
anti-tobacco campaign. *See* tobacco issues
anti-war movement, 193
APEC Summit (Vancouver, 1997). *See* Vancouver protest
Arron, Laurie, 206
arts and culture, 63, 64
Arusha Centre, Calgary, 190
Atlantic Canada Opportunity Agency, 47
Atlantic Salmon Federation, 134
attracting media attention, 32–33, 35
  ALERT and, 138
  Canadian Taxpayers Federation and, 32–33, 56, 57
  de Villiers case and, 199
  Duff Conacher and, 229, 241–42
  education issues and, 83–84, 88
  fishing issues and, 247
  Gas Tax Honesty Day and, 47–50
  Greenpeace and, 24–25, 29, 123
  pesticide use and, 127
  poverty issues and, 31–32
automobile safety, 4
Azzopardi, Ken, 61, 65

Bachmann, John, 75, 76
bank mergers, 42, 44, 224, 229–31, 234, 236
Barlow, Maude, 6, 16, 43, 99, 253
barter systems, 190–92
Bassani, Teresa, 184

Battle of Seattle. *See* Seattle protest
bear hunting, 14
Behrens, Matthew, 83
Belaney, Archie, 5
Berlin, Rosalee, 38, 163
Blackett, Kathryn, 84
"blame the victim," 162
Blanchard, Bill, 153
Bleyer, Peter, 43
Bow Chinook Barter Community,
  190–91
bracket creep, 50, 56, 60
Bread Not Circuses, 31, 253
"Bricks for Wendy" campaign, 220
British Columbia Civil Liberties
  Association, 18, 39, 212–15, 240
Brockovich, Erin, 244, 245
Brown, Colin, 52
budgets
  activists', 33, 38–39, 41, 43, 55,
    106, 143, 204, 238, 240
  advertising, 41–42
  alternative, 48
  balanced, 46, 51
  bank-merger, 240
  federal, secrecy, 26
  federal (1999), 59
  federal (2000), 46, 60
Burdett, Christine, 152–59, 236
burnout, 205, 234, 245, 248

Cadman, Chuck, 51
Calderhead, Vince, 186–89
Calgary protest, 30, 116–21, 190, 191
Campaign Life Coalition, 52
Campaigns & Elections, 13, 27,
  145, 231
Campbell, Gordon, 179, 195
Campbell, Kim, 9, 214, 215, 216, 217

Canada Family Action Coalition,
  51, 52
Canada Pension Plan, 53
Canadian Alliance Party, 10, 51, 53,
  54–55, 218
Canadian Auto Workers, 229
Canadian Bankers Association,
  229, 230
Canadian Broadcasting Corporation,
  29, 58, 92
Canadian Cancer Society, 162, 167,
  168, 174
Canadian Centre for Policy
  Alternatives, 48
Canadian Coalition on Acid
  Rain, 234
Canadian Community Reinvestment
  Coalition, 224–30, 234–36, 241
Canadian Council on Smoking and
  Health, 167
Canadian Environmental Law
  Asssociation, 163, 164
Canadian Environmental
  Network, 106
Canadian Federation of
  Independent Business, 19, 33, 229
Canadian Federation of
  Students, 229
Canadian Health Coalition, 132, 153
Canadian Peace Alliance, 39
Canadian Taxpayers Federation, 15,
  18, 20, 26, 46–68, 236
  media and, 32–33
Canadian Wheat Board, 52
Canadians Against Violence Every-
  where Advocating its Termination
  (CAVEAT), 51, 200–205, 215
Canadians for Gun Control, 219
capital punishment, 201–2

Casey House, 173–74

CAVEAT, 51, 200–205, 215

censorship, 210, 214

charitable status, 41, 130, 144

Charter of Rights and Freedoms, 52, 137, 140, 209

Charter Revolution and the Court Party, The, 140

Chavez, Cesar, 193

Check Your Head, 12, 97, 105–8

Chicago Seven, 2

Chow, Olivia, 30, 182

Chrétien, Jean, 6, 9, 98, 110, 112, 240
    pepper spray and, 93
    Pie Brigade and, 100

Church, Matthew, 256–57

Churley, Marilyn, 158

cigarettes. *See* tobacco

Citizens' Oil and Gas Council, 122, 143

Citizens Utility Boards, 228

citizenship, 5, 90, 112–13, 227–28, 231, 244–59. *See also* democratic issues

civil disobedience, 102, 104, 118, 140, 145, 146, 147

civil liberties, 212–15. *See also* democratic issues; police

civil-rights movement, 3, 140, 192

Clarke, John, 181–82

Clayoquot Sound, 146, 191–92

Co-Motion, 118

Coalition for Gun Control, 19, 20, 27, 136, 215–21

Coastal Forest Conservation Initiative, 149

Cohn, Josh Raisler, 117–18

Committee for an Independent Canada, 94

Committee on Legal and Constitutional Affairs (Senate), 215

Conacher, Duff, 62, 66, 67, 224–42, 252, 253–54

Conacher family, 231–33

Concerned Parents of Etobicoke, 71

Conference Board of Canada, 57

Conservative Party
    Alberta, 153
    federal, 25, 56, 98, 218
    Ontario, 14, 25, 77, 85, 86, 89

conservatives, 62, 214
    activists and, 50–52
    fiscal, 54
    legal system and, 140, 141, 189
    social, 52

consumer associations, 228, 231

Corbett, David, 208

Corcoran, Terence, 171–72

Corporate Responsibility Coalition, 240

corporate welfare, 48, 49, 57–59

corporations. *See also* tobacco issues
    brand names and, 105, 106, 112
    court challenges and, 141
    as donors, 130, 131, 133, 204
    lobbyists and, 7, 10, 19, 102, 165
    power of, 41, 250–51
    sponsorship and, 99
    sweatshops and, 99, 106–7
    as targets, 35–37, 102, 146–49, 150
    youth culture and, 99

Council of Canadians, 6, 16, 42–43, 98, 99, 229

court challenges, 41, 53, 137, 139, 140–42, 174, 175, 186–89, 209–10, 218

Court Challenges Program, 174

Covenant on Economic, Social and
   Cultural Rights, 188
Crampton, Bob, 219
credibility, 18, 33, 40–41, 57, 84
Crooks, Andrew, 17, 52
Crosbie, John, 206
Cukier, Wendy, 19, 27, 136, 215–22,
   258, 259

Dare, Malkin, 20, 70–73, 74–78, 83
David Suzuki Foundation, 28,
   40, 144
Davies, Darryl, 219
Davies, Libby, 194, 195
de Villiers, Nina, 198, 199, 215
de Villiers, Priscilla, 51, 198–205, 215
debt-reduction issue, 26, 63
decision-making, 122–23
Decline of Deference, The, 21, 255
deep ecology, 120, 128–30, 131
Democracy Street, 109, 110–11
Democracy Watch, 62, 66, 224–33,
   238, 240–41
democratic issues, 4, 5, 10, 21–22,
   94–95, 109, 112–13, 195, 248–55.
   See also citizenship
Dheer, Bani, 13, 95–96, 102
Do It, 2
Douglas, Shirley, 153, 154, 158
Douglas, Tommy, 153, 221
Downtown Eastside Residents
   Association, 178, 182–83, 194–96
"driving the agenda," 20, 60
Dufay, Jo, 231
Duplisea, Brad, 132
Dyson, Rose, 51

Earth Action, 99, 131–32, 134
Ecker, Janet, 86, 88

eco-terrorism, 121, 123
École Polytechnique, L', 215, 219
ecology
   deep, 120, 128–30, 131
   shallow, 128
Economic Summit (1988), 32
education issues, 20–21, 52, 70–90
   Alberta and, 79–81
   Ontario government and, 75–76,
      77, 88
Edward, Suzanne Laplante, 215
Edwards, Gavin, 145–49
Edwards, Henrietta Muir, 4–5
Egan v. Canada, 209
elections, 13–14, 76, 254. *See also*
   democratic issues; electoral reform
   federal (1988), 98
   federal (1993), 9, 98
   federal (2000), 9, 10, 13–14, 40, 53
   gag laws and, 41, 52, 53, 240
   Ontario (1990), 24–25, 41
Elections Canada, 237
electoral reform, 62, 66–67,
   236–38, 240
Elves Against the Cuts, 83
End of Oil Action coalition, 117, 118
Energy Probe, 25
Environmental Assessment Act
   (Ontario), 164
Environmental Coalition of Prince
   Edward Island (ECO-PEI), 126,
   130–34
environmental issues, 16, 41–42,
   163–64, 235, 245
   Alberta and, 124–25
   British Columbia and, 35–36, 124
   court challenges and, 21
   globalization and, 95–97, 106
   government jurisdiction and, 141

law and, 139, 163, 164
media and, 33, 34
poverty and, 190
Prince Edward Island and,
99–100, 125–27, 130–37
social conservatives and, 52
Equality for Gays and Lesbians
Everywhere, 21, 40, 206–11
Erickson, Arthur, 183, 185
Eriksen, Bruce, 194, 195
ethics codes for MPs, 240
euthanasia, 175
Evans, Liz, 183, 185, 186
Expo 86, 31, 178, 194

Fair Vote Canada, 67
Family Law Act (Ontario), 209
Famous Five, the, 4–5
Firearms Act, 218
Fisher, John, 21, 40, 206–11
fishing issues, 133, 134–37, 245–47
focus groups, 8, 9, 27, 228
Forest Action Network, 146
Forest Alliance, 145
forest issues, 35–36, 133, 142, 145–50
Forest Stewardship Council, 148
Forum on Health Care Reform, 158
Foundation for Equal Families, 208
Four Corners Community Savings,
178, 180, 195, 196
Four Sisters Housing Co-op,
184, 196
"framing the debate," 20, 58, 60
Fraser Institute, 48, 54, 56, 214
Free Trade Agreement, 97, 98
Free Trade Area of the Americas,
7, 103
free-trade protests, 6–7, 97–98
free trade vs. fair trade, 101

Freeman, Aaron, 233, 240
Friends of Leduc Hospital, 155
Friends of Medicare, 152–57,
155, 236
Friends of the Oldman River
Society, 139
Fry, Lorraine, 37, 170, 182,
251–52, 255
fundraising, 27, 28, 39, 42–43, 157,
168, 204, 210, 238
charitable status and, 41, 130, 144
corporations and, 130, 131,
133, 204
foundations and, 143–44
government sources and, 41, 133,
171, 183

Gabelmann, Doug, 225–26, 241
Gandhi, Mohandas, 4, 140
Gas Tax Honesty Day, 40, 46–50,
56, 66
Gay and Lesbian Educators, 214
gay issues. *See* sexual
orientation issues
genetic engineering issues, 35, 100,
102, 240–41
globalization issues, 6, 12, 13,
92–113. *See also* Check your Head;
Quebec City/Seattle/
Vancouver protests
Globe and Mail, 67, 171, 172–73, 253
Goldman, Emma, 12
Gorman, Mary, 244–49, 259
Governing from the Centre, 9
Government Ethics Coalition, 240
government spending, 47, 52,
56–60, 63
on advocacy groups, 41, 133,
171, 236

on hockey teams, 46, 50,
59–60, 63
"grassroots movement," 19
Great Bear Rainforest, 35, 145–49
Great Canadian Puck-off, 60
Green, Jim, 21, 31, 33, 178–80,
182–84, 192–96, 258
Green Web, 128
Greenpeace, 5, 11, 28, 42
forest products and, 145–49, 240
media and, 24–25, 29, 33, 34,
123, 253
Grey, Deborah, 54
Grey Owl, 5
Group Against Smoking
Pollution, 163
gun-control issue, 18, 19, 20, 27, 52,
136, 215–22

Harper, Stephen, 53
Harris, Mike, 83, 86
Hate Crimes Bill, 207
Hayne, Percy, 246
Health Canada, 19, 168, 169
health care issues, 9, 20, 124,
152–75
Alberta, 152–59
anti-medicare ad and, 52
marijuana and, 173–75
Hein, Gregory, 141
Heintzman, Tom, 239
Henderson, Paul, 253
hockey subsidies, 46, 50, 59–60, 63
Holmes, Mark, 74, 89
Home Depot, 36, 148
home schooling, 79–81
homelessness/housing, 30, 180–81,
189, 194–95

*How to Get the Right Education for
Your Child,* 75
Howe, Paul, 17
human rights, 96–97, 188–89.
See also poverty issues; sexual
orientation issues
Human Rights Act, 21, 206, 207,
208, 209
Human Rights Committee
(U.N.), 188
Hurley, Adele, 234
Hyde, Betty, 239

IKEA, 36, 148
Imagine Democracy, 62
Imperial Tobacco, 164
Industry Canada, 58–59
Infotab, 170
Institute for Research on Public
Policy, 17
*Interest Group Litigation and
Canadian Democracy,* 141
interest groups, 15, 17–22. *See also*
activism/activists; lobbyists
court challenges and, 141
International Farmers Union, 134
International Forest Products,
147, 149
International Fund for Animal
Welfare, 14
International Monetary Fund,
94–95
Internet. *See* technology
Island Nature Trust, 134
Island Residents Against Toxic
Environment, 100

Jacobs, Jane, 19
John Howard Society, 216, 219

Jones, Craig, 18, 211–15, 254
justice issues, 198–222

Keane, Alan, 118
Kennedy, Gerard, 51
Kenney, Jason, 51
Kerr, Sarah, 40, 189–92, 236
Kidder, Annie, 71–73, 81–90, 251
King, Martin Luther, 4
Klein, Naomi, 6, 106, 109
Klein, Ralph, 152, 154, 157, 158
Koleszar, Aaron, 99–103, 132
Kostuch, Martha, 21, 138–43
Kraft, David, 33, 34, 35, 42, 43
Kyle, Ken, 162

Labchuk, Sharon, 125–28, 130–34
labour standards, 97, 101
Lanigan, Troy, 51, 61, 65
Layton, Jack, 253
Lee, Ian, 62
"left" *vs.* "right," 18, 50–51, 62,
  156, 237
left wing, 36, 41, 54
  nuts, 154, 155, 159
Lepine, Marc, 215
libel actions, 171
Liberal Party
  federal, 13, 25–26, 98, 238
  Ontario, 24, 55
lobbyists, 10, 236, 252–53. *See also*
  interest groups
  Canadian Cancer Society, 162
  corporate, 7, 10, 19, 102, 165
  government tactics and, 123
  registration of, 231
lockdowns, 104
logging. *See* forest issues
Ludwig, Weibo, 124

Luther, Martin, 4
Luther L. Terry Award, 172

M. v. H & Ontario, 209
Machiavelli, 76
MacMillan Bloedel, 146
MacPhail Woods Ecological
  Forestry Project, 133
Mahood, Garfield, 16–22, 38,
  159–73, 252
Mair, Rafe, 226, 239
Mandela, Nelson, 4
Manifest Communications, 27
Manley, John, 46, 59–60, 229
marijuana, 173–75
marine issues. *See* fishing issues
markets campaigns, 145–50
Marshall, Donald, 137, 247
Martin, Paul, 26, 46, 60, 66, 234
McAfee, Les, 206–7
McClung, Nellie, 4, 5
McDermott, Dan, 28
McDonald, Valerie, 82, 83, 84
McKinney, Louise, 5
McLellan, Anne, 218
McPhedran, Marilou, 16, 224
McQuaig, Linda, 62, 241
media, 9, 20
  activism/activists and, 15–16,
    28–34, 104, 110–11, 170–73
  attracting attention and (*See*
    attracting media attention)
  badges, 30
  editorialists, 215, 253–54
  government finances and, 47
  growth of outlets in, 29
  independent, sites, 30
  investigative reporting in, 31

journalists, 16, 120, 159–60, 170
  technology and, 30, 39–40, 42
media training, 27–28
medicare. *See* health care
Metro Parent Network, 82, 84
Milke, Mark, 56
Millsip, Kevin, 106
Money in Politics Coalition, 240
Monkey Wrench Gang, The, 129
Monsanto, 241
Morton, F.L. (Ted), 140, 141
Mullins, Garth, 30–31, 93–94,
  97–99, 108–13, 259
Multilateral Agreement on
  Investment, 6, 44, 99, 103
Murphy, Emily, 5

Nader, Ralph, 4, 224, 225. 226,
  233, 240
Naess, Arne, 120, 128, 129
National Action Committee on the
  Status of Women, 62
National Citizens' Coalition, 33,
  52–53
National Energy Board, 144
National Firearms Association, 218
National Hockey League, 59, 63
National Post, 54, 141, 171, 182,
  215, 253
Nature of Things, The, 16
Network, 95
Nevitte, Neil, 21, 255
New Democratic Party, 28, 54, 55,
  158, 237
  Ontario, 25, 34, 37, 62, 182
New Hawk nation, 147
Newsworld, 29, 30, 226
Nike, 99, 105, 112

*No Logo: Taking Aim at the Brand
  Bullies,* 6, 106, 109
Non-Smokers' Rights Association,
  17, 37, 159, 164–65, 167, 170–72
North American Free Trade
  Agreement (NAFTA), 43, 98
North Shore Environmental
  Web, 128
Northrup, David, 17
Nova Scotia Legal Aid, 187
Novaczek, Irene, 32, 132,
  134–37, 245

offenders' rights, 203, 216
Office for Victims of Crime
  (Ontario), 204
O'Hare Airport protest, 4
oil issues, 116–18, 122, 123, 142–44.
  See also Calgary protest; Gas Tax
  Honesty Day
  east coast, 136–37, 245
  sour gas and, 124, 138
Old Age Security Act, 209
Oldman River Dam, 139, 141, 142
Olympics (1996), 32, 253
Ontario Coalition Against Poverty,
  29, 181–82
Ontario Medical Association, 19
Organization for Economic
  Development, 99
Organization for Quality Education,
  20, 71, 73, 75–79
Organization of American States,
  96, 103
  protest (*See* Windsor protest)
organization styles, 42–44, 87–88,
  110, 131–32, 136–37, 219–20, 235
Orton, David, 128–30, 136, 137

Parents for Learning, 71, 75, 77
Parlby, Irene, 4
peace movement, 11
Penner, Bob, 11–12, 27–29, 38–39, 43–44
pensions, 44, 53
    MPs', 52, 54–55, 66
People for Education, 72, 82–90, 251
People or Planes, 164
pepper spray, 92, 101, 181
Perks, Gord, 24–25
Perley, Michael, 234
pesticides, 126–27, 131–32, 252
Peterson, David, 24–25, 34, 35, 41
Physicians for a Smoke-Free Canada, 168
Pickering Airport, 164
Poaps, Lyndsay, 12–13, 14, 97, 105–8, 254–55
police, 32, 99, 186, 250
    Alberta, 53
    Calgary protest and, 116–21, 191
    de Villiers and, 198, 199
    gun control and, 220
    Quebec City protest and, 7, 211
    Seattle protest and, 99, 101, 111
    Toronto protest and, 181–82
    Vancouver protest and, 92–93, 110, 211–12
Police Services Board (Toronto), 30, 182
Policy Centre for Victim Issues, 204
politics
    activism and/or, 14, 17–22, 51–57, 195, 204, 251, 257
    power and, 8–11, 12, 15, 17, 67
Pollution Probe, 234
Portland Hotel, 183–86, 196
potato industry, 125–27

poverty issues, 18, 21, 29–32, 178–96
    children and, 220–21
    Toronto protest and, 181–82, 190
"power model," 123, 124, 150
Prague protest, 6
Prince, The, 76
prison sentences, 202
pro-democracy movement, 6, 21–22
Progressive Conservative Party. *See* Conservative Party
property damage. *See* tactics; training
property rights, 52
proportional representation. *See* electoral reform
protectionism, 97, 101
protests. *See* various cities
Public Complaints Commission, 109, 111
public opinion, 19–20, 44
    mobilizing, 216, 221–22, 225, 248
    polls, 8, 9
public servants protests, 108–9

Quebec City protest, 6–8, 54, 211
Quebec Public Interest Research Group, 239
Queen's Park protest. *See* Toronto protest

Radikal Cheerleaders, 118, 119, 120
Raging Grannies, 119
Rainforest Action Network, 148
rainforests, 35–36, 145–49
rape victims, 203
Rath, Dan, 25, 27–29
Rathjen, Heidi, 215–17, 219
Real Toronto Tour, The, 32
"reason model," 122, 123

Rebick, Judy, 62, 67
Reform Party. *See* Canadian
  Alliance Party
Residential Tenancies Act (Nova
  Scotia), 187
Resolution One, 55
Reveille for Radicals, 4
Revenue Canada, 41, 130, 144
Riot at the Hyatt, 110
Robinson, Svend, 11, 214
Robinson, Walter, 15–16, 17, 20, 26,
  33, 40, 50–68, 73, 237, 255
  Gas Tax Honesty Day and, 46–50
Robson, Bill, 75, 77, 83
Roche, Douglas, 16
Rock, Allan, 167, 174, 175, 200, 206,
  207, 217
Rocky Mountain Ecosystem
  Coalition, 143, 144
Ronald McDonald, 100
Roosevelt, Franklin Delano, 20
Round Table on Resource Land Use
  and Stewardship, 133
Royal Canadian Mounted Police, 92,
  93, 109, 146, 212
Rubin, Jerry, 2
Rubin, Norm, 25
Ruckus Society, 117
Rules for Radicals, 4

SafetyNet Conference (1994), 200
Saskatchewan Taxpayers
  Federation, 55
Save Our Seas and Shores Coalition,
  32, 136–37, 245, 247
Savoie, Donald J., 9
Sawyer, Mike, 120–25, 142–44,
  150, 236
Schneider, Gary, 130–31, 132–34

schools. *See also* education issues
  boards and, 71, 76, 80, 81, 82, 84,
    89, 90
  home, 78, 79–81
  kinds of, 77, 90
  workshops at, 12–13, 105–7
Scott Paper, 244
Sea Shepherd Society, 123
seal hunt, 136
Seattle protest, 6, 40, 54, 93–94, 99,
  100–101, 107, 111, 192
sexual orientation issues, 21, 40,
  79–80, 174, 175, 206–11
  public education and, 209
Shapcott, Michael, 31–32, 253
Sierra Club of Canada, 28, 240
Sierra Legal Defence Fund, 28,
  139, 239
Sierra Youth Coalition, 100
Simpson, Jeffrey, 96
Sinclair, Rob, 14
Singh, Jaggi, 211
Sir George William University, 128
Smith, Merran, 149
smoking. *See* tobacco issues
Smoking and Health Action
  Foundation, 171
Somerville, David, 52, 53
SOS². *See* Save our Seas and
  Shores Coalition
sour-gas issue, 124, 138
Spadina Expressway, 19
Sparks, Irma, 186–87
"special interest groups," 19
"spouse," 209
Spring Cleaning, 238
Stewart, Hugh, 92
Stewart, Ron, 165
Stock, Peter, 51

Strategic Communications, 27–28, 34, 39, 42
Strategic Counsel, The, 13, 95
Strengthening Canadian Democracy, 17
Strom, Ray, 79–81
Students for Life, 215
Summit of the Americas, 6–9, 211, 249
    protest (*See* Quebec City protest)
Surrey School Board, 214
Sutherland, Kiefer, 153, 154
Suzuki, David, 16
Sweanor, David, 171

tactics, 89, 102, 104, 111–12, 121, 124–25, 129. *See also* attracting media attention; training; various issues and protests
    strategy disputes and, 125, 128–31, 134, 135, 162, 209–10
talk radio, 61–62
Task Force Report on the Future of the Canadian Financial Services Sector, 226
Tax Freedom Day, 48
tax issues, 26, 252. *See also* Canadian Taxpayers Federation; Gas Tax Honesty Day
    Alberta and, 53
    deficit and, 63
    income, 56, 60, 63
    western, 55
teach-ins, 103–5
technology, 30, 39–40, 42
Technology Partnerships Canada, 59
Ted Weatherill Awards. *See* Teddies, the

Teddies, the, 48, 49, 56
terminology, 104
"terrorists," 19
Tevlin, Tom, 145
tobacco issues, 17, 18, 19, 21, 159–73, 212
    Toronto City Council and, 165
"Tobacco OR Kids" campaign, 168
Tobacco Products Control Act, 161, 166
Toronto Disarmament Network, 28, 38–39
Toronto Island homes, 37
Toronto protest, 29–30, 181–82, 190
tourism, 127
Townsend, Mark, 183, 184, 185–86
trade agreements, 6, 7, 36–37, 41, 43, 94
    concerns with, 95–98, 101, 103, 106
training, 13, 27–28, 103–5, 145, 231
Trudeau, Pierre Elliott, 8, 9, 11, 14, 15, 221

unions, 87, 157, 194
    labour, 157
    teachers, 76, 78, 80, 89
United Farm Workers, 193
university courses, 27
University of British Columbia. *See* Vancouver protest

Vancouver protest, 6, 30, 39, 92–94, 211–12
    inquiry, 109–10
    media and, 93–94
    Prime Minister's Office and, 93
Vancouver's Downtown Eastside, 178–80, 182–86, 193–96

victims' rights, 51, 52.
  See also CAVEAT
violence, 51, 111–12, 121, 123, 124,
  127, 140. *See also* CAVEAT; police
voting-reform coalition, 237
Vrsnik, Victor, 47

Wagner, Nancy, 75, 77
Wakeford, Jim, 173–75
Wallace, Rick, 241
Walsh, Mary, 153, 154
Wamback, Joe, 51
War Room, The, 234
water exports, 42
Watson, Paul, 123
western issues, 53
White, Randy, 54
White Owl Conservation
  Award, 164
Wigand, Jeffrey, 170
Willis, John, 5, 12, 33–37, 41, 42, 251
Wilson, Michael, 26, 56
Winchester, Bruce, 46, 49, 50

Windsor protest, 96, 103
Windsor Star, 104
Winnipeg General Strike, 11–12
Woman's Christian Temperance
  Union, 5
Women's Legal Education and
  Action Fund, 28, 209–10
World Petroleum Congress, 29, 30,
  116, 142, 190, 191
  protest (*See* Calgary protest)
World Trade Organization, 40, 93,
  94, 100, 107, 254
  protest (*See* Seattle protest)
World Wildlife Fund, 144
Wynne, Kathleen, 82, 83

Xtra, 210

Yeo, Jonathan, 198, 202, 205, 215
Young, Alan, 174

Zapatista uprising, 98